WALKING THE MOURNE MOUNTAINS

30 HIKES IN NORTHERN IRELAND'S HIGHEST MOUNTAINS, INCLUDING SLIEVE DONARD AND THE MOURNE WALL

by Kieron Gribbon

CICERONE

JUNIPER HOUSE, MURLEY MOSS,
OXENHOLME ROAD, KENDAL, CUMBRIA LA9 7RL
cicerone.co.uk

First edition 2026
ISBN: 978 1 78631 262 4
eISBN: 978 1 78765 275 0

MIX
Paper | Supporting responsible forestry
FSC® C014138

Printed in Czechia on behalf of Latitude Press Ltd on responsibly sourced paper.
A catalogue record for this book is available from the British Library.
All photographs are by the author unless otherwise stated.
Route maps are reproduced with permission from Harvey Maps harveymaps.co.uk

Overview mapping by Lovell Johns lovelljohns.com

Contains OpenStreetMap.org data © OpenStreetMap contributors, CC-BY-SA. NASA relief data courtesy of ESRI. Please be aware that the overview map in this guide was created using open-source data and has not undergone the checking procedures of an official mapping agency.
Cicerone's EU representative for GPSR compliance is Easy Access System Europe, Mustamäe tee 50, 10621 Tallinn, Estonia. Email gpsr.requests@easproject.com

Updates to this guide

While we strive to ensure that our guidebooks are as up to date and accurate as possible, changes can occur during the lifetime of an edition. Facilities, accommodation, transport and even rights of way can change, so if you find any inaccuracies in this book or have any feedback, please let us know by email at updates@cicerone.co.uk. Updates will be published on the Cicerone website (cicerone.co.uk/1262/updates), so please check before planning your trip.

To receive free updates, special offers and GPX files where available, don't forget to **register** your book at the 'My Account' tab at cicerone.co.uk.

Front cover: The Mourne Wall snaking its way off Bearnagh and over the North Top towards Donard (Routes 13, 17, 25 and 27)

CONTENTS

ROUTE SUMMARY TABLE

Rte	Route name	Start/finish	Distance	Ascent/ descent	Grade	Time	Pg
1	Tollymore Forest Park highlights	Tollymore Forest Park car park	11.5km (7.1 miles)	315m (1035ft)	Easy	3hr 30min	41
2	Tollymore Forest Park and the Brandy Pad	Donard car park, Newcastle	20.2km (12.6 miles)	835m (2740ft)	Moderate	6hr 30min	46
3	Slieve Donard and Slieve Commedagh from Newcastle	Donard car park, Newcastle	11.6km (7.2 miles)	995m (3265ft)	Hard	4hr 45min	54
4	Slieve Donard and Chimney Rock Mountain	Bloody Bridge car park	12.7km (7.9 miles)	945m (3100ft)	Hard	4hr 45min	61
5	The Brandy Pad – Bloody Bridge to Trassey	Bloody Bridge car park (start)/ Trassey car park (finish)	11.7km (7.3 miles)	570m (1870ft)/ 430m (1410ft)	Moderate	4hr	67
6	Annalong River, Hare's Castle and Rocky Mountain	Dunnywater parking spot	9.8km (6.1 miles)	415m (1360ft)	Moderate	3hr 15min	73
7	Annalong Valley Horseshoe	Carrick Little car park	21.3km (13.2miles)	1635m (5365ft)	Very hard	8hr	78
8	Slieve Binnian from Carrick Little	Carrick Little car park	11.2km (7 miles)	600m (1970ft)	Moderate	4hr	87
9	Lamagan, Cove and Beg from Carrick Little	Carrick Little car park	15.5km (9.6 miles)	720m (2360ft)	Hard	5hr 15min	91
10	Slieve Binnian from Silent Valley	Silent Valley car park	11.4km (7.1 miles)	675m (2215ft)	Hard	4hr	96
11	Beg, Cove and Lamagan from Silent Valley	Silent Valley car park	20.2km (12.6 miles)	770m (2525ft)	Hard	6hr 30min	102
12	Silent Valley floor	Silent Valley car park	18.8km (11.7 miles)	420m (1380ft)	Moderate	5hr 30min	108
13	Silent Valley Horseshoe	Silent Valley car park	27.1km (16.8 miles)	2265m (7430ft)	Very hard	11hr	114

Rte	Route name	Start/finish	Distance	Ascent/ descent	Grade	Time	Pg
14	Slieve Muck, Carn Mountain and Slievenaglogh	Banns Road car park	14.9km (9.3 miles)	685m (2245ft)	Hard	5hr	126
15	Doan, Ben Crom, Slieve Loughshannagh and Carn Mountain	Ott car park	14.2km (8.8 miles)	575m (1885ft)	Moderate	4hr 30min	131
16	Slieve Meelbeg and Slieve Loughshannagh	Happy Valley car park	8.3km (5.2 miles)	540m (1770ft)	Moderate	3hr	136
17	Bearnagh, Meelmore and Meelbeg	Meelmore Lodge car park	11.4km (7.1 miles)	780m (2560ft)	Hard	4hr 15min	140
18	Commedagh and Donard from Meelmore Lodge	Meelmore Lodge car park	15.1km (9.4 miles)	925m (3035ft)	Hard	5hr 30min	146
19	Spelga Horseshoe	Spelga Dam car park	15.6km (9.7 miles)	955m (3135ft)	Hard	5hr 30min	153
20	Eagle Mountain and Shanlieve	Sandy Brae parking spot	9.6km (6 miles)	525m (1720ft)	Hard	3hr 30min	161
21	Slievemeen, Slievemartin and Crenville	Rostrevor Forest car park	10.5km (6.5 miles)	405m (1330ft)	Moderate	3hr 30min	165
22	Tievedockaragh, Tornamrock and Rocky Mountain	Leitrim Lodge car park	11.8km (7.3 miles)	485m (1590ft)	Moderate	4hr	172
23	Rocky River Horseshoe	Hen Mountain car park	18.3km (11.4 miles)	1175m (3855ft)	Very hard	6hr 30min	177
24	Hen Mountain, Cock Mountain and Slievenamiskan	Hen Mountain car park	7.8km (4.8 miles)	450m (1475ft)	Moderate	2hr 45min	183
25	The Mourne Wall Challenge	Dunnywater parking spot	32km (19.9 miles)	2555m (8385ft)	Very hard	12hr 30min	194
26	Newcastle to Trassey Track (TMU1)	Donard Park car park	24.3km (15.1 miles)	1240m (4070ft)	Very hard	8hr 30min	214
27	Trassey Track to Ott Track (TMU2)	Meelmore Lodge car park	14.9km (9.3 miles)	885m (2905ft)	Hard	5hr 15min	223

Rte	Route name	Start/finish	Distance	Ascent/ descent	Grade	Time	Pg
28	Ott Track to Rocky River (TMU3)	Ott car park	18.5km (11.5 miles)	860m (2820ft)	Very hard	6hr 15min	229
29	Rocky River to Yellow Water River (TMU4)	Leitrim Lodge car park	19.8km (12.3 miles)	880m (2885ft)	Very hard	6hr 30min	235
30	Yellow Water River to Rostrevor (TMU5)	Yellow Water car park	18km (11.2 miles)	680m (2230ft)	Moderate	5hr 45min	243

Mountain safety

Every mountain walk has its dangers, and those described in this guidebook are no exception. All who walk or climb in the mountains should recognise this and take responsibility for themselves and their companions along the way. The author and publisher have made every effort to ensure that the information contained in this guide was correct when it went to press, but, except for any liability that cannot be excluded by law, they cannot accept responsibility for any loss, injury or inconvenience sustained by any person using this book.

International distress signal *(emergency only)*
Six blasts on a whistle (and flashes with a torch after dark) spaced evenly for one minute, followed by a minute's pause. Repeat until an answer is received. The response is three signals per minute followed by a minute's pause.

Helicopter rescue
The following signals are used to communicate with a helicopter:

Help needed: raise both arms above head to form a 'Y'

Help not needed: raise one arm above head, extend other arm downward

Emergency telephone number
999 (112 can also be used)

Weather reports
The Met Office mountain forecast
weather.metoffice.gov.uk/specialist-forecasts/mountain/mourne-mountains

Silent Valley and Ben Crom reservoirs from the summit of Slievenaglogh (Routes 14 and 25)

INTRODUCTION

Purple-flowering heather carpets the Mournes in summer

Referred to by locals and most visitors as 'the Mournes', the Mourne Mountains are one of the best hillwalking areas in Ireland – if not THE best. Tucked away in the southern corner of County Down, between Dundrum Bay and Carlingford Lough, this compact little mountain range offers hillwalkers more opportunities per square kilometre than any other Irish upland area. Large chunks of land in the Mournes are publicly owned (Northern Ireland Water and Northern Ireland Forest Service) and charity owned (National Trust), plus there are plenty of permitted access routes from the many purpose-built car parks dotted along surrounding roads. This, along with the Mournes' proximity to the island's two largest cities – Belfast and Dublin – makes them one of Ireland's most popular hillwalking destinations.

Rising steeply to 850m from the Irish Sea coastline just 3km away, Slieve Donard is the Mourne summit that draws the big crowds. It is not only the highest in the Mourne Mountains but also in County Down, in Northern Ireland, in the province of Ulster and in the two-thirds of Ireland north of the 53° latitude line. Its closest higher neighbour, Lugnaquillia Mountain (also spelled Lugnaquilla in some sources), in the Wicklow Mountains, is almost 140km south.

The Mourne summits vary in character, from the rounded peat-clad granite domes of Donard and Commedagh to the rugged rocky tors of Binnian and Bearnagh. Fourteen summits in the Mournes qualify as official mountains (i.e. Hewitts), all of which feature in the routes described throughout this book. In comparison with Slieve Donard, the other mountains attract far fewer walkers. Some can be very quiet indeed, even on the best summer weekends.

An extensive network of clear tracks and paths throughout the Mournes connects the summits, cols, ridges and valleys to give hillwalkers an unrivalled selection of routes to choose from. Using the primary routes and alternatives described in this book as a foundation, along with a hard-copy map (see the 'Maps' section), hillwalkers can easily plan hundreds of their own bespoke walks – enough for a lifetime of hillwalking.

Walkers visiting the Mournes are among the best catered for in Ireland. Accommodation and other facilities are abundant in the surrounding lowlands, especially in towns and villages like Newcastle and Rostrevor, further reinforcing the Mournes' place among Ireland's premier walking-holiday destinations.

Slieve Donard Hotel in Newcastle is just one of many local places you can stay

PLANNING INFORMATION

Donard and Commedagh towering behind the busy seaside town of Newcastle

Whether you are going for a day walk, a weekend break or a longer walking holiday in the Mournes, the following planning information will help to make everything run as smoothly as possible.

WHEN TO GO

The Mournes are beautiful all year round. While the endless cycle through the changing seasons creates a dynamic landscape for walkers to enjoy, it also introduces factors that must be taken into consideration when planning walks.

Spring

The spring months (March, April and May) are when the Mournes start to get busy. Three-season hillwalkers bring their boots out of hibernation as they return to the hills after a winter break. The number of daylight hours increases most rapidly each day, peaking around the spring equinox (about 21 March), when day and night are the same length. With rising temperatures thawing the ground, boggy areas firmed up by winter frosts become soft again; this can make walking difficult in places. It is the time of year when life returns to the Mournes in the form of humans, other animals and plants.

Summer

The summer months (June, July and August) are by far the busiest and best time to go to the Mournes, when the days are longest (about 17hr at the summer solstice), warmest and – hopefully – sunniest. As a result, the dry ground is also firmer to walk on, opening up some routes that are too boggy the rest of the year. On clear days, haze and glare can limit the views, especially towards the south. Look for the vast blankets of blooming heather purpling the landscape. On very hot days, consider taking a walk in one of the cool, shady forests. It might also be worth bringing your swimwear and a towel in case you are tempted to take a refreshing dip if passing a lake or rocky river pool.

Autumn

The autumn months (September, October and November) are when the Mournes start to get quieter. The number of daylight hours decreases most rapidly each day at this time of year, peaking around the autumn equinox (about 21 September), when day and night are the same length. With less sunlight but temperatures still above freezing, boggy areas are likely to be at their softest; this can make walking difficult in places. The decrease in haze and glare allows three-season hillwalkers to enjoy some long-distance views before putting their boots away for the winter. At lower levels, you can expect to see some dramatic colours in the forests as the trees prepare for the approaching winter.

Winter

The winter months (December, January and February) are the quietest time to go to the Mournes, when the days are at their shortest (about 7hr 30min at the winter solstice) and coldest. With most of the colour gone, and the possibility of snow and frost, the Mournes can often transform into a monochrome landscape during this time. As a result, frozen ground becomes firm to walk on, opening up some routes that would otherwise be too boggy. However, extra care needs to be taken when stepping on smooth hard surfaces, as these can become very slippery. There are usually just a handful of snowfall days each year, but the white stuff tends to lie a few days longer on the higher summits. Beware of road conditions in the mountains and at low level when driving. On clear days, long-distance views are possible through the crisp, clean air.

Getting there

Lying 50km south of Belfast and 120km north of Dublin, the Mournes are well positioned just off the main transport corridors connecting Ireland's two most-populated cities. As you approach from the northern side, the town of Newcastle, at the foot of Slieve Donard, serves as the main gateway to the range. From the south and west, the village of Rostrevor, at the foot of Slievemartin, is another popular entry point.

Public transport

As the main northern gateway into the Mournes, the town of Newcastle can be easily reached using scheduled public transport services. On the

Newcastle bus station is the local public transport hub

south side, the village of Rostrevor is also well served.

Buses

Newcastle bus station is the public transport hub for the Mourne Mountains. Regular services connect with surrounding cities, towns and villages, including Belfast, Newry, Downpatrick, Banbridge, Kilkeel and Bryansford. Buses on the Belfast to Dublin route stop at Newry bus station, from where connecting services depart for Newcastle, Rostrevor and Kilkeel. A taxi from Newry bus station to your walk start point or base is also an option.

Regular bus transfers are also available from the three closest airports: Belfast International Airport (BFS), Belfast City Airport (BHD) and Dublin Airport (DUB). Services from BFS and BHD bring arriving air passengers to Grand Central Station in Belfast city centre. From here, direct bus services depart for Newcastle and Newry bus stations, as well as trains to Newry. From DUB, direct bus services depart for Newry bus station and Belfast Grand Central Station.

Trains

In the past, a train station near the north end of Newcastle promenade was the last stop on the Belfast and County Down Railway. The line closed in 1950 and a branch to Castlewellan closed in 1955, at which point Newcastle train station itself became redundant. The old red-brick station building and its B1 listed clock tower can still be seen on Railway Street, beside the access roads to the Royal County Down Golf Club and Slieve Donard Resort and Spa.

Today, the nearest train station is at Newry, just to the west of the Mournes, on the Belfast to Dublin line. An 8min bus connection from the train station brings rail passengers to Newry bus station, from where services depart for Newcastle, Rostrevor and Kilkeel. A taxi from Newry train station to your walk start point or base is also an option.

Driving

Having access to a car maximises your flexibility for getting around in the Mournes and the surrounding areas. If you are travelling from England, Scotland, Wales, the Isle of Man or mainland Europe, you can bring your own car to Ireland on a ferry then drive to the Mournes from the port. If flying in, you can rent a car at any Irish airport.

Please remember to drive on the left-hand side of the road in Northern Ireland and the Republic of Ireland. It is also worth noting that tolls are charged on the motorways in the Republic of Ireland, which are paid at booths along the routes, so it is worth having some euros and cents close to hand. Fuel filling stations are abundant throughout Ireland, and many of these have shops on site where you can buy hot beverages, sandwiches and cooked meals.

Here are some basic directions for driving to the Mournes:

To Newcastle

- From Belfast, take the A24 south.
- From Lisburn, take the A49 south.
- From Banbridge, take the A50 south-east.
- From Newry, take the A25 east.

To Newry

- From Belfast, take the M1 south-west to junction 8, then A1 south-west.
- From Lisburn and Banbridge, take the A1 south-west.
- From Dublin and Drogheda, take the M1 north, then N1 and A1 north.
- From Dundalk, take the N1 and A1 north.

To Rostrevor

- From Newry, take the A2 south-east.

The Mourne Coastal Route

Strategically placed brown road signs guide drivers along the scenic coast road connecting the cities of Belfast and Newry. Seven of the walking routes described in this book can be accessed directly from the section between Newcastle and Rostrevor. The Mourne Coastal Route also connects with the world-famous Wild Atlantic Way via the Causeway Coastal Route.

Ferries

Ports dotted along the east and south coasts of Ireland are popular entry points for incoming sea passengers travelling from England, Scotland, Wales, the Isle of Man and mainland Europe. From north to south, in a clockwise direction, the passenger ferry ports in Ireland are located at Larne, Belfast, Dublin, Dún Laoghaire, Rosslare and Cork. The first four of these are more conveniently located for a walking holiday in the Mournes. If you arrive at one of the more southerly ports, your land journey to the Mournes will require you to travel via Dublin.

See theirelandwalkingguide.com/getting-to-ireland.html#BookFerries.

Flights

Ireland is served by flights from a wide variety of airports in Great Britain, mainland Europe and further afield. Of the nine airports in Ireland, the closest ones are Belfast International Airport (BFS), Belfast City Airport (BHD) and Dublin Airport (DUB). Each of these airports has good public transport connections from right outside their terminal buildings. However, do not expect there to be a direct service to Newcastle and Rostrevor; this would require at least two separate buses and possibly a train journey or taxi (depending on your arrival airport and your chosen destination). Public transport options from airports are described in an earlier section. All airports in Ireland offer car rental offices.

See theirelandwalkingguide.com/getting-to-ireland.html#BookFlights.

Bloody Bridge car park (Routes 4 and 5) on the A2 Kilkeel Road 4km south of Newcastle

GETTING AROUND

Some of the routes in this book start and finish within walking distance of Newcastle and Rostrevor, but the majority require motorised transport to get you there. Having access to a car provides the greatest flexibility, but there are other options for getting around in the Mournes.

Public transport and taxis

During the summer months, the Mourne Rambler bus service travels a loop through the range, connecting Newcastle with many of the most-popular walk start points. This expands route options for walkers who do not have a car or who are undertaking linear routes that start and finish at different places. Bus stops are marked on the maps and listed in the routes, with information on stops at or near car parks in Appendix A. Taxi services based in the surrounding towns can also be used. These will be considerably more expensive than public transport but may be a good option for groups, who can split the cost.

See theirelandwalkingguide.com/mourne-mountains#PublicTransportAndTaxis.

Driving and parking

If you are using your own car or a rental car to get to walk start points, you will find a good selection of parking places on the roads around and throughout the Mourne Mountains. The biggest of these are located at Donard Park in Newcastle, Kilbroney Park in Rostrevor, Tollymore Forest Park and Silent Valley Mountain Park. The more rural car parks vary in size and are likely to fill up quickly at weekends and on public holidays, especially if the weather forecast is good. Please always park considerately. A small number of rural car parks (e.g. Meelmore Lodge and Carrick Little) also provide on-site accommodation and cafés.

Where possible, leave your car in an official car park or roadside parking spot. If there is no space available, you should consider starting from a different car park. Do not block gates or laneways. If parking at the side of a quiet country road, leave plenty of room to allow lorries, large agricultural machinery and emergency service vehicles to pass unhindered. When walking away from your car, look back and imagine a large vehicle trying to get past it. Reposition your car accordingly. Do not leave any valuables in your car – thieves are more likely to target cars parked in isolated areas.

Every route start and finish point in this book is located at an official car park. A list of these, plus Google Maps QR code, is provided in Appendix A.

See theirelandwalkingguide.com/mourne-mountains#Parking.

Car rental

Whether you need a car for just a day or for the duration of your holiday, you have plenty of options to rent one in Ireland. Car rental offices can be

Meelmore Lodge (Routes 17, 18 and 27)

found at every airport and in many of the bigger towns and cities.

See theirelandwalkingguide.com/car-rental.

LOCAL ACCOMMODATION

The Mournes and the surrounding lowlands offer a wide variety of places to stay, including hotels, guest houses, B&Bs, self-catering, hostels, glamping and camping. Whatever your budget, you can find a place to suit. Most accommodation options are concentrated in nearby towns and villages, such as Newcastle, Bryansford, Rostrevor, Kilkeel and Annalong, but there is also a good selection in the more rural areas. Newry is the closest city, and day trips to the Mournes can easily be made from Belfast and Dublin.

See theirelandwalkingguide.com/mourne-mountains#PlacesToStay.

FOOD AND DRINK

You will not go hungry or thirsty through a lack of places to eat and drink. Whatever your budget and taste, the nearby cities, towns and villages will provide. There you will find a wide range of options, including hotels, restaurants, cafés, takeaways, tea shops, coffee shops and ice-cream parlours. Many of the larger fuel filling stations now serve hot food and made-to-order sandwiches. Some trailheads also offer food and drink. The most notable of these is the Hare's Gap Bistro at Meelmore Lodge, which is located a short distance off the Mourne Way. Check their website in advance for the bistro menu and opening times (meelmorelodge.co.uk). If you fancy a wee Guinness (other drinks are available) after your walk, you will find plenty of places to drink in the nearby cities, towns and villages.

MONEY

The Mournes are in Northern Ireland, where the official currency is the UK pound sterling (£). Banks in Northern Ireland issue their own banknotes, which may be unfamiliar to visitors from England, Scotland and Wales. These local banknotes have the same value as, and are completely interchangeable with, their Great Britain equivalents.

Cash machines (ATMs) are generally easy to find in the surrounding cities, towns and villages. The best places to look for them are at banks and in supermarkets, as well as other on-street locations. Fuel filling stations, including those in rural locations, often have ATMs located in their forecourts or inside their shops.

Most retailers and many accommodation providers now accept payments using major debit and credit cards. However, some businesses in rural areas and smaller accommodation providers may not have card-payment facilities. If in doubt, ask them in advance.

Tipping is not compulsory, but it is very much appreciated. This practice is commonplace in – but not necessarily limited to – restaurants, cafés, coffee shops and other dining establishments. If you receive good service, leaving a tip lets the staff know they have done a good job. Tips are usually left on the table as cash upon departure, but some places allow you to add it to the total when making a

Group descending Slieve Loughshannagh towards Carn Mountain and Slieve Muck (Routes 13, 15, 16, 25 and 27)

card payment. Generally, 10% is the norm but you can choose your own amount. Some places may add a service charge to the bill before they bring it to you, for example, if your group size exceeds a certain number of people. In these cases, there is no need for any additional tip.

Being close to the border with the Republic of Ireland, some businesses may also accept cash and card payments in euros. If you choose to pay in euros, where the option is available, it is worth checking the current rate of exchange to make sure you are getting the best deal.

MULTI-DAY ITINERARIES

The Mournes are the perfect choice for a hillwalking holiday in Ireland. However, the wide selection of fine walks makes it difficult to recommend one general multi-day itinerary to meet everyone's needs.

If you are planning a few days in the area, here are some suggestions:

Best of the Mournes

If you want to sample the very best walking opportunities in the Mournes, this selection of eight hand-picked routes is the ideal starting point for planning an itinerary. Each route features at least one best, one highest or one largest in the range:

- Route 1 – Tollymore Forest Park (best in woodland)
- Route 3 – Slieve Donard (highest summit) via Glen River (best river)
- Route 8 – Slieve Binnian (best big mountain)
- Route 12 – Silent Valley to Ben Crom Dam (best on road)
- Route 14 – Lough Shannagh (largest natural lake)
- Route 15 – Slieve Loughshannagh (best small mountain) and Doan (best big hill)
- Route 21 – Slievemartin (best in the west)
- Route 24 – Hen Mountain (best small hill)

The mountains of Mourne

According to the list of Irish Hewitts, there are 209 official mountain summits in Ireland, 14 of which are in the Mournes. If you want to bag all mountain summits in the range over a few days, there are numerous itineraries to choose from. Here is one option:

- Route 4 (with extension) – Slieve Donard, Slieve Commedagh and Chimney Rock Mountain
- Route 8 – Slieve Binnian and Slieve Binnian North Tor
- Route 11 – Cove Mountain and Slievelamagan
- Route 14 – Slieve Muck
- Route 20 – Eagle Mountain and Shanlieve
- Route 27 – Slieve Loughshannagh, Slieve Meelbeg, Slieve Meelmore and Slieve Bearnagh
- Alternatively, you could try one of the one-day versions of the Mourne Mountains Challenge (see theirelandwalkingguide.com/mourne-mountains-challenge).

The full Mournes

Experienced hillwalkers looking for a challenge and an unforgettable hillwalking holiday should consider the following itinerary:

- Routes 26 to 30 – five interconnected loops covering the Mourne Ultra (TMU). This five-day itinerary is a great way to experience most of the range's finest hillwalking and viewing opportunities. If you have fewer days available, and are up for an even bigger challenge, adjoining TMU loops can be linked together to form longer walks. Connection points are included in each loop's route description.
- Route 15 (partial) – an out-and-back detour to the summit of Doan (Route 15) when walking loop two of the Mourne Ultra (Route 27).
- Route 7 – a full circuit of the Annalong Valley Horseshoe.
- Route 12 – a day exploring Silent Valley.

Plan your own

Of course, you can also plan a bespoke itinerary of your own by browsing all routes and variations described in this book, selecting those which appeal most and can be fitted into your schedule. One route from this book per day is probably plenty, although multiple short out-and-back sections from different routes in the same day are also an option.

From Round Seefin, you can follow the wall (left) or the high line (right) (Route 7)

PRACTICAL INFORMATION

Winter in the Western Mournes (Routes 22 and 23)

The Mournes really are one of the best hillwalking areas in Ireland, if not THE best. Before setting off to explore, please consider the following practical information. This will help to make your day more enjoyable and more memorable for all the right reasons.

CLIMATE AND WEATHER

Ireland is one of the first European landmasses to receive weather systems from the Atlantic. These generally bring intermittent spells of rain at any time of year, and most rainfall occurs where they meet the mountain ranges along the west coast. Being on the east coast, the Mournes tend to receive less rain than western ranges. There are no defined wet or dry seasons in Ireland, so it is advisable to be prepared for rain at any time of year.

Ireland's summer falls during the months of June, July and August, when maximum daytime temperatures can reach about 25°C. Unfortunately, a dry summer is never guaranteed. Bear in mind that prolonged periods of wet weather during the summer months are not uncommon.

The Irish winter is during the months of December, January and February. On average, there might only be two or three days of significant snowfall during the year in low-lying areas. On higher ground, however, snow may remain for a few weeks.

Despite sharing the same latitudes as parts of Canada and Russia, Ireland experiences severe wintry conditions only occasionally; this is due to the Gulf Stream – a warm water current originating near Florida – which travels in a general north-east direction across the Atlantic. An extension of the Gulf Stream – the North Atlantic Drift – passes Western Europe, thereby maintaining Ireland's temperate climate.

DAYLIGHT HOURS

Located just north of 54° north, the Mournes experience a wide range of daylight hours throughout the year. The amount of daylight available needs to be considered before planning a long walk, otherwise there is an increased risk of finishing in darkness during the winter months. The winter solstice, or the shortest day, occurs every year on or near 21 December. It is the day on which the sun spends the shortest time above the horizon. In the Mournes, on the shortest day, the sun rises at about 8.40am GMT and sets at about 4.00pm GMT, providing almost 7hr 30min of daylight. The summer solstice, or the longest day, occurs every year on or near 21 June. It is the day on which the sun spends the longest time above the horizon. In the Mournes, on the longest day, the sun rises at about 4.50am BST and sets at about 10.00pm BST, providing more than 17hr of daylight.

CLOTHING AND EQUIPMENT

Always dress sensibly before setting off on a walk. In the Mournes, it is best to assume that it could rain on any day, so always carry a waterproof layer. Windproof clothes can significantly reduce the cooling effects of the wind on exposed summits. It is advisable to wear several thin layers of clothing rather than a few thick ones, as it provides you with options and more control over your body temperature. Never assume that it will be a hot day at the summit of Slieve Donard just because it is 25°C at sea level in Newcastle. It will be a few degrees colder up top, and a strong, chilling wind could easily bring temperatures down to single figures. It is best to be over-prepared than under-prepared. Always keep a hat and gloves in your rucksack, just in case. In the mountains, walking boots will provide support for your ankles when crossing uneven terrain. A good, well-fitting rucksack will prevent injury to your back and shoulders. For crossing boggy ground, waterproof gaiters are a worthy investment. Walking poles can make things easier by transferring some of the burden from your

legs to your arms, especially on longer walks – don't forget to shorten poles for uphill walking and extend them for downhill sections (or reposition your hands on longer grips).

Always carry spare food and plenty of water, especially on a hot day. When venturing into the hills or forests, always carry a map and compass – and know how to use them! A handheld GPS can be a useful backup device if you need to pinpoint your location in an emergency, but never rely solely on a GPS device or a phone app for navigation. In case the worst should happen, always pack a fully charged mobile phone – although it is worth bearing in mind that a clear signal is not guaranteed in remote locations.

In addition to extra water on hot sunny days, it is also a good idea to wear a sun hat and sunglasses. Apply suncream on any exposed skin pre-walk and reapply throughout the day as required. If you are planning to be out for a while, it is a good idea to carry some toilet paper and a plastic bag (you get the picture). Bring ALL waste home with you. Carrying a first aid kit stocked with in-date items is also encouraged. This advice is most applicable to the moderate, hard and very hard walks described in this book, and all may not apply to the easier low-level walks.

To help you find the start point of a walk, a smartphone app or in-car satnav can be useful.

Always carry a printed map and a magnetic compass when walking in the Mournes

MAPS

A paper map and a traditional magnetic compass are essential items in every hillwalker's backpack. These simple tools provide the most satisfying solution for route planning and on-route navigation. The hillwalker who can use these tools, and who does not rely on GPS to navigate, really is a skilled outdoor enthusiast.

Three published maps each cover the area of the Mourne Mountains and all the routes described in this book:

- Harvey Maps – 1:25,000 Superwalker series – Mourne Mountains
- Ordnance Survey of Northern Ireland – 1:50,000 Discoverer series – Sheet 29
- Ordnance Survey of Northern Ireland – 1:25,000 Activity series – Mournes including Slieve Croob

The route illustrations in this book are based on the Harvey map and are reproduced at a scale of 1:32,000.

See theirelandwalkingguide.com/mourne-mountains#RecommendedMaps.

ACCESS

Few Irish upland areas offer as much access to hillwalkers as the Mournes do. However, it is important to be aware that there are very few legal rights of access in the range and recreational walking is generally permitted through the goodwill of private and public landowners. Their collective goodwill is widely appreciated and supported by the local and wider hillwalking community.

The famous Mourne Wall encloses more than 9,000 acres of publicly owned land in the Eastern

Mournes and is owned by Northern Ireland Water. Of the 14 official mountain summits in the Mournes, 11 are either crossed or enclosed by 'the Wall'. Large chunks of publicly owned forestry around the edges of the range belong to the Northern Ireland Forest Service, while other areas of charity-owned mountainside and ancient woodland belong to the National Trust and the Woodland Trust. Between them, this extensive area of countryside provides abundant walking opportunities. Walkers are generally allowed to go wherever they please within these properties but are encouraged to stick to the established network of paths and tracks for safety and environmental reasons.

The Mourne Way is a long-distance waymarked trail linking the town of Newcastle in the north-east to the village of Rostrevor in the south-west and is a Quality Section of the Ulster Way. This route has been agreed by the Northern Ireland Environment Agency, Northern Ireland Forest Service, private landowners, and Newry, Mourne and Down District Council.

The public are also welcome to walk in many areas of privately owned high ground throughout the range where there has been a tradition of use. Permission to walk is generally indicated by the presence of stiles, which have been installed either by the local landowners or with their formal approval. It is worth pointing out that there are no legal rights of access on the higher ground of the Mournes generally, and permission to walk in these areas is entirely at the relevant landowner's discretion.

Access to higher ground in the Mournes can be made via tracks and paths leading from the numerous car parks dotted around the range. Most of these access routes cross private land, but the presence of a car park with an unhindered path or track leading towards high ground generally indicates that there is at least some kind of informal arrangement in place that allows walkers to proceed. Always keep an eye out for signage placed by landowners and obey any declared instructions.

Most of the routes described in this book pass only through land where there is a widely accepted long tradition of use by walkers. Progress along these routes is facilitated by clear paths and tracks with gates and stiles installed. Please note, however, that a couple of locations on the more challenging routes may require you to cross fences where gates and stiles are currently not present. By their nature, these routes are more suited to capable, highly experienced hillwalkers, so are unlikely to attract high levels of footfall. Even so, stiles at these locations would be welcome additions.

WAYMARKINGS

There are very few waymarked trails in the Mournes. The most notable of these is the Mourne Way, which

Waymarker post in Tollymore Forest Park (Routes 1, 2 and 26)

connects the town of Newcastle and the village of Rostrevor. Other shorter waymarked trails, ranging from a few hundred metres to several kilometres, can also be found in Tollymore Forest Park, Rostrevor Forest, Kilbroney Park and Silent Valley Mountain Park.

The Mourne Wall runs alongside many of the most popular high-level route sections, where it has become a very handy navigational aid. As such, it could be regarded as a type of waymarking.

ETIQUETTE

When in the countryside, use your common sense and be on your best behaviour at all times. This makes the countryside a more pleasant place to be, and helps to maintain good relationships between walkers, landowners and other land users.

Leave no trace

This is fairly self-explanatory: do not leave any rubbish in the countryside. Take your rubbish home or dispose of it carefully in a public bin. Do not leave food waste at a lunch stop or picnic site. Apple cores, orange peel and banana skins take longer to decompose than you might think.

Prevent fires

Wild fires can have disastrous effects on the plants and animals living in the Mournes. Avoid starting fires in the first place, especially in dry conditions. Consider precooked food and boiled water in insulated flasks rather than using a stove or lighting a campfire in the wild. Do not leave glass behind that could focus the sun's rays. If you really must undo the benefits of fresh mountain air by smoking, bring your butts home. If you see a wild fire, report it immediately: call 999 or 112 and ask for the fire service.

Livestock and dogs

Never take a dog into an environment where you are likely to encounter livestock at close distance. Even when on a lead, a dog can worry livestock, which may be enough to cause damage to unborn lambs and calves. There is also the additional risk of walkers with dogs coming under attack from livestock, especially from bulls and protective cows with newborn calves. Even without a dog, never enter a space containing a bull. Other male livestock, including sheep, can also be protective of their territory. Never assume that you can outrun a bull or ram – they move surprisingly quickly!

If walking a dog, you must consider ground-nesting birds living and rearing their chicks among the heather, sometimes only a short distance from paths and tracks. By always keeping your dog under control (i.e. on a lead), you are helping to protect these vulnerable little creatures.

Stiles, gates and fences

Always remember that gates and fences have been put in place for practical reasons that far outweigh a walker's need for unhindered access through farmland. Fences are there to allow farmers to maintain control of livestock. Climbing over fences can cause damage that may allow livestock to enter fields they are not supposed to be in. Never forget that farming is a meticulously planned business and you are the end user of its produce on a daily basis. The industry deserves full respect.

Before attempting to cross a fence, look for a stile first. If there is a stile, use it. Keep an eye out for rocks close to fences; these may have been placed there by the landowner to aid crossing. If there's no stile, look for a gate. If the gate is open, pass through it and leave it open. If the gate is closed but can be opened, open it, pass through, then close it behind you.

Obey instructional signs (e.g. 'Please close the gate'). If the gate is locked and sturdy, climb over at the hinged end to avoid damage. If there is no alternative but to climb a fence, cross at a sturdy post. Place your hands on the top horizontal surface of the post and apply as much of your weight as possible down through the post's axis to minimise any burden imposed on the wire strands or mesh. Take extra care if the post is wet.

The walks described in this book have been designed to keep the need for fence crossings to an absolute minimum. Please note, however, that a small number of fences without gates or stiles are unavoidably encountered in some of the more challenging routes. By their nature, these routes will not appeal to most hillwalkers and will attract only the elite few.

Say 'Hello'

When crossing farmland, always acknowledge passers-by you encounter – there is a good chance that one of them could be the landowner. A friendly 'hello' (or a wave from a distance) can make all the difference between being asked to get off the land and being allowed to proceed across it. If instructed to leave by the landowner for any reason, always respect his/her wishes and leave immediately without protest.

Noise

People go walking in the Mournes for different reasons. Whatever your reason, it is always worth remembering that most people go there to enjoy some well-earned peace and quiet. For them, walking in the Mournes is what they do to escape their busy lives for a few hours. It is their chance to immerse themselves in the sounds of nature and to get the headspace they need for contemplation. This is their precious 'me time', so please minimise any acoustic intrusions.

Keep your voice down. The only time you need to shout in the Mournes is when you get into difficulty and require assistance. If walking with a group, the people you are chatting with are likely to be close by, so there is no real need for others to hear you half a kilometre away.

Keep your sounds to yourself. If you must listen to music, news or podcasts while hillwalking, use headphones or earphones.

Consider not flying your drone in the Mournes. Is it really worth spoiling other people's quiet time for a few likes on your social media?

STAYING SAFE

You are responsible for your own safety and for the safety of those you are leading, so know your limits and the limits of your group. Only choose walks you are fit enough to undertake on the day and for which you have the necessary skills. Each of the 30 routes described in this book has been graded as easy, moderate, hard or very hard (more about these grades in the 'Using this guide' section).

If you are new to hillwalking, throwing yourself into a challenging route straightaway is not advisable. Start off with easy and moderate walks first and progress from there. Walking with your hillwalker friends or joining a local walking club are great ways to gain experience in the hills. Attending a mountain-skills course is also a highly recommended investment.

Bring a printed map and compass

Relying solely on a phone app or GPS device for navigation is not advisable. Always carry a printed map (listed in the 'Maps' section), a traditional magnetic compass and a copy of this book when walking in the Mournes.

Tell someone where you are going

Always let a responsible person know where you are going and give them clear details of your intended route in advance. If you are following a walk described in this book, lend them your spare copy and tell them which route you are taking. Keep them informed of your progress throughout the day. This will allow them to provide detailed positional information to the Mourne Mountain Rescue Team (Mourne MRT) if anything should happen to you on the hills.

What to do in an emergency

Stop walking if you sustain an injury, become lost or are too tired to continue. Rest and take a moment to assess your situation. Members of the Mourne MRT are always on call if you need assistance, and can be contacted by calling the emergency number 999 and asking for the police (112 connects to the same service). They will pass you through to a member of the Mourne MRT. Always carry a fully charged phone for this scenario and minimise its use during your walk to ensure it can be used when needed.

Mourne MRT (mournemrt.org) operates as a charity and does not charge for call-outs. Hillwalkers visiting the Mournes are encouraged to make a donation to help cover the team's running costs, especially after a call-out. As well as one-off payments, regular visitors to the Mournes can also set up recurring monthly, quarterly or annual donations.

what3words

This is a very useful app (what3words.com) to have on your phone in the event of an emergency. Its positioning system uses a 3m x 3m virtual grid that covers the entire planet. Each square on the grid has a unique three-word reference, which is easier to relay than a long string of numerical digits. The what3words positioning system is recognised worldwide by emergency services, including Mourne MRT.

An icy Crannoge Quarry (Routes 4 and 5)

BACKGROUND INFORMATION

Taking a short out-and-back detour along the top of Ben Crom Reservoir's dam wall (Routes 10, 11 and 12)

This section is not required for planning or practical purposes, but provide an additional layer of information that may be of special interest to walkers exploring the Mournes.

GEOLOGY

Six hundred million years ago, the northern half of Ireland, along with the northern half of Great Britain, started out near the South Pole, wedged between what would eventually become North America's north-east coast and South America's west coast. The opening of the Iapetus Ocean sent the northern halves north, still attached to North America. Meanwhile, the southern halves of Ireland and Great Britain broke away from Gondwanaland to begin their own journey across the Iapetus.

About 400 million years ago, the northern and southern halves of Ireland and Great Britain docked, closing the Iapetus Ocean and locking in the seven terranes that now form the geological base of Ireland. The area that would eventually become the Mourne Mountains was on one called the Southern Uplands–Down–Longford Terrane. Over the next 300 million years, continents around the world continued to collide and rip apart while new oceans opened up and old ones closed. Ireland moved around the world, carried by these tectonic movements, sinking beneath the waves on occasions and rising again along the way, building up layers of sedimentary rock as it went.

Around 60 million years ago, as North America was splitting away from Europe, creating the North Atlantic Ocean, the crust thinned beneath Ireland to produce massive local volcanic events, causing vast amounts of lava to flood what is now County Antrim.

Around 56 million years ago, bubbles of magma were on the rise beneath County Down. However, their upward journey was blocked by the overlying sedimentary rocks, which were forced upwards by the pressure underneath. As a result, the trapped magma bubbles were forced to cool slowly underground over a long period of time, which allowed their minerals to develop into large crystals of felspar, mica and quartz. This process repeated in pulses, producing a slightly different variation of granite each time. Two distinct areas of granite formed: the Eastern Mourne Complex and the Western Mourne Complex. Their boundary was roughly the same as today's recognised topographical split between the Western and Eastern Mournes.

Over the last 100 millennia, ice ages have progressively scraped away the overlying sedimentary rock to expose the underlying granite. It should be noted that the Mourne Mountains are not composed entirely of granite. For example, the bedrock along parts of the main ridge, near Rostrevor and around the Spelga Dam catchment area, includes sandstone, mudstone, conglomerates and greywacke. This would also have been exposed during the ice ages.

The advancing and retreating ice sheets carved the U-shaped valleys we see in the Mournes today. The moving ice ground the rock beneath it into sands and gravels that were deposited along the way. We can see evidence of this along some of the rivers in the Mournes and the surrounding areas where moraines have formed. A good example of this can be seen on Route 6, where Annalong River has cut its own path through glacial sands and gravels. Other evidence of local glacial activity includes the Cloughmore, commonly known as the 'Big Stone'. This 50-tonne granite erratic, perched on 400-million-year-old sandstone at the southern end of the Mournes' main ridge, high above the village of Rostrevor, is believed to have been carried there from Scotland by ice 10,000 years ago.

Throughout the Mournes, the overlying drift deposits are primarily peat. The depth of this varies widely across the region, from zero, where the bedrock is exposed, to several metres deep along valley floors and on some higher areas surrounded by summits, where the topography is flat enough for the peat to build up. On summits where the bedrock is not exposed, you can expect a very shallow layer of peat, perhaps only a few centimetres, but enough for grasses and heathers to grow.

In recognition of their geological value, in 2023 the Mournes were included in the new Mourne Gullion Strangford UNESCO Global Geopark.

WILDLIFE

At first glance, the Mourne Mountains can appear rather lifeless. If this is the case, it is either winter or you are not looking hard enough. When out walking, stop every once in a while to have a good look and listen around you. The sights and sounds of nature will reveal themselves soon enough.

Animals

The most visible animals in the Mournes are sheep, cows and us humans. The most common wild animals you will see are birds. With a lack of trees on the higher ground, small birds will build their nests among the low-growing plants. These ground-nesting birds are at particular risk from predators, and you will often see and hear them in defensive mode when you pass close to their nests, which is one of the reasons dogs, where permitted, must ALWAYS be kept on leads. A dog on the loose could easily discover a nest full of chicks and cause irreversible, but avoidable, damage.

Larger birds, usually crows and ravens, journey up to the summits from their lowland homes. Raptors, including buzzards and peregrine falcons, are also a common sight as they hover above their prey before swooping down for the kill. Keep your ears open for their warning calls during late spring and early summer. They are known to occasionally swoop at humans who get too close to their nests.

Red squirrel in Tollymore Forest Park

Wild deer also live in the Mournes, but you are unlikely to see them as they tend to stay hidden in the low-level forests. Tollymore Forest Park supports a controlled population of up to 200, but even there they are hard to spot. The forest park is also home to a fluctuating population of red squirrels. However, any squirrels you see in the forests of Mourne are more likely to be of the grey variety.

Insects are widespread throughout the Mournes from March until September; these include butterflies, dragonflies, bees, beetles and those pesky biting midges and horseflies. It is worth carrying insect repellent and a fine-mesh head net during the summer, especially on calm days, just in case the wee biters are out and about. Avoid disturbing any plant life where they otherwise tend to hang out.

There is a good chance you will see some frogs hopping about, although they usually remain very still in order to blend in with their surroundings. Frog spawn season is in February and March, so try not to disturb shallow ponds and ditches during this time. You may spot the occasional newt or even a lizard in the Mournes if you keep your eyes

Flowering gorse between Tollymore Forest Park and Donard Forest (Route 2)

peeled. Thankfully, there are no snakes, so a big thank you to Saint Patrick for that!

Plants

Most of the trees in the Mournes can be found on the lower slopes in state-owned forests, the largest of which are Tollymore Forest Park, Rostrevor Forest, Donard Forest and Annalong Wood. These mostly comprise non-native coniferous species planted to be harvested for their long, straight timber. Pockets of native deciduous trees are also present within these forests, most notably in Tollymore. In October and November, their leaves turn vibrant shades of yellow, brown and red as they prepare for winter.

Forest floors comprise a variety of plants, including grasses, ferns and brambles. Tollymore is a good place to see spectacular bluebell displays during May. Gorse is a common sight in the Mournes; they flower throughout the year but most widely during spring and early summer, when they give off a sweet coconut-like scent.

On the higher ground, trees are few and far between. Here the dominant plant species is heather, which turns the landscape purple when it flowers in summer. Bog cotton, commonly found on peat, develops its conspicuous white tufty seed heads in late spring and summer. Walkers are advised to stick to established paths as much as possible to protect the delicate plant life.

BUILT HERITAGE

The most notable human-made structures visible in the Mourne Mountains today are associated with water collection and storage. As well as the Mourne Wall, there are four reservoirs in the range: Fofanny (1906), Silent Valley (1933), Ben Crom (1957) and Spelga (1957). Lough Shannagh, the largest natural lake in the Mournes, also acts as a feeder reservoir for Silent Valley. A low embankment, constructed across the lough's outflow at its north-east corner, has artificially raised the surface level by about a metre. Water from Annalong Valley has also been diverted into neighbouring Silent Valley through the 3.5km-long Binnian Tunnel (1952), which passes almost directly under the summit of Slieve Binnian.

Most of the catchment area of Silent Valley Reservoir and its various tributaries is owned by Northern Ireland Water, whose main property in the Mournes is enclosed by the Mourne Wall (often referred to in this book as 'the Wall'). This dry-stone wall took 18 years to construct (1904–1922) and is 31.4km (19.5 miles) long. It links 10 official summits and passes within 300m of 3 others. From a hillwalking perspective, the Wall is the single most-visited built structure in the entire range. Many popular walks in the Eastern Mournes follow, cross or meet the Wall at some point, and it features in 21 of the 30 primary routes described in this book.

How the Mournes became a major water source for Belfast and County Down is an interesting and epic endeavour that took over a century to fully unfold. Surprisingly, this is the first walking guidebook to give the story the attention it deserves, identifying and explaining the various related historical sites in route descriptions; these include reservoirs, air wells, tunnels, overground sections of water pipeline and staff housing. Further information is available at theirelandwalkingguide.com/mourne-water-projects.

Other examples of local built heritage include Batt's Wall in the Western Mournes and a restored ice house beside Glen River, which served Donard Lodge – a former hotel demolished in 1966. Gated entrances, bridges and other historical structures are also located throughout Tollymore Forest Park.

Old granite quarry workings can also be found in the upper Bloody Bridge River valley, where remnants of an old railway line lead down off Chimney Rock Mountain. Other quarries can also be seen on the slopes of Thomas's Mountain and Millstone Mountain, from where stone was transported down to the harbour on bogies along what is now known as the Granite Trail.

Meelmore (right) and Meelbeg (left) from corner of the Mourne Wall on Slieve Bearnagh (Routes 13, 17, 25 and 27)

USING THIS GUIDE

Walking alongside Ben Crom River toward the 511m col (Meelbeg pictured) (Route 15)

This is the most comprehensive guidebook to the Mourne Mountains ever produced. It has been set out in a way that allows readers to split routes into shorter walks or combine them with neighbouring routes to form longer ones: shortcut turn-offs and connection points are identified in the descriptions as they occur. The 30 primary walks and 70+ variations described give readers more than 100 unique routes to choose from and form a solid base for planning hundreds of bespoke walks in the Mournes.

The routes have been grouped into four main sections: Eastern Mournes, Western Mournes, Mourne Wall and Mourne Ultra.

Each of the first two sections focuses on one half of the Mourne Mountains either side of the main north–south road, which splits the range pretty much straight down the middle. The walks in the Eastern Mournes and Western Mournes sections of the book vary from easy lower-level rambles to challenging high-level horseshoe ridge walks. Each route typically focuses on a specific forest, a single summit, a small group of neighbouring summits or a valley.

The third section of the book focuses on the range's longest-established hillwalking challenge – the Mourne Wall Challenge – and the impressive 31.4km (19.5 mile) structure upon which it is based. Normally undertaken over one or two days, this is one of Ireland's most epic and best-known hillwalking challenges.

The final section of the book introduces the newly created, never-before-published, Mourne Ultra – a monster of a challenge combining the Mourne Way and the Mourne High Ridge Traverse (HRT) routes. The Mourne Ultra is presented in this book as a set of five interconnected one-day loops that together cover the full challenging route. This format opens it up to all hillwalkers who can navigate with confidence. The five loops are set out in a way that allow hill runners and experienced challenge hillwalkers to combine them over fewer days (or even a single day!).

For each primary route, an information box provides a grade, the overall distance, the total ascent/descent and an indicative time for the walk. Figures related to variations are stated in the Options line, with a minus value indicating a reduction and a plus value indicating an increase on the overall route figures.

QR codes to a Google Maps pin locating every car park in this guide are contained in Appendix A.

Grades

Based on their total length, total ascent, types of terrain covered, path/track conditions and navigation, all routes have been graded as follows:

- Easy – suitable for all recreational walkers
- Moderate – suitable for all hillwalkers with basic navigation skills
- Hard – suitable for regular hillwalkers with good fitness and navigation skills
- Very hard – suitable for challenge hillwalkers with excellent fitness and navigation skills

The primary routes in this book comprise 1 easy, 11 moderate, 11 hard, and 7 very hard walks. Additional easy and moderate out-and-back options are possible by extracting initial or final sections from the more challenging routes, where you decide when to turn and retrace your steps to the start point.

Distances

The distances provided in this book have been taken from accurate GPX tracks and are displayed in kilometres.

Ascent/descent

The ascent/descent values provided in this book have been obtained from accurate GPX tracks and are displayed in metres.

Times

All route times provided are indicative only and do not include stops. They have been calculated using Naismith's Rule, allowing 15min for every 1km walked plus an additional 10min for every 100m of ascent. Calculated times are rounded up to the nearest 15min. It must be noted that hillwalkers move at different speeds and should adjust the numbers accordingly to match their own walking pace.

Ascending the Yellow Water River gorge (Routes 22 and 29)

Alternate start/finish locations

All alternate start/finish points are marked on the route maps and mentioned in route descriptions. A note will also appear at a point near the end of the main route description, reminding you to continue past the main start/finish. When using an alternate start/finish, remember to jump back to the corresponding point near the start of the main route description and follow directions from there.

CICERONE APP AND GPX FILES

This book is available in the Cicerone app on your phone, where you can view GPS-enabled maps that can be downloaded for offline navigation, check route details and local points of interest and plan your adventure with confidence. GPX files are also available to download. See cicerone.co.uk/1262.

FURTHER INFORMATION

Only so much information can be included in a guidebook. For this reason, a selection of useful trusted links can be found in Appendix C at the back of this book. Some of these links have already been mentioned in the introduction, but they have also been brought together in their own dedicated 'Useful links' pages along with QR codes, allowing you to access the information you need much more quickly using your smartphone.

EASTERN MOURNES

Glen River valley (Routes 2 and 3)

Stretching from the Dundrum Bay coastline just south of Newcastle to the main north–south B27 Moyad Road, the Eastern Mournes are the most popular and best-catered-for hillwalking area in the whole of Ireland. This is due to the large areas of publicly- and charity-owned land making up most of the Eastern Mournes, throughout which there is a long-established and widely accepted tradition of recreational walking. Access across much of the surrounding privately owned land is also permitted, thanks to the ongoing goodwill of landowners and the trustees of historical estates.

Of the Mourne Mountains' 14 official mountains, 12 are in the Eastern Mournes – including the 11 highest – and its most popular attractions include Tollymore Forest Park, Silent Valley and the summits of Slieve Donard, Slieve Binnian and Doan. Outside of these, you can expect to encounter fewer people. The 18 routes presented in this section lie entirely within the Eastern Mournes.

Hore's Bridge spans the Spinkwee/Cascade River, a tributary of the Shimna (Routes 1, 2 and 26)

ROUTE 1

Tollymore Forest Park highlights

Start/finish	Tollymore car park
Time	3hr 30min
Distance	11.5km
Ascent/descent	315m
Grade	Easy
Options	White Fort extension (+0.5km/+15m/+15min); omitting Drinns Trail (-4.8km/-160m/-1hr 30min)
Bus stop	Year-round local Ulsterbus services and the Mourne Rambler summer bus service stop in Bryansford village

Usually referred to as 'Tollymore', these 630 hectares of woodland became a forest park in 1955. Native deciduous trees, including beech, ash, birch and oak, can be found in its arboretum and close to Shimna River. The rest of the forest park is mainly populated by coniferous species. The Shimna can be crossed at several points as it flows through Tollymore, including at the 300-year-old Old Bridge and two stepping-stone weirs.

Photo opportunities are in abundance, so keep your camera ready. If you are lucky, you might even spot one of the 100+ fallow deer who reside among the trees. This route combines the best parts of the waymarked River, Mountain and Drinns Trails.

From the information panel at the south-west corner of Tollymore car park, follow the red arrow waymarkers west along the path. The first section of this route follows the River Trail (red arrows), so keep an eye out for markers on posts. Continue to follow the path as it branches left downhill with azaleas on both sides. As you begin to descend through the azaleas, take a final look at the Mourne peaks ahead of you. The next 2km of walking will make you temporarily forget they are even there.

After 100m, pass under **Horn Bridge** (built 1770), an ornate single-arched stone bridge, beyond which the path splits with two options separated by a stream. Both walled paths converge 60m further down the slope, so you can choose either. Proceed south downhill for 70m to a junction. Continue straight ahead for 30m to meet another path with Shimna River flowing alongside it.

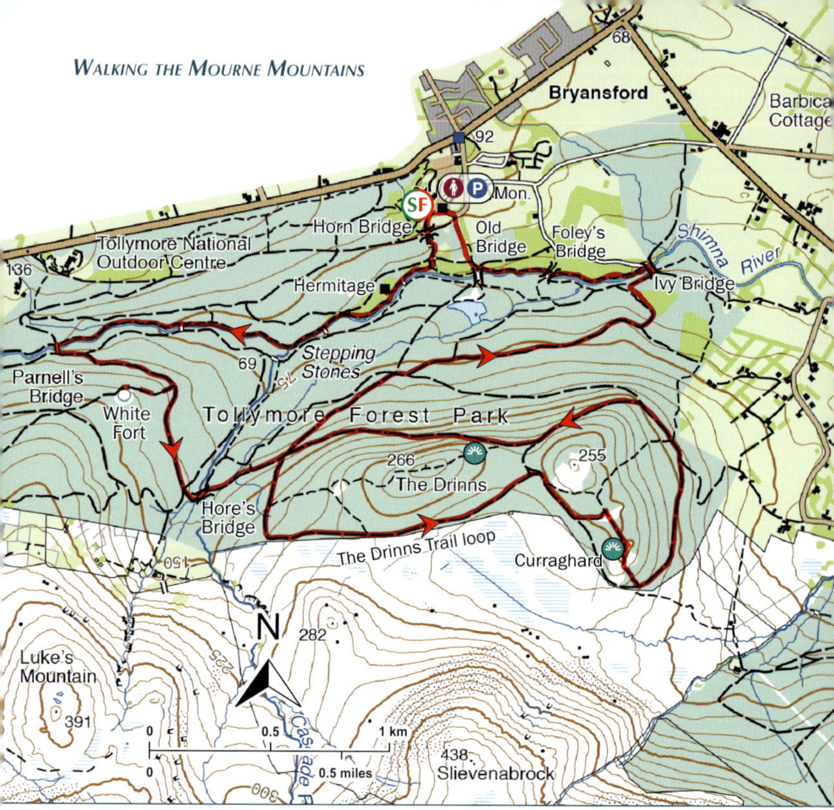

Turn right, as directed by the red arrow, and follow the river upstream through mature deciduous woodland. Stay on this path for 200m until you come to the **Hermitage**. Climb the stone steps to walk through this curious little stone structure overlooking a small gorge. Ascend the stone steps on the other side to rejoin the main path. Turn left to follow this path high above the waterfalls and rock pools below. After 500m, come to the first of two sets of purpose-built stepping stones.

The **stepping stones** are effectively weirs, with the gaps along the top allowing water to flow through as people walk across. The overspilling water produces a mini waterfall between each stone, making this a popular photography spot. Feel free to carefully cross the stones to the south bank before returning to the north. Take extra care if the stones are wet or covered with leaves. Avoid if icy or covered in snow.

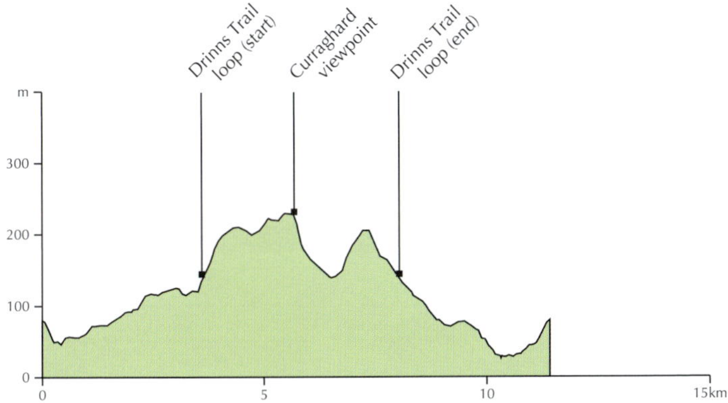

Continue upstream for 1.1km, with Shimna River still on your left, passing bridges and the second set of stepping stones until you meet a wide forest track at **Parnell's Bridge** (built 1842). Turn left, as directed by the red arrow, along this track to cross the bridge. At a track junction just beyond the bridge, take a left and head east. After 110m, bear right along the higher track at a fork. Keep on this for 400m to come to a sidetrack signposted 'White Fort'. If taking the short out-and-back detour to White Fort, turn right here.

One of two sets of stepping stones crossing the Shimna

Curraghard on the Drinns Trail offers views over Newcastle and Dundrum Bay

Ignore the sign and follow the main track as it bends right. Up ahead, the Mourne peaks now come back into view as you head south for 450m to a junction with waymarkers for the Mourne Way. Ignore the red arrow pointing left and proceed straight ahead. You have now joined the Mountain Trail (black arrows) and the Mourne Way. Follow the track as it curves left to cross Spinkwee River at **Hore's Bridge**. Continue on the main track for 420m, ignoring all side paths, to another junction with a selection of waymarkers. If omitting the Drinns Trail, turn left here.

The next stage is the 4.8km Drinns Trail loop (black 1 arrows). Turn right at the junction to follow the black 1 arrow and the Mourne Way uphill. The track continues to rise as it curves left to follow the forest park's southern boundary wall. It descends slightly before rising again to meet a couple of other tracks on the left. Ignore these and follow the main track as it curves right. Ignore a path on the left marked 'To the summit' and continue along the track until a black 1 arrow directs you left up another side path.

Take this and follow it uphill to reach a crossroads of paths. This is the highest point on the route. Turn right here and proceed through the trees to reach **Curraghard viewpoint** with stone seating. The view from here takes in the mountains to the south and Newcastle town to the east with Dundrum Bay beyond.

Take the grassy path south from the viewpoint and descend carefully through trees and over some rocks to rejoin the main track. Turn left along the track and follow as it curves left.

Ignore all side paths, including the one where the Mourne Way departs to the right, to arrive at a fork in the track. Take the track on the right, as directed by the black 1 arrow, and proceed downhill. Views over the forest on the right stretch to the village of Castlewellan and to the Dromara Hills beyond. Close out the Drinns Trail by arriving back at the junction you passed through earlier. Turn right here to resume the Mountain Trail (black arrows without the 1).

The remainder of the route follows this trail. Black arrows guide you east for 2km to Shimna River at **Ivy Bridge** (built 1780). Cross the bridge and turn left at the other side. Follow the river west for 750m, passing **Foley's Bridge** (built 1787) and a stunning section of gorge to reach a junction beside **Old Bridge** (built 1726). Turn right here and ascend a path for 280m to finish at **Tollymore car park**.

Other walks in Tollymore Forest Park

The main route described above combines sections from the various waymarked trails in Tollymore. You can stick to one of the waymarked trails if you prefer. These are all marked on a free map, which you can request from a staff member upon arrival. The trails are also displayed on an information panel close to the start point. A photo of this would be a handy reference along the waymarked trails. At the time of writing, all the maps provided on site were oriented with north pointing down the page, so please be aware of this.

BRYANSFORD HOUSE AND TOLLYMORE PARK

Between about 1730 and 1952, the lower section of the present-day car park was occupied by a Georgian mansion called Bryansford House (Tollymore Park House on historical mapping). Over the centuries, the house and its surrounding land (then known as Tollymore Park) passed down through successive generations of Hamiltons (Earls of Clanbrassil and Lady Clanbrassil) and Jocelyns (Earls of Roden). During this time, Bryansford House was modified and enlarged around its central courtyard, and the wide variety of follies and bridges we see today were built in the grounds.

The upper section of the present-day car park was a walled garden back then. Much of its enclosing wall still surrounds the car park, next to some of the original outbuildings, including a stable block resembling a church complete with spire. Tollymore Park was sold as forestry to the Ministry of Agriculture in 1930 and 1941, and Bryansford House was demolished in 1952. The park became a forest park three years later.

ROUTE 2

Tollymore Forest Park and the Brandy Pad

Start/finish	Donard car park, Newcastle
Alt starts/finishes	Trassey car park and Meelmore Lodge car park
Time	6hr 30min
Distance	20.2km
Ascent/descent	835m
Grade	Moderate
Options	Via Meelmore Lodge (+0.8km/+25m/+15min); via Commedagh (+0.9km/+190m/+30min)
Bus stops	Year-round local Ulsterbus services and Mourne Rambler summer bus service stop 100m from Donard car park. Mourne Rambler stops 1.4km from Trassey car park.

This woodland and upland loop from the bustling seaside town of Newcastle passes through Donard Forest and Tollymore Forest Park, follows an old smugglers' route and passes over two of the Mourne's finest cols. Paths are clear and relatively flat along most of the route. The only difficult section is a steep pathless ascent through a boulder field on the approach to Hare's Gap.

From the south-west corner of Donard car park, at the entrance to the overflow car park, head south-west alongside a tarmac road. A short distance after passing a private access on the left, enter Donard Park. Continue south-west, with a tall perimeter fence on your left, for 150m to an information map displaying the forest's trails.

Follow the path into Donard Forest. To your left, you will hear Glen River. Take care when walking over the exposed tree roots along this section, especially in wet conditions. After 150m, arrive at a junction of forest tracks beside the arched **Donard Bridge**. Turn right here to take the surfaced access road uphill. Watch out for passing cars. You will soon come to a junction with a 'Greenhill YMCA' sign pointing to the right. Follow this sign and proceed west-north-west along the avenue, past the various buildings and outdoor activity apparatus.

Continue straight ahead, keeping the large buildings on your left and ignoring all bends and turn-offs, to arrive at a gate and metal barrier. Walk past the barrier and follow the forest track straight ahead. Come to a fork after 730m. Keep left

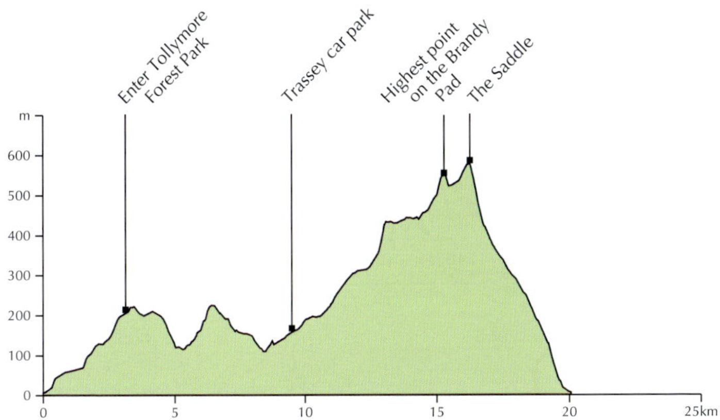

and ignore all turn-offs for 830m until you reach a junction with a metal barrier. Pass the barrier and turn right along the track for 130m, ignoring a barriered track on the left, to arrive at the gated entrance to a long single-storey building. This is marked as '**Shepherd's Lodge**' on historical maps.

Bend right with the track and head north for 40m to a metal gate in a stone wall. If the gate is closed, follow the path to the right to a nearby pedestrian gate close to a metal security fence. Pass through the gate, continue along the path and turn right to rejoin the track. A structure behind the metal security fence to your right here is one of 97 air wells dotted along the Mourne Conduit – a historical water supply line from Silent Valley to Belfast.

Leaving Donard Forest behind, follow the track north for 100m through gorse bushes and over a stream to a junction. Take a left here then an immediate left to pick up a rough path heading west. As it curves right, you will see the south-east corner of Tollymore Forest Park directly ahead. This is where you are aiming for. The path through jaggy gorse splits and remerges to arrive at the forest park's boundary wall after 420m. Bear left, keeping the wall on your right, and follow it west for 500m initially, curving right before straightening north-west to a corner in the boundary wall.

Pass through a gap in the wall here to enter Tollymore Forest Park. Take the path curving right to pass through a collapsed section of an adjoining wall. Follow this path north uphill for 50m through the trees to meet a forest track. Turn left along the track. From here, until instructed otherwise, you are following Newcastle Way and Mourne Way markers. Ignoring all right turns, follow the track bending left to descend west. The boundary wall comes in close on the left for a while before the track descends

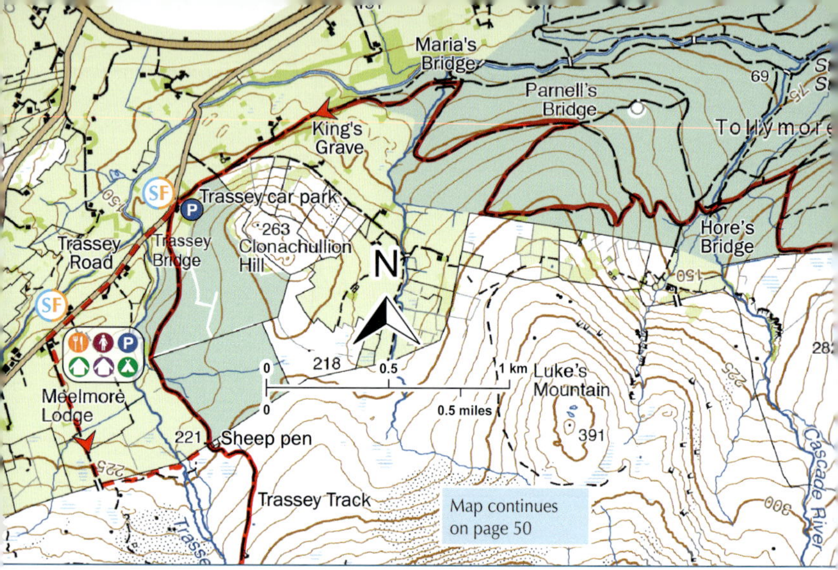

Map continues on page 50

again more steeply and bends right, heading north. After 1.7km, come to a major track junction with various waymarkers.

Take a sharp left here to follow a forest track west-southwest for 420m to **Hore's Bridge**. Continue across this and curve right to another major junction with waymarkers 70m further along. Take a sharp left and follow the track zigzagging west uphill. You have now departed from the Mourne Way but are still following the Newcastle Way. After 900m, level out to pass over a crest, then descend for 280m to a viewpoint where the track bends right. Take the bend and descend north-east for 560m to a crossroads of tracks. Take a sharp left here.

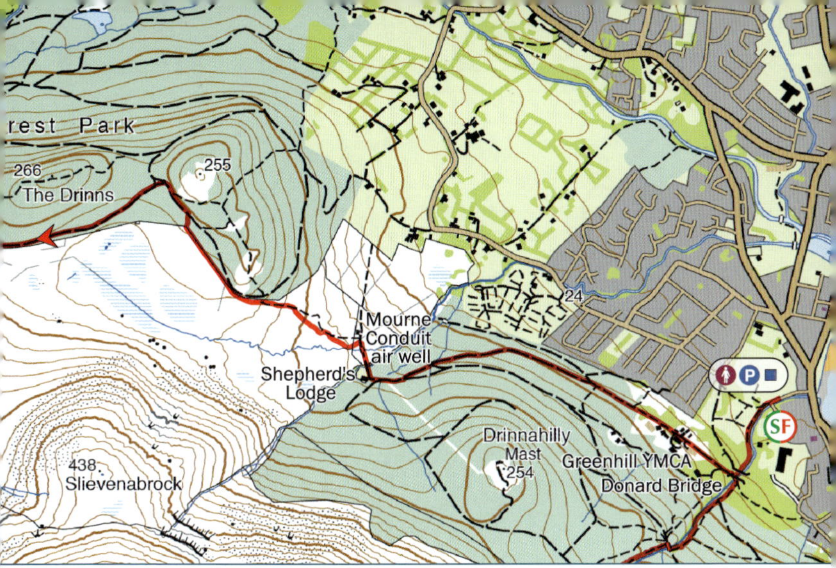

Follow the track west, curving north-east for 1km, ignoring all side paths, to a major track junction. Leave the Newcastle Way by turning left here to rejoin the Mourne Way, heading west. Follow this path west past the **King's Grave** and avoiding all turn-offs. Pass through several boundaries, using the gates and stiles provided. After 1.3km, meet Trassey Road close to Trassey car park. This can be used as an alternate start/finish. Turn left here to follow the road uphill for a few metres to where it bends right.

Variant route to Meelmore Lodge

To make a detour via Meelmore Lodge, bear right here and follow Trassey Road for 0.7km. Meelmore Lodge can serve as an alternate start/finish or halfway lunch stop. It is worth checking the opening hours of the on-site Hare's Gap Bistro in advance. From the rear of the bistro, follow the track south-south-east for 600m to a dry-stone wall. Cross the stile and turn left. Follow the Mourne Way east-north-east for 500m, alongside the wall and across a couple of streams, to join the main route near a stone **sheep pen**.

Main route continues

Follow the Mourne Way through the gate on the left at this bend. There is also an option to cross the wall to the left of the gate, using the built-in stone steps. You are now on Trassey Track. Continue south along the track for 1.1km, passing through a couple of pedestrian gates, to enter open mountain

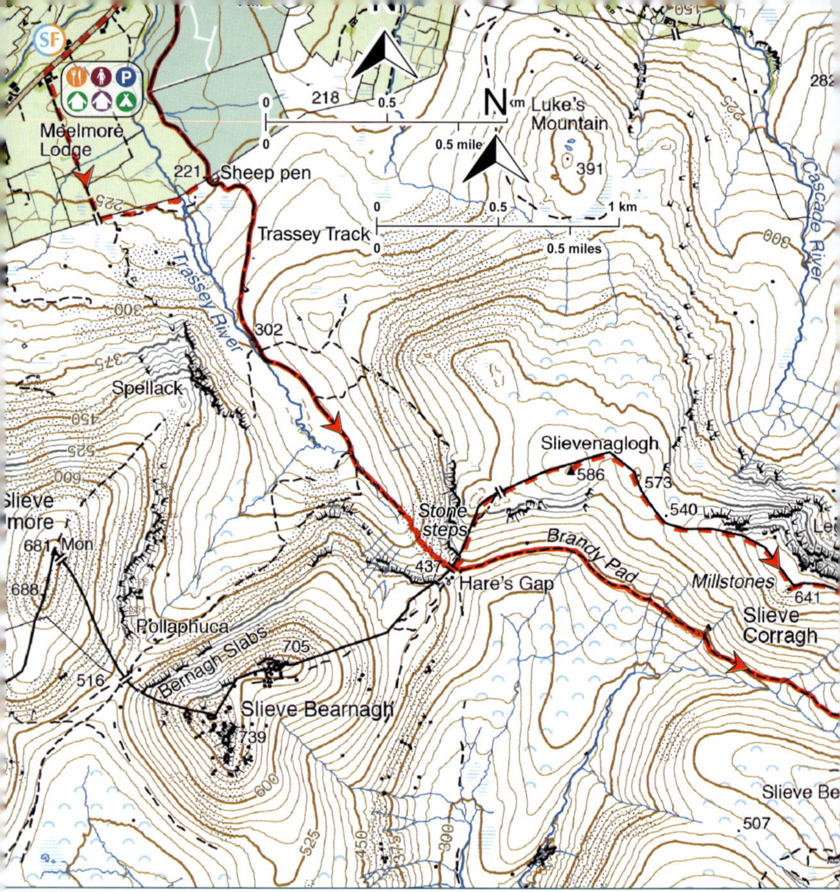

land beside a stone **sheep pen**. Leave the Mourne Way here. Pass the sheep pen on your left and continue along Trassey Track as it gently ascends the Trassey River valley.

With Spellack's cliffs on your right, proceed towards the dramatic steep-sided col of Hare's Gap directly ahead. Stick to the track, avoiding all turn-offs. After 1.5km, ford a shallow stream, then keep left at two forks in the track. As the valley narrows, the track splits into faint paths that all lead steeply through rough bouldery ground. Take care along this 500m section, especially if the ground is wet. Choose your own path south-east, keeping close to the centreline, to meet the Mourne Wall at **Hare's Gap** (437m). Cross the stile.

Variant route alongside the Mourne Wall

For a higher-level diversion, turn left to ascend a stepped path steeply through rocks. Follow a fine section of the Wall east to a stone shelter near the summit of **Slieve Commedagh** (765m). The summit cairn is just 270m to the north-east of here if you fancy the short out-and-back detour. Continue straight along the Wall, past the shelter, and descend south-east to the **Saddle** (583m).

Main route continues

Directly ahead lie the Silent Valley and the central Mournes. Turn left here to pick up the Brandy Pad, ignoring the stepped path ascending steeply through rocks to the left of it. Follow the Brandy Pad east, curving south-east for 2.2km as it contours conspicuously around the southern slopes of Slievenaglogh to a 553m col. Continue straight for 600m, passing **The Castles** rock formation on your left along the way. Take any of the paths branching off to the left immediately after The Castles and ascend north-east for 300m to meet the Mourne Wall at the **Saddle** (583m).

THE BRANDY PAD

Starting at the Bog of Donard col and finishing at Hare's Gap, the Brandy Pad was crucial for smuggling contraband during the 18th century. 70km east of the Mourne coast, out in the middle of the Irish Sea, the Isle of Man had much lower taxes on goods compared to Great Britain and Ireland. Everybody loves a bargain, and so cheap goods made their way secretly across to the beaches of County Down for onward transport inland by horse via the Mourne Mountains. Goods transported would have included alcohol (including brandy), tobacco, tea, coffee and other high-tax items.

Tracks like the one along Bloody Bridge River would have been used to access the higher ground. From there, the Brandy Pad became the main thoroughfare as it crossed the source tributaries of the Annalong and Kilkeel rivers. Upon arrival at Hare's Gap, goods would have been taken in the direction of their final destinations or hidden for later retrieval. There is little doubt that Trassey Track would have been used as a departure route from the Brandy Pad at Hare's Gap, and the village of Hilltown a likely distribution hub.

Gate on Trassey Track

The highest point on the Brandy Pad, with the Castles further along on the left

Cross the Wall using the wooden stile. Proceed north, away from the Wall, along an obvious path to start the Glen River valley descent. Expect to see lots of people along here. Follow the constructed path for 600m to meet Glen River. Cross the river at some **stepping stones** and continue along the path with the river on your right. After 870m, exit National Trust property as you meet Donard Forest on the left. Continue along the path for 1.1km, passing an **ice house** perched on the opposite bank of the river, to meet a forest track.

Bear left along the track for a few metres to locate a path on the right. Take this and follow it north-east for 380m, with the river still on your right, to meet another forest track. Turn right here, cross a bridge, then descend a path immediately on the left. With the cascading Glen River now on your left, follow it downstream for 430m along another constructed path. After a brief cobbled section of path, come to a junction beside a bridge. Turn right here and cross **Donard Bridge** to arrive immediately at a junction of forest tracks. If using an alternate start/finish, bear left here.

Turn right to follow a path for 150m through the trees, with Glen River on your right. Take care when walking over the exposed tree roots along this section, especially in wet conditions. Exit Donard Forest and re-enter Donard Park. Continue north along the boundary path and access road for 240m to finish at **Donard car park**.

ROUTE 3

Slieve Donard and Slieve Commedagh from Newcastle

Start/finish	Donard car park, Newcastle
Time	4hr 45min
Distance	11.6km
Ascent/descent	995m
Grade	Hard
Options	Millstone Mountain ascent (+0.2km/+30m/+15min); Commedagh only (-1.7km/-250m/-1hr); Donard only (-2.2km/-170m/-1hr); Shan Slieve descent (-1.1km/+5m/-15min)
Bus stop	Year-round local Ulsterbus services and Mourne Rambler summer bus service stop 100m from Donard car park

Visit the two highest summits in the Mourne Mountains to enjoy far-reaching views across the entire range, as well as the surrounding lowlands and the Irish Sea, taking in Glen River's waterfalls and cascades along the way. Much of the route follows an obvious out-and-back path along Glen River and also a section of the Mourne Wall, making it the most popular choice among walkers of all abilities. The route includes some long steep sections. Confident navigators can escape the crowds by combining the described alternate ascent and descent sections into a circular route.

From the south-west corner of Donard car park, at the entrance to the overflow car park, head south-west alongside a tarmac road. A short distance after passing a private access on the left, enter Donard Park. Continue south-west, with a tall perimeter fence on your left, for 150m to an information map displaying the forest's trails. Follow the path into Donard Forest. To your left, you will hear Glen River. Take care when walking over the exposed tree roots along this section, especially in wet conditions.

After 150m, come to a junction of forest tracks beside the arched **Donard Bridge**. Turn left to cross the bridge, then turn right at the other side to follow a cobbled path, with the river now on your right.

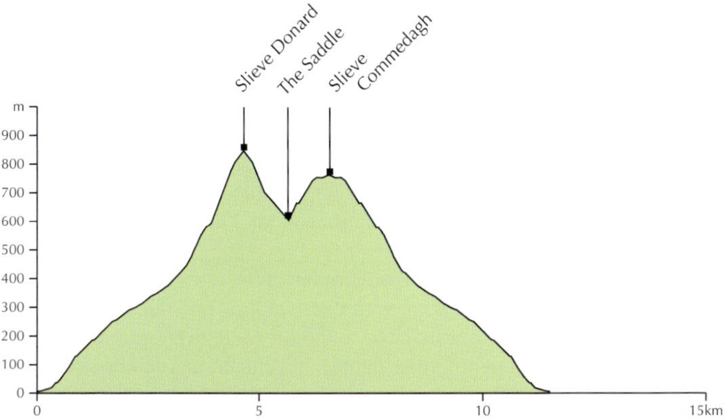

One of the many waterfalls along Glen River as it flows through Donard Forest

In the trees to your left is the overgrown site of **Donard Lodge**. Built around 1830 as a hotel, it was destroyed by fire in 1941 and demolished in 1966. A surviving gate lodge is now used as a private residence.

About 100m along the cobbled path, you will see a forest track with a metal barrier branching off to the left. If ascending Slieve Donard via Millstone Mountain, take the forest track on the left here (Variant 1). To continue on the main route, when the cobbles run out, a constructed path continues straight ahead alongside the river. Follow this south-west for 330m until you meet a forest track close to another bridge.

Turn right to cross the bridge, then turn left at the other side to follow a constructed path south-west for 380m, with the river now on your left. For this section, you have the option to walk close to the tumbling river or to follow a more heavily walked parallel path further right of it. Whichever you choose, you will arrive at another forest track. You have just passed over a tunnel section of the Mourne Conduit – a historical water supply line from Silent Valley to Belfast – which lies about 55m below your feet.

Turn left along the track for a short distance to where it starts bending left towards a bridge. Bear right here along a path as you pass an information panel, keeping the river on your left. As you follow this path south-west, the forest stops on the left to reveal an **ice house** perched on the opposite bank of the river.

Long before the days of fridges and freezers, this little **domed structure**, built about 1840 and restored by the National Trust between 1996 and 1997, was originally used to store ice for Donard Lodge.

As you continue, with the river on your left, the forest eventually ends on the right and you enter the open mountains. After 1.1km, a small sign announces your arrival on National Trust property. Continue along the constructed path, with the river on your left, for 870m. Carefully cross the river at a set of **stepping stones**, then ascend steeply along the obvious path curving up the left-hand side of the valley for 600m to meet the **Mourne Wall** at the Saddle (583m). If walking Commedagh on its own, turn right to ascend along the Wall here.

Turn left to follow the Wall east, keeping it on your right to benefit from the constructed path. Ascend steeply to the trig-adorned stone shelter and summit cairn on **Slieve Donard** (850m) – the highest point in the Mourne Mountains and County Down. Descend west from the summit cairn, with the Wall on your left, back to the Saddle. If walking Donard on its own, turn right here for the Glen River descent. See Route 2 for directions.

SF
The Bogie Line
Shoddy hut
Donard Bridge
Donard Forest
Gate
Black Stairs (waterfalls)
Ice House
Thomas's Mountain
Potentially boggy col
460
Millstone Mountain
Crossone
544
Drinnahilly Mast
254
Glen River
Eagle Rock
Stone shelter with roof-mounted trig
850
Slieve Donard
Stepping stones
Stepping stones
The Mourne Wall
The Saddle
583
The Castles
553
Slievenamaddy
Shan Slieve
683
Slieve Commedagh
765
Mon.
Stile and stone shelter
622
641
Pot of Legawherry
438
Slievenabrock
N
1 km
0.5 miles
0.5
0
282
596
Cascade River

VIEWS FROM DONARD SUMMIT

Most people tend to hang around on the summit of Slieve Donard for a while to admire its long-distance views. Many will find a spot against the sheltered side of the Wall to sit and eat their lunch. To the west, the Wall can be seen passing over Slieve Commedagh on its way to the jagged tors of Slieve Bearnagh and the far side of Silent Valley. In the far distance lies Slieve Gullion, the highest point in neighbouring County Armagh. Panning south down the opposite side of Annalong Valley, you can see Slieve Beg – split from top to bottom by its Devil's Coachroad gully – followed by Cove Mountain, Slievelamagan and Slieve Binnian. Further south is the rugged profile of Slieve Foye, the highest point in County Louth, and the Wicklow Mountains rising from the southern edge of Dublin city, 100km away. In the immediate foreground sits Chimney Rock Mountain, Donard's quiet southern neighbour. Further to the left, the sea views are spectacular. On a clear day, these extend down the east coast of Ireland to Howth Head and across the Irish Sea to the Isle of Man, with Saint John's Point and its lighthouse jutting across the foreground, marking the end of Dundrum Bay. Further north, the south-west coast of Scotland can be seen across the North Channel. To the left across the northern land horizon, look for the sea inlet of Strangford Lough, as well as Scrabo Tower, the Belfast Hills, the Dromara Hills, Lough Neagh and the Sperrin Mountains.

Continue straight on through the Saddle and ascend north-west for 780m beside the Wall. Turn right at a **stone shelter** to follow a worn path north-east across the grassy plateau for 270m to the summit cairn on **Slieve Commedagh** (765m). If descending via Shan Slieve, bear left here, north, along the ridgeline (Variant 2). Retrace your steps to the **stone shelter**, then keep left alongside the Wall back down to the **Saddle**. Turn left for the Glen River descent (see Route 2).

Variant 1: Millstone Mountain ascent

Turn left off the cobbled section of path, passing a metal barrier to access a forest track. Follow the track south-east as it contours through the forest, passing an arched stone shelter (dated 1842) and avoiding all turn-offs. After 980m, meet the Granite Trail at an information panel where a slipe – a timber sledge used for transporting rock – is on display. Turn right at the slipe and ascend the steep, straight path south-west for 450m to the southern edge of the forest at a timber **shoddy hut**. The steep straight you have just ascended is now referred to as the Bogie Line (see Route 26), which is part of the Granite Trail.

Stone shelter on the Mourne Wall seen from the summit of Commedagh

Pass through the nearby gate and continue straight along a rough track. Follow it uphill as it bends right and pass an old quarry on your left. After 350m, arrive at a fence with two gates. Turn left before the gates and follow the fence uphill, south, curving right for 100m to meet another fence with a gate. Pass through this and continue straight for about 40m. Turn left before a small river and head south to pick up a ridgeline. Ascend the high line of the ridge, heading south, for 650m to a cairn marking the subsidiary top of **Millstone Mountain** (460m).

Turn right at the cairn. With the sea behind you, Slieve Donard now dominates the skyline in front. Head directly towards Donard summit, descending west for 170m into a shallow col. Depending on rainfall in recent days and weeks, this col may be quite boggy with large (and possibly deep) puddles to negotiate. Find the driest route across and begin to ascend, continuing west. As you gain height, Slieve Donard appears again above the slope you are ascending.

Aim for where the bottom of Donard's right-hand slope appears to meet the top of the slope you are on. As more of Donard appears, the point you are aiming for will shift right. Adjusting your course to match keeps you roughly on the high line of the ridge, thereby avoiding any loss of elevation. After 500m, as the incline eases slightly for a bit, continue straight towards the right-hand side of Donard. When the slope steepens again, gradually curve left towards Donard summit.

This 700m section is steep and bouldery, so proceed carefully. Be aware that some of these rocks may be unstable and could move when stepped on. There may also be deep gaps between rocks, some of which could be hidden by heather. Maintain a central high line on this ridge as best you can to a large cairn. As the ground noticeably flattens, continue south-west straight past this cairn for 230m to the summit cairn on **Slieve Donard** (850m) and a trig-adorned stone shelter right next to it.

Variant 2: Shan Slieve descent

Please note that this option should be avoided during windy conditions, especially strong westerly crosswinds. From the summit cairn on **Slieve Commedagh** (765m), the worn grassy path continues north. Follow this as the initial descent curves left to avoid cliffs above the Pot of Pulgarve. After about 150m, the path comes close to the clifftop. If it is windy or if you have a fear of heights, take a parallel course further to the left. Continue downhill along the path as it now curves right along the clifftop for 300m. A short ascent brings you to the top of **Shan Slieve** (683m).

Ignore any paths heading left. Continue over the subsidiary top of Shan Slieve, along a faint path bearing right. This may not be obvious in places due to heather. For the next 1.4km, you need to descend on a grid bearing of roughly 70° along the right-hand side of the ridge. Depending on rainfall in recent days and weeks, this section may be quite slippery. Keep to the faint path as closely as possible as it drifts towards the high edge of the forest on the right.

At the end of the ridge, beyond the minor top of **Slievenamaddy**, the descent gets steeper and rockier. A couple of sections can be tricky, so take care. Head east for 200m to a fence junction at an inner corner of Donard Forest. Pass through a gap in the fence to enter a firebreak. Immediately turn right through a gap in the adjoining fence to follow a winding path east through the trees.

When you encounter a stone wall after 200m, pass straight through a collapsed section and head north-east for another 180m to meet a forest track. If the track to your left (north-west) is straight, you need to turn right (south-east). Locate a side path heading north-east off a bend on the track. Follow the Glen River descent (see Route 2) to finish at **Donard car park**.

ROUTE 4

Slieve Donard and Chimney Rock Mountain

Start/finish	Bloody Bridge car park
Time	4hr 45min
Distance	12.7km
Ascent/descent	945m
Grade	Hard
Options	Chimney Rock only (-3.1km/-320m/-1hr 15min); Commedagh extension (+2.1km/+170m/+1hr); Chimney Rock omitted (-1.3km/-120m/-30min)
Bus stop	Year-round local Ulsterbus services and Mourne Rambler summer bus service stop at Bloody Bridge car park

This alternative way up Slieve Donard, with its out-of-town start/finish, sees far fewer walkers than the Glen River approach described in Route 3. Here you get a chance to pass the site of a 17th-century massacre, follow part of an old smuggling route and visit the crash site of a WW2 bomber on Donard's quiet southern neighbour – Chimney Rock Mountain.

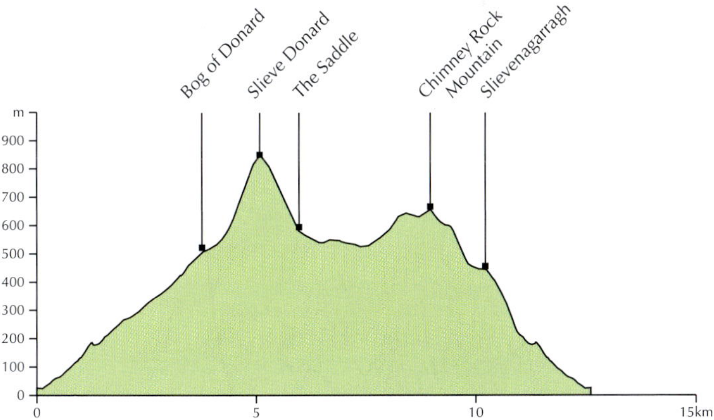

From the south end of Bloody Bridge car park, follow the roadside footway south for 40m to where it ends at a small wooden gate. You need to cross the A2 Kilkeel Road at this point. The Mourne Coastal Route is a waymarked scenic drive that mostly follows the A2 road between Belfast and Newry. Only cross when it is safe to do so, bearing in mind any walkers who are with you or others who may be influenced by your timing. Please be aware that traffic moves quickly along this busy stretch of road.

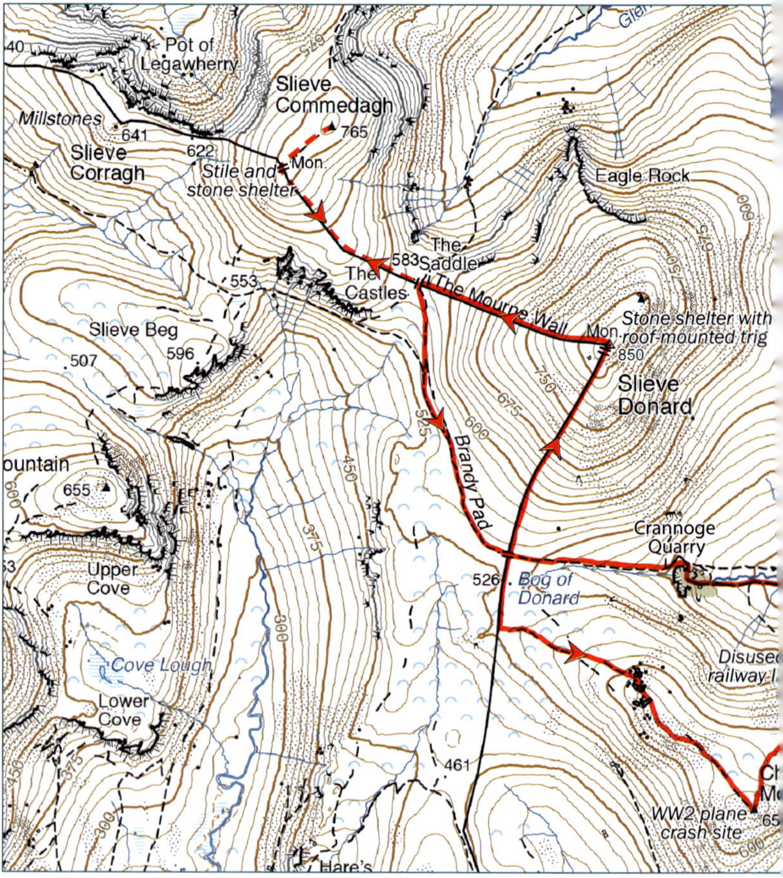

Once safely across, you are faced with two gates. Pass through the smaller gate on the left to enter the National Trust's Bloody Bridge property (see Route 5). Follow the path straight ahead. After 70m, the old stone-arched **Bloody Bridge** appears on the left. Continue west along the path for 700m, keeping Bloody Bridge River on your left. Cross a tributary (Glen Fofanny River) using the footbridge and continue west. The pipelines seen crossing Bloody Bridge River are the Mourne Conduit – a historical water supply line from Silent Valley to Belfast.

Mourne Conduit pipes crossing Bloody Bridge River

Chimney Rock Mountain from the Bog of Donard

After this, the path splits and merges but try to keep as close to the river as possible. Look for a stone track up ahead on the opposite (south) side of the river. You need to walk slightly upstream of this track to find the location where you can walk down to the river and cross safely. Take care if the rocks are wet. Once across, climb the track on the south side. After 80m, cross a stile and continue uphill along a 300m section of zigzagging track.

The track then straightens and continues parallel to the river, with Chimney Rock Mountain on your left and Slieve Donard up ahead on the right.

Notice the diagonal straight line descending the steep slope on the left. This was formerly a **mineral railway** used to transport granite from Carr's Face Quarry. Parts of the deteriorated railway line are still visible.

Stay on the track alongside Bloody Bridge River for 1.5km to the disused **Crannoge Quarry**. Turn right to follow the track north through the quarry and pick up a path on the opposite side. Continue along this path as it bends left and rises above the north side of the quarry. With Bloody Bridge River (now just a stream) on your left, ascend along the well-worn path for 750m through peat to meet the **Mourne Wall** in the Bog of Donard (526m). If walking Chimney Rock Mountain on its own, turn left here.

Turn right and follow the Wall north, uphill, for 1km. The ascent is steep and rough in places. Arrive at the trig-adorned stone shelter – where the Wall bends left (west) – and the summit cairn on **Slieve Donard** (850m) – the highest point in the Mourne Mountains and County Down. Most people tend to hang around on the summit of Slieve Donard for a while to admire its long-distance views (see Route 3).

Descend west from the summit cairn, with the Wall on your left, for 850m to the **Saddle** (583m). If adding Slieve Commedagh, continue straight across the Saddle and follow the Wall (Variant 1). Turn left to cross the Wall at the stile. Head south, away from the Wall. Worn paths go in various directions from here. Pick one bearing left and follow it to contour around Donard for 400m. When it meets the **Brandy Pad** (see Route 2), continue left.

Keep contouring for 800m, avoiding any side paths on the right, to arrive back at the Wall in the Bog of Donard. Cross the stile. If omitting Chimney Rock Mountain, continue straight here and retrace your steps down the Bloody Bridge River valley. Turn right to follow the Wall south. After a 300m section of bogginess alongside the Wall, come to a crest. Do not follow the Wall any further when it begins to descend. Instead, locate a path on the left heading south-east along a ridge leading to Chimney Rock Mountain.

Follow this and proceed uphill. The path splits occasionally but all are good as long as you keep close to the high line and aim for the rock outcrop 650m directly ahead. Pass through or around these impressive granite formations on the north-west subsidiary top. After this, the incline decreases. Continue along the high line for 730m, passing a couple of rocky hummocks along the way, to reach the summit cairn on **Chimney Rock Mountain** (656m). Leave the summit by heading north initially. You may find a faint path to follow.

AMERICAN B-26 BOMBER CRASH SITE

On the south side of Chimney Rock Mountain, just metres from the summit itself, is the crash site of an American World War Two B-26 Marauder bomber. On 10 April 1944, three of these aircraft took off from Toome airfield, 75km away at the northernmost tip of Lough Neagh, for a routine mission over the Irish Sea just off the County Down coast. During the mission, one of the aircraft got separated from the others in thick cloud and struck the mountain's summit. All five crewmen on board were killed. A memorial plate has been installed on a rock just south of the summit cairn.

Curve right for 500m to avoid the top of Carr's Face, which you observed earlier from the track below. The goal now is to descend along the east ridge. The northern skyline beyond the Bloody Bridge River valley is dominated by Donard and its subsidiary top, Crossone (544m). As you proceed along the ridge, the descent steepens. Directly ahead, see if you can spot the cairn marking the end of the ridge, about 700m to the east. This is your target. The descent flattens for the final approach to **Slievenagarragh** (452m).

Bear left past the cairn and descend north-east for 750m to the section of zigzagging track you walked up earlier. Negotiate the rocks carefully along this descent. Be aware that some of these rocks may be unstable and could move when stepped on. There may also be deep gaps between the rocks, some of which could be hidden by heather. Maintain a north-east descent to meet the track. Follow this downhill and retrace your steps east alongside the river to finish at **Bloody Bridge car park**.

Variant 1: Slieve Commedagh extension

Continue straight through the **Saddle** (583m) and ascend north-west along the Wall for 780m to a stone shelter. Turn right, away from the Wall, and follow a worn path north-east across the grassy plateau for 270m to the summit cairn on **Slieve Commedagh** (765m). Retrace your steps to the stone shelter and turn left to follow the Wall back down to the Saddle. Turn right across the stile to rejoin the main route.

Bloody Bridge with Slieve Donard rising beyond

ROUTE 5

The Brandy Pad – Bloody Bridge to Trassey

Start	Bloody Bridge car park
Finish	Trassey car park
Alt finishes	Meelmore Lodge car park and Bloody Bridge car park
Time	4hr
Distance	11.7km
Ascent	570m
Descent	430m
Grade	Moderate
Options	Return (+11.7km/+430m/+570m/+3hr 45min); return via Meelmore Lodge (+12.5km/+455m/+595m/+4hr); return via Mourne Wall (+13.5km/+895m/+1035m/+5hr)
Bus stops	Year-round local Ulsterbus services and Mourne Rambler summer bus service stop at Bloody Bridge car park. Mourne Rambler stops 1.4km from Trassey car park

Walk in the footsteps of smugglers from the Irish Sea coast and follow their well-trodden path as it contours beneath towering peaks and over high cols. Described here from east to west, the Brandy Pad can be walked in either direction or as an out-and-back with the option to visit the range's two highest summits on the return leg.

From the south end of Bloody Bridge car park, follow the roadside footway south for 40m to where it ends at a small wooden gate. You need to cross the A2 Kilkeel Road at this point. The Mourne Coastal Route is a waymarked scenic drive that mostly follows the A2 road between Belfast and Newry. Only cross when it is safe to do so, bearing in mind any walkers who are with you or others who may be influenced by your timing. Please be aware that traffic moves quickly along this busy stretch of road.

Once safely across, you are faced with two gates. Pass through the smaller gate on the left to enter the National Trust's Bloody Bridge property. Follow the path straight ahead. After 70m, the old stone-arched **Bloody Bridge** appears on the left. Continue west along the path for 700m, keeping Bloody Bridge River on your left. Cross a tributary (Glen Fofanny River), using the footbridge, and

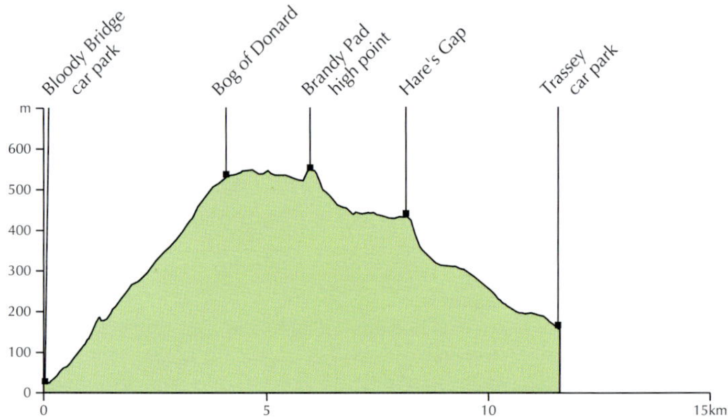

continue west. The pipelines seen crossing Bloody Bridge River are the Mourne Conduit – a historical water supply line from Silent Valley to Belfast.

The path soon splits and remerges but try to keep as close to the river as possible. After about 300m, look for a stone track on the opposite (south) side of the river. You need to walk slightly upstream of this track to find the location where you can walk down to the river and cross safely. Take care if the rocks are wet. Once across, climb the track on the south side. After 80m, cross a stile and continue uphill along a 300m section of zigzagging track.

The track then straightens and continues parallel to the river, with Chimney Rock on your left and Slieve Donard up ahead on the right.

Notice the diagonal straight line descending the steep slope on the left. This was formerly a **mineral railway** used to transport granite from Carr's Face Quarry. Parts of the deteriorated railway are still visible.

Stay on the track alongside Bloody Bridge River for 1.5km to the disused **Crannoge Quarry**. Turn right to follow the track north through the quarry and pick up a path on the opposite side.

Continue along this path as it bends left and rises above the north side of the quarry. With Bloody Bridge River (now just a stream) on your left, ascend along the well-worn path for 750m through peat to meet the **Mourne Wall** in the Bog of Donard (526m). Cross the wooden ladder stile and continue straight ahead. You are now on the **Brandy Pad** (see Route 2).

The Smuggler's Head *sculpture at Bloody Bridge car park requires precision viewing*

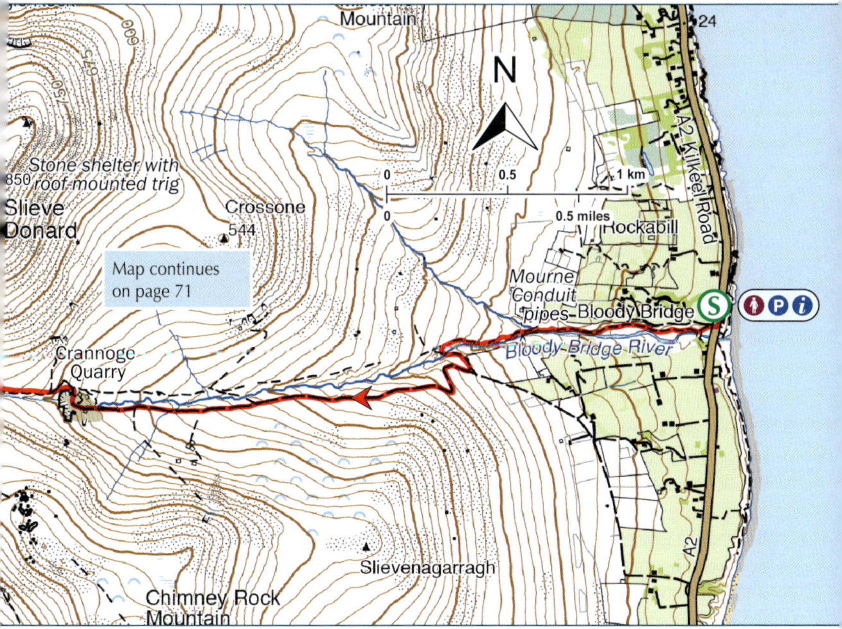

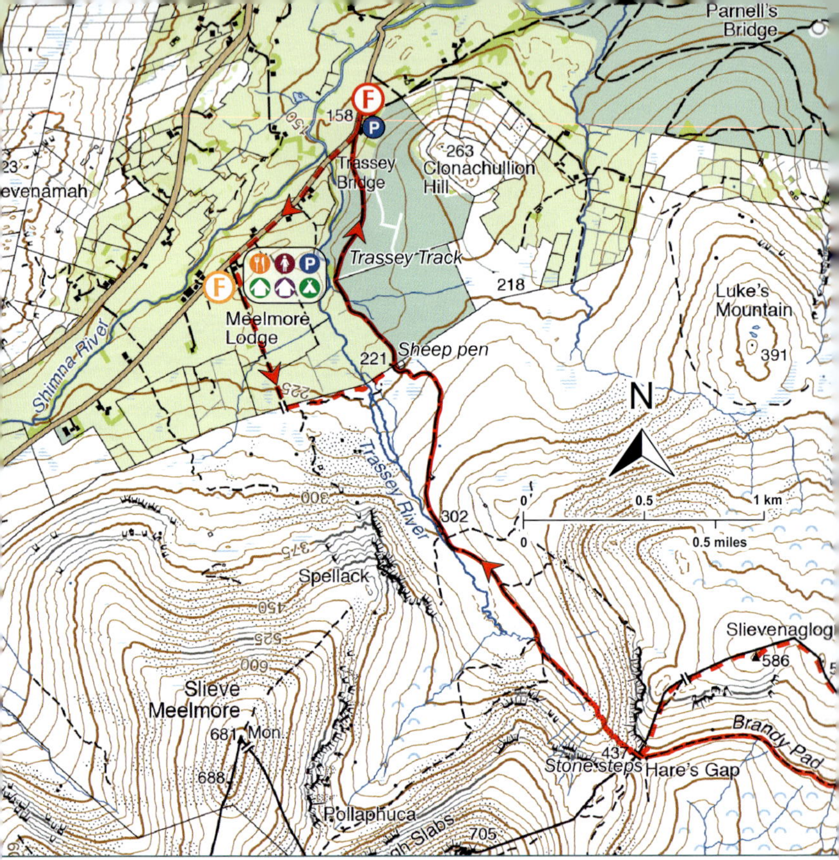

Follow this path as it curves right to contour around the base of Slieve Donard. With Slieve Commedagh dominating the view directly ahead, note the location of The Castles rock formations at its base, just left of the Saddle (583m). Ignore any sidetracks, especially those heading right and up towards the Saddle. Keep to the obvious line of the Brandy Pad, heading north-west for 1.9km past **The Castles** to a 553m col.

Up ahead, the view becomes dominated by the rugged granite tors of Slieve Bearnagh. Continue along the obvious path for 2.2km to meet the Mourne Wall again at **Hare's Gap** (437m). Cross a stile and make your way carefully down the initial rough section of the valley. Find your own path north-west, keeping slightly left of the centreline. After 500m, pick up a track at the bottom of the slope.

Follow this north-west for 1.6km down the Trassey River valley to a gate beside a stone **sheep pen**. Pass through the gate and follow the track north for 1.1km. You are now on the Mourne Way. Continue along the track, passing through a second gate and a third with stone steps built into a wall beside it. Keep straight along Trassey Road for 100m to finish at **Trassey car park**. Retrace your steps if returning to Bloody Bridge car park. Variations 1 and 2 describe optional sections along the return leg.

Variant 1: return section via Meelmore Lodge

Meelmore Lodge can serve as an alternate start/finish or halfway lunch stop. It is worth checking the opening hours of the on-site Hare's Gap Bistro in advance. Turn left out of Trassey car park to follow Trassey Road uphill. Continue along the road as it bends right. Stick to the road for about 0.7km until you arrive at **Meelmore Lodge** on the left. Follow the track from the rear of Meelmore Lodge south for 600m to a dry-stone wall. Cross using the stile and turn left. Follow the Mourne Way for 500m alongside the wall and across a couple of streams to meet

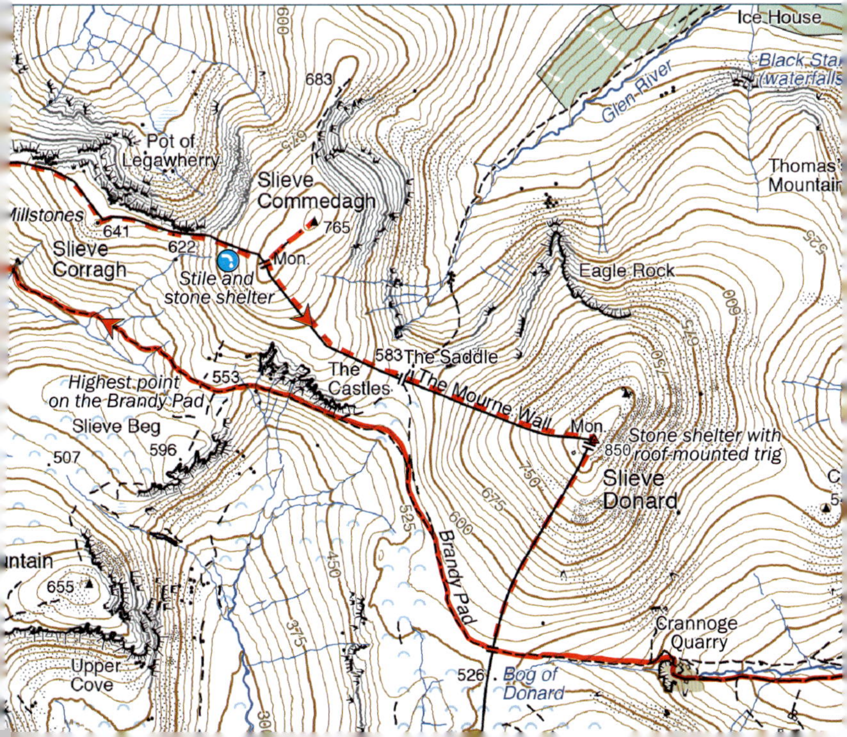

The Brandy Pad heading towards Hare's Gap

a gated track, entering open ground near a stone **sheep pen**. Turn right here and head south, retracing your steps up the track towards **Hare's Gap**.

Variant 2: return section via the Mourne Wall

On the return leg, turn left at **Hare's Gap** (437m) to follow a fine section of the Wall over the summits of **Slievenaglogh** (586m), **Slieve Commedagh** (765m) and **Slieve Donard** (850m). From Donard, turn right at its stone shelter to descend south-west alongside the Wall to arrive back at the **Bog of Donard** (526m), which you crossed on the outward leg. Turn left, away from the Wall, and head east, retracing your steps towards the coast to finish at **Bloody Bridge car park**.

BLOODY BRIDGE

Of the various stories that have been told over the centuries, the accepted one today tells of a group of prisoners who were being transported from Newry to Downpatrick in October 1641. Upon arrival, they were due to be exchanged for a group of prisoners being held there. But as they were rounding Slieve Donard, along the coast, their captors found out that the prisoners in Downpatrick had been hanged. In response, the jailers took their prisoners to a bridge spanning Midpace River, massacred them and threw their remains over the side, turning the river red with blood. The bridge and Midpace River have since become known as Bloody Bridge and Bloody Bridge River.

ROUTE 6

Annalong River, Hare's Castle and Rocky Mountain

Start/finish	Dunnywater parking spot
Time	3hr 15min
Distance	9.8km
Ascent/descent	415m
Grade	Moderate
Bus stop	The Mourne Rambler summer bus service stops 220m from the Dunnywater parking spot

Annalong River flows down a wide glacial valley, having carved a path for itself through sands and gravels deposited by retreating ice sheets. This route allows you to see the resulting moraine riverscape up close as you walk right through it. Other highlights along the way include a reservoir that never happened, the Binnian Tunnel and a fine section of the Mourne Wall.

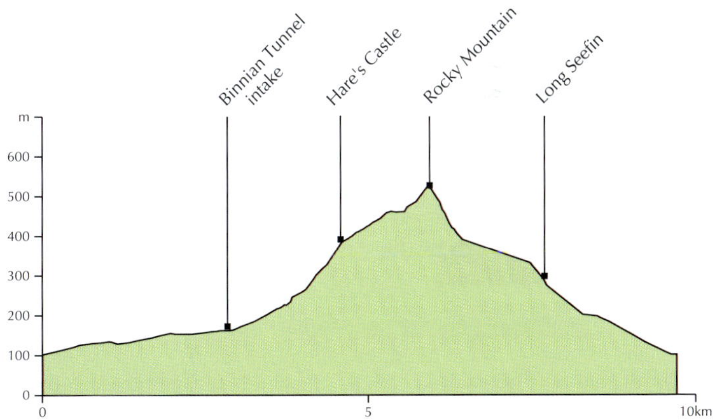

From the Dunnywater parking spot, pass through a gate in the ornate stone-walled entrance to the Dunnywater Track. Proceed north-west along the track, passing a couple of houses on the right after about 300m.

The first of these was built in 1900 to house the superintendent who was in charge of **water-related projects** in the Annalong Valley, including the Mourne Conduit – a historical water supply line from Silent Valley to Belfast – which can be seen crossing Annalong River below on your left.

A further 800m along, just before reaching a stone building, look for the **Mourne Wall** crossing the track. Proceed past the stone building on the right-hand edge of the track. The building housed an inlet well where water from Annalong River was diverted to the Belfast-bound Mourne Conduit. Had the Annalong Valley Reservoir not been cancelled, it would have been built across the valley close to this building. Continue north-west, heading straight along the track for 1.5km through Annalong Wood to a turning circle. Beyond this is a walled section of Annalong River. You can cross the two bridges here for a micro loop past the **Binnian Tunnel intake** (see Route 10), where water is diverted to Silent Valley.

ANNALONG VALLEY RESERVOIR

Water from Annalong River enters the Binnian Tunnel here

In the very earliest days of the 20th century, long before construction started on the Mourne Wall, plans were afoot to build a reservoir in the Annalong Valley to store water for Belfast; this is one of the main reasons the Mourne Wall cuts across the valley so far south. This phase of the Mourne water masterplan, however, was cancelled due to difficulties encountered during the construction of the Silent Valley Reservoir. If it had gone ahead, the reservoir wall would have been built across Annalong Valley close to the inlet well house, which remains on site to this day, and a large area of the wide valley above would have been flooded.

The cancellation of the Annalong Valley Reservoir disrupted the masterplan: without it, there would not be enough water to supply Belfast. This problem was later solved with the Binnian Tunnel and the Ben Crom Reservoir. If the Annalong Valley Reservoir had been built, its catchment area would have been approximately 14.2km^2. Its tunnel replacement collects rainfall from a 9km^2 section of the valley. Additional water can also be collected downstream from the remainder of the valley through the inlet well and diverted into the Belfast-bound Mourne Conduit.

Cove Lough
Lower Cove
Chimney Ro
Mountain
656
600
525
461
300
375
Ruined stone structures
Hare's Castle
525
Rocky Mountain
The Mourne Wall
Moraine
225
Bysshe
Spences Mountain
515
450
165
Binnian Tunnel intake
Spences River
Long Seefin
Stone pillar
Annalong River
300
e Mourne Wall
225
Inlet well house
231
Round Seefin
215
Carrick Big
150
Straining well
Mourne Conduit pipes
Quarter Road
N
SF
P
Dunnywater Bridge
Head Road
Carrick Little
0
0.5
1 km
0
0.5 miles
Gla

From the turning circle, proceed north along a track, heading upstream for 100m to where it bends right. Continue straight onto a side path beside a field gate. Follow the path parallel to the river on the left and a fence on the right for 300m to a stile. Cross the **stile** and continue along the path, keeping the river close on your left. As you progress upstream, the rocky riverbed produces some small waterfalls. After 350m, enter a moraine landscape where the river has carved its own path through glacial sand and gravel deposited by retreating ice. A similar landscape on Kilkeel River was flooded by Silent Valley Reservoir.

Perched up ahead, Hare's Castle is nicely framed by the steep sides of the moraine channel. When the river bends left 170m further on, continue straight, in the direction of Hare's Castle, up a short, steep path to the top of the bank. Turn left here and follow a path north-east through a broken wall and onwards to ascend beside a tributary stream on the right. After 450m, as you approach **Hare's Castle**, feel free to explore some ruined path-side structures on its left-hand side (west), keeping in mind that the onward route passes on the right-hand side (east). When you reach the quarried south face, locate a path between it and the stream heading north-east.

Walking through the moraine landscape of Annalong Valley towards Hare's Castle

Follow the path uphill between the stream and the ridgeline behind Hare's Castle for 180m. The ridgeline offers good views across Annalong Valley if you fancy the short detour along a faint side path. Follow the path as it bends right towards the stream. When it is close, turn right to meet the stream. Find a safe place to cross just downstream from a waterfall, bearing in mind the wet rocks may be slippery. Ascend the opposite bank to locate a path parallel to the stream.

Turn left to follow the path upstream, with Slieve Donard directly ahead. Your next target is Rocky Mountain on the right but keep straight on along the path beside the stream for now. When the path bends sharply right after 390m, follow it away from the stream. After a couple of zigzags, continue along the path for 400m, passing close to a 461m col, to reach a corner in the **Mourne Wall**. Turn right onto a path ascending south-west, away from the Wall. Follow this for 410m to a cairn and continue roughly 100m south-east to the unmarked summit of **Rocky Mountain** (525m).

Continue straight past the summit and descend south-west along a zigzagging path for 500m to a stile over the Mourne Wall. Ignore this stile and follow the Wall south-south-east for 1.2km. Pass another stile, then arrive at a corner embellished with a small ornate pillar at **Long Seefin**. Turn right and carefully descend south-west beside a wall for 600m to a stile. If you look over the wall along here, you will see the Mourne Wall itself branching off to the left. Cross the stile, turn left and follow a track south-east for 160m. Pass through the **Mourne Wall** at a gate and continue straight along the track.

A walled area on the right encloses a **straining well** on the Belfast-bound Mourne Conduit. This was an important junction where water piped separately from Silent Valley and Annalong Valley was brought together for the onward journey to Belfast.

After 1.1km, meet Head Road. Turn right along the road for 90m to finish at **Dunnywater parking spot**.

ROUTE 7

Annalong Valley Horseshoe

Start/finish	Carrick Little car park
Alt start/finish	Dunnywater parking spot
Time	8hr
Distance	21.3km
Ascent/descent	1635m
Grade	Very hard
Options	West loop (-1.3km/-340m/-45min); east loop (-5.2km/-815m/-2hr 30min)
Bus stops	The Mourne Rambler summer bus service stops at Carrick Little car park and 220m from Dunnywater parking spot

Walk one of Ireland's most iconic horseshoe routes. Following the upper Annalong Valley's enclosing ridgeline, you will pass over (or very close to) eight summits, including six official mountains. Eastern, northern and southern sections of the route include some fine sections of the Mourne Wall, deviating from it slightly in places to follow the valley's true catchment boundary. The western section is a north–south traverse of the Western Mournes' central ridge. This route could be linked with the Silent Valley Horseshoe (Route 13) as an alternative to the Mourne Wall Challenge (Route 25).

From the entrance of Carrick Little car park, turn left along Head Road and follow it north-east for 1.4km. If walking the west loop only, head north from the car park instead (Variant 1). There is no footway so be careful along the road as it is quite narrow with a few blind bends. Take extra care at a twisting section where it drops to cross Annalong River at the single-lane **Dunnywater Bridge**. From there, ascend along the road to Dunnywater parking spot. This can be used as an alternate start/finish. Continue straight alongside the road for 260m to where it bends sharply right.

Bear slightly left to pick up a track heading north-east. Follow this for 240m to where it finishes at a field gate. Turn left up some steps and follow a path north-west for 330m along a field boundary. Along the way, pass a concrete structure

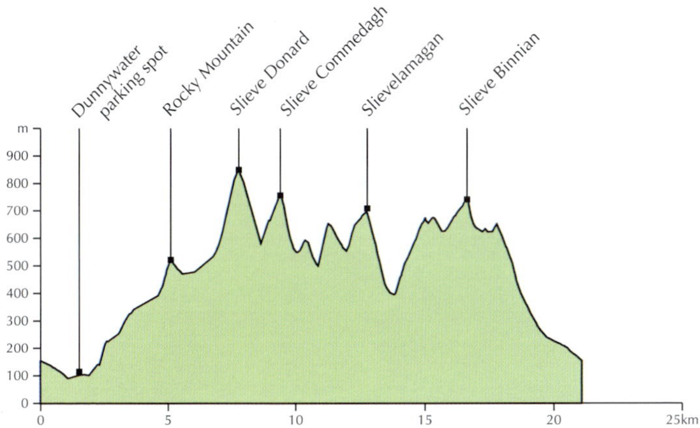

which almost blocks the path. This is one of 97 air wells dotted along the Mourne Conduit – a historical water supply line from Silent Valley to Belfast. Turn right to follow the path east for 60m to a gate and stile. Cross the stile then turn left immediately.

Ascend north through trees and ferns for 300m, keeping as close to a stone wall on the left as the paths allow. Negotiate your way up the left side of a rocky section beside the wall. After some more ferns, come to a mini cliff face. The wall passes straight over this, but you need to find an easier alternative to the right. Keep an eye out for possible strands of wire on the ground here to avoid tripping. Turn left along a broken wall at the top of the face to reach the subsidiary top of **Round Seefin** (231m).

Step over the broken wall. Bear right slightly to follow the true ridgeline north for 970m, curving left along its high line to a wall junction just north of a wooden stile at **Long Seefin**. Cross the Wall at a built-in stone stile here. If visibility is poor or you are not strict about keeping to the route, stay alongside the wall between Round Seefin and Long Seefin, pass a decorative pillar at a wall junction, cross the wooden stile, turn right and continue north along the Wall to its built-in stone stile.

You are now beside the Mourne Wall. Follow it north to another wooden stile beside Rocky Mountain. Turn left, away from the Wall, and zigzag up the paths on Rocky's south-east slope. After 500m, pass over the unmarked summit of **Rocky Mountain** (525m), then aim for its north cairn 100m away. You have the option to

Leaving the Mourne Wall to ascend Rocky Mountain

bear right at the cairn to descend a path off the ridge to a corner on the Wall. Turn left to follow the Wall north. Follow the true ridgeline from the cairn for 900m by keeping straight initially before curving right to maintain the high line across a **461m col** to meet the Wall.

Turn left to follow the Wall north. After 700m, come to a stile in the **Bog of Donard** (526m). Before continuing north, decide which side of the Wall to ascend along, using the stile if necessary. This ascent is steep and rough in places. After 1km, arrive at the trig-adorned stone shelter where the Wall bends left west.

The nearby stone cairn marks the summit of **Slieve Donard** (850m) – the highest point in the Mourne Mountains and County Down (see Route 3). From the summit cairn, descend west with the Wall on your left to the **Saddle** (583m). If walking the east loop only, turn left here across the stile (Variant 2).

Continue straight through the **Saddle** and ascend north-west beside the Wall for 780m to a stone shelter. (The summit cairn on Slieve Commedagh, 765m, is just 270m to the north-east of here if you fancy the short out-and-back detour.) Cross the stile beside the stone shelter and descend south-west, away from the Wall. Zigzag carefully down this steep grassy slope for 620m to meet the **Brandy Pad** (see Route 2) at a 553m col.

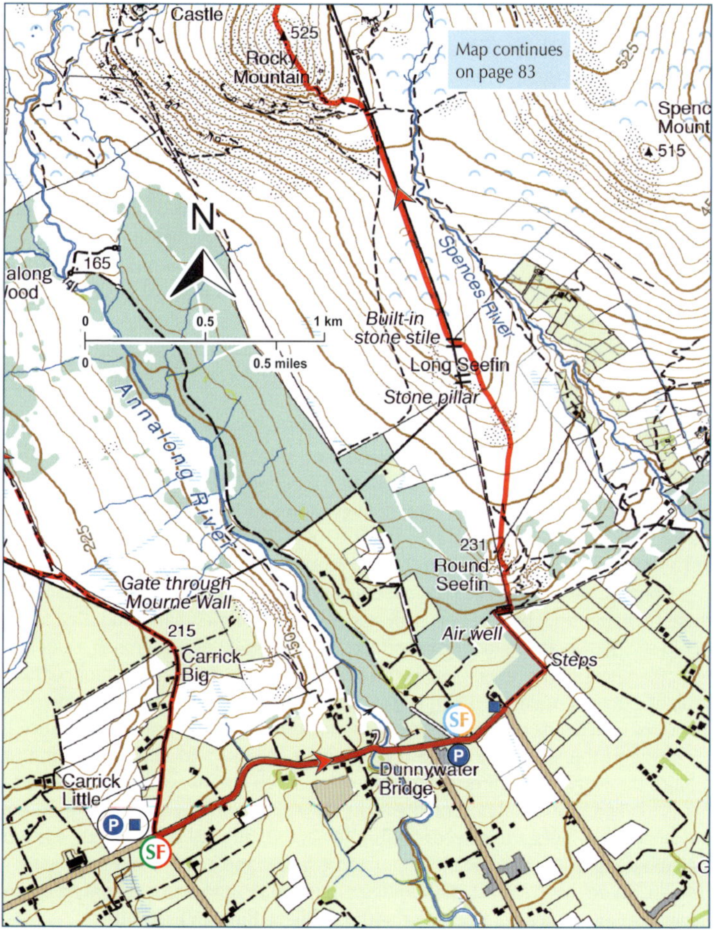

Alternative descent off Slieve Commedagh

You can bypass the steep zigzagging descent off Commedagh's south side by retracing your steps from the stone shelter along the Wall to the **Saddle** (583m), turning right across the stile and bearing right of centre onto the Brandy Pad, past The Castles, to the **553m col**. Turn left here to join the main route.

Main route continues

Continue straight across the col to ascend south-west along a path for 360m to the summit of **Slieve Beg** (596m). A short distance past the summit, pause for a look down the gully. Continue straight past the top of the Devil's Coachroad gully, then curve right to descend west on a path for 370m to meet a stream left of a 507m col. Strict horseshoe challenge walkers will bear to the right of the path along the high line to pass over the 507m col.

Turn left across the stream and ascend south along a path for 450m, keeping away from the steep slope and cliff edge on the left, to the summit cairn on **Cove Mountain** (655m). Turn right to descend west-south-west on a path for 620m. Pass a cliff edge on the left, cross a 553m col and ascend south along the path for 780m to the summit cairn on **Slievelamagan** (702m). Continue straight over the summit and descend the zigzagging path for 1km to a junction at a **398m col**.

Continue straight across the col to ascend south-west on a constructed path curving south.

Pause every now and then to take in the views behind you over Ben Crom Reservoir. After 1.4km, arrive at the right-hand side of **Slieve Binnian North Tor**. (Its 683m summit is accessible, but care is needed.) Cross the path and head west for 200m to the subsidiary top of **Slieve Binnian North Top** (677m). Turn left across low heather, heading south-east for 300m, then rejoin the path to a **627m col** – the highest col between two official mountain summits in the Mournes.

Come to the first in a chain of interesting ridgeline rock formations. You can pass these on either side, but the best path stays close to their left-hand side. Be careful not to stray down a path forking left off the ridge. After 400m, go through a gap in a wall, then pass another rock formation – either side is fine. With the summit tor now in sight, continue south for 350m across the grassy plateau, past a couple of smaller formations, including one where the top slab looks to be quite precariously balanced.

Ascend the summit tor of **Slieve Binnian** (747m) and take some time to admire the views in all directions. Descend south to a mini col. (The actual summit is marked by a metal post on the rocks above you, directly ahead to the south. It is accessible, but care is needed.) Turn left at the mini col and descend east on the Annalong Valley side, bearing right immediately and keeping close to the tor's base to where the Wall restarts. Turn left along the Wall to a stile. Cross this, turn left and follow a path south-east for 440m to **Slieve Binnian East Top**.

This is as far along the ridge as you can go without entering private land or having to reascend. Retrace your steps to the stile. Cross it, turn right and descend for 1.9km beside the Wall to a path junction. Continue south-east for 300m, with a fence on your left and the Wall on your right, passing through a couple of gates to access a track. Follow this for 1km to finish at **Carrick Little car park**. If finishing at the Dunnywater parking spot, turn left along the road here.

Map continues on page 85

Slieve Binnian's South Tor from the summit

Variant 1: west loop

From Carrick Little car park, head north along the track just beside it. Follow the track for 1km to where it passes through the **Mourne Wall** at a gate. Continue through this and another gate a short distance directly ahead to enter open mountain land. Continue north-west for 200m to a junction. Bear right along a path beside the fence. Stick to the path as it bends right with the fence to rejoin the track. Beyond the fence lies Annalong Wood. Part of this area would be flooded today had a reservoir project not been cancelled (see Route 6).

Follow the track for 1.4km alongside the fence to meet a dry-stone wall at the north-west corner of the forest. Keep straight ahead through the gap in the wall and continue north-west along the path for 110m to where an obvious side path branches off to the right.

Bear right and continue north-east for 670m to another side path on the right. Follow this, heading east initially for 90m before a sharp left bend. Now heading north, ignore all side paths to pass under the dramatic **crags of Cove Mountain**. The path becomes less obvious from here. Try not to stray too far left onto any higher paths.

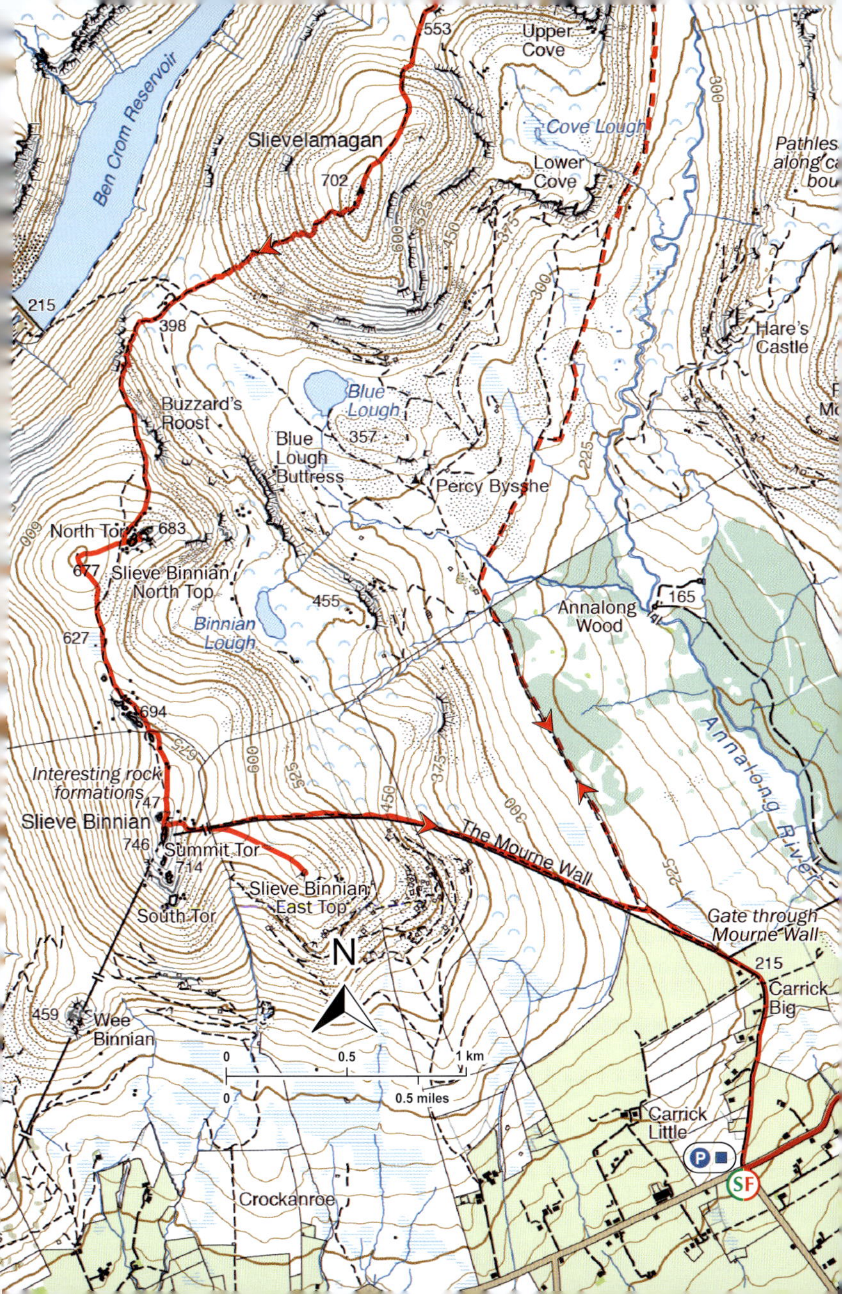

553
Upper Cove
Ben Crom Reservoir
Cove Lough
Slievelamagan
Lower Cove
Pathles along c bou
702
215
398
Hare's Castle
Buzzard's Roost
Blue Lough
Blue Lough Buttress
357
Percy Bysshe
North Tor
683
677
Slieve Binnian North Top
455
Annalong Wood
165
Binnian Lough
627
694
Annalong River
Interesting rock formations
747
Slieve Binnian
746
Summit Tor
714
The Mourne Wall
Slieve Binnian East Top
South Tor
Gate through Mourne Wall
215
Carrick Big
N
459
Wee Binnian
0
0.5
1 km
0
0.5 miles
Carrick Little
SF
Crockanroe

The **Devil's Coachroad** divides Slieve Beg's east face and is regarded as the most intimidating gully in the Mournes. Ascending it is challenging, so only attempt it if you and your group are confident scramblers. If you fancy an ascent, consider doing so now as a shortcut up Slieve Beg. Please note that it is not safe to descend this gully.

After 3km, ascend what has now become a faint path up a steepening section where several tributaries of Annalong River are flowing. You will soon meet the **Brandy Pad**. Turn right to follow the Brandy Pad east-south-east for 300m. Towards the end of **The Castles** rock formation on your left, start curving left uphill wherever side paths permit. Continue to ascend north-east for 350m to meet the Wall at the **Saddle** (583m). Cross the stile here and turn left to join the main route.

Variant 2: east loop

Having arrived at the **Saddle** (583m) from Slieve Donard, turn left across the stile and head south, away from the Wall. Several paths radiate from the stile on the south side of the wall. Aim slightly right of centre before descending. If you can see the tor-studded profile of Slieve Binnian ahead, use that as your initial line. After 350m, meet a clear path contouring left to right. Turn right here to follow it west-north-west. This is the **Brandy Pad**.

Proceed along the Brandy Pad for 300m, passing **The Castles** rock formations on your right, to locate a faint side path on the left descending steeply south into Annalong Valley. This may not be obvious among the tributary streams also descending across the Brandy Pad here. Turn right onto this side path and proceed down it. Take care when stepping on exposed rock, loose gravel and peat to avoid slipping on this descent.

The path becomes clearer as you descend the valley. Try not to stray too far right onto a higher path towards the Devil's Coachroad gully (see Variant 1). Continue south, passing under the dramatic crags of **Cove Mountain** and ignore any side paths. After 3km, the path bends sharply right for 90m to a junction. Turn left and follow the path south-west for 670m to meet a broader path. Bear left here for 110m to meet a dry-stone wall.

Keep straight through a gap in the wall and follow the track alongside a fence for 1.4km to a junction. Bear left, south-east, along the path for 300m, with the fence on your left and the Mourne Wall on your right, passing through a couple of gates to access a track. Follow this for 1km to finish at **Carrick Little car park**.

ROUTE 8

Slieve Binnian from Carrick Little

Start/finish	Carrick Little car park
Time	4hr
Distance	11.2km
Ascent/descent	600m
Grade	Moderate
Options	Combine with Route 9 (+5.9km/+465m/+2hr 30min)
Bus stop	The Mourne Rambler summer bus service stops at Carrick Little car park

When asked which mountain in the Mournes is their favourite, most hillwalkers will answer 'Binnian' and it is easy to see why. The views from its tor-studded summit and north ridge across Silent Valley and Annalong Valley are spectacular on a good day. Even though it has a special place in the hearts of so many local hillwalkers, Slieve Binnian does not attract anywhere near as many visitors as Slieve Donard. The summit can be approached from both sides, but this route from Carrick Little in the Annalong Valley is by far the most popular way up Binnian. Route 10 describes a more difficult option from Silent Valley Mountain Park.

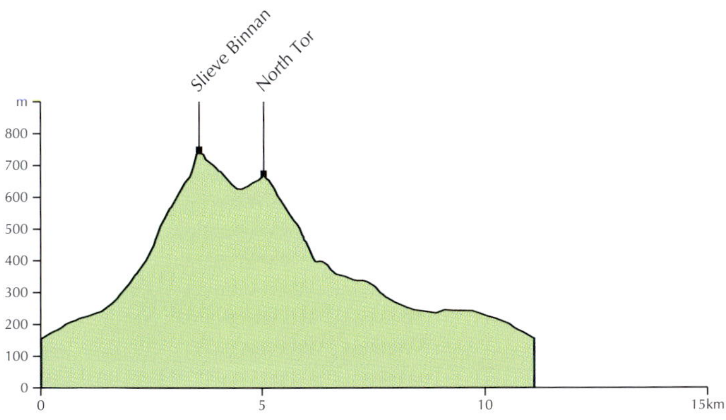

The view over Annalong Valley from the summit of Slieve Binnian

From Carrick Little car park, head north along the track just beside it. Follow the track for 1km to where it passes through the **Mourne Wall** at a gate. Continue through this and another gate a short distance directly ahead to enter open mountain land. Continue north-west for 200m to a junction. You will pass this point again later in the walk. For now, bear left along a path beside the Mourne Wall. Ascend north-west, close to the Wall as it gradually curves left for 1.9km.

Bear right, away from the Wall, past a stile along a path bringing you to a mini col near the summit of **Slieve Binnian** (747m). From here, you can look down the other side over Silent Valley Reservoir. (Binnian's actual summit is marked by a metal post nearby on the rocks to your left, south. It is accessible, but care is needed.) Turn right at the mini col, ascend north onto the rocks and take some time to admire the views in all directions.

Continue north across the grassy plateau, past a couple of interesting formations, including one where the top slab looks to be quite precariously balanced. Bypass a larger granite outcrop – either side is fine. After 350m, go through a gap in a wall. Pass the last in this chain of ridgeline rock formations on either side. The best path stays close to their right. After 400m, continue north across the **627m col** – the highest col between two official mountain summits in the Mournes.

Ascend the path for 450m to the left side of **Slieve Binnian North Tor** (683m). (Its summit is accessible, but care is needed.) Continue straight along the path and descend north for 1.4km. Pause every now and then to take in the views over Ben Crom Reservoir as you descend this constructed path to a junction at a **398m col**.

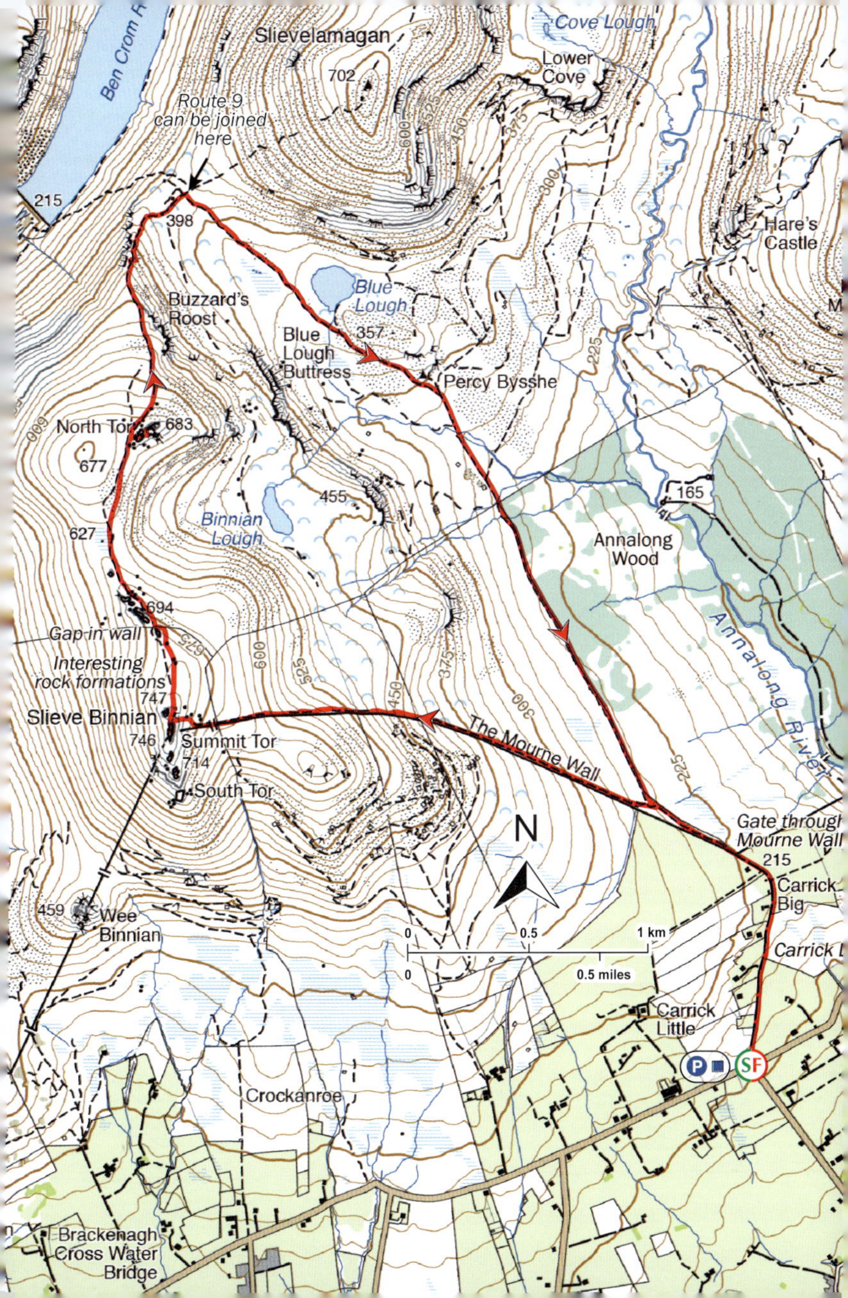
Slievelamagan
Cove Lough
Lower Cove
Ben Crom R
702
Route 9 can be joined here
215
398
Blue Lough
Buzzard's Roost
Blue Lough Buttress
357
Percy Bysshe
Hare's Castle
North Tor
683
677
Binnian Lough
455
165
Annalong Wood
627
694
Gap in wall
Interesting rock formations
747
Slieve Binnian
746
Summit Tor
714
South Tor
The Mourne Wall
Annalong River
Gate through Mourne Wall
215
Carrick Big
N
0
0.5
1 km
0
0.5 miles
459
Wee Binnian
Carrick Little
P
SF
Crockanroe
Brackenagh Cross Water Bridge

Epic views over Ben Crom Reservoir and the north-west section of Silent Valley on the descent

If combining with Slievelamagan, Cove Mountain and Slieve Beg, divert to Route 9 here. Turn right here and descend south-east along a clear path for 1.9km, past **Blue Lough**, ignoring all turn-offs to meet a dry-stone wall.

Keep straight ahead through a gap in the wall and follow the track alongside a fence for 1.4km to a junction. To your left is Annalong Wood (see Route 6). Bear left, south-east, along the path for 300m, with the fence on your left and the Mourne Wall on your right, passing through a couple of gates to access a track. Follow this for 1km to finish at **Carrick Little car park**.

ROUTE 9

Lamagan, Cove and Beg from Carrick Little

Start/finish	Carrick Little car park
Time	5hr 15min
Distance	15.5km
Ascent/descent	720m
Grade	Hard
Options	Combine with Route 8 (+1.6km/+345m/+1hr 15min)
Bus stop	The Mourne Rambler summer bus service stops at Carrick Little car park

Of the six mountains in the Mournes higher than 700m, Slievelamagan is the only one not crossed by the Mourne Wall. Of the other five, the Wall passes directly over three and within 300m of two. In fact, Slievelamagan is the most centrally placed summit within the area enclosed by the Wall. As such, there are very few short routes from which to approach it. The one described below is the shortest loop to feature Slievelamagan, two of its northern neighbours and a section of the Brandy Pad. Route 11 describes a longer option from Silent Valley Mountain Park.

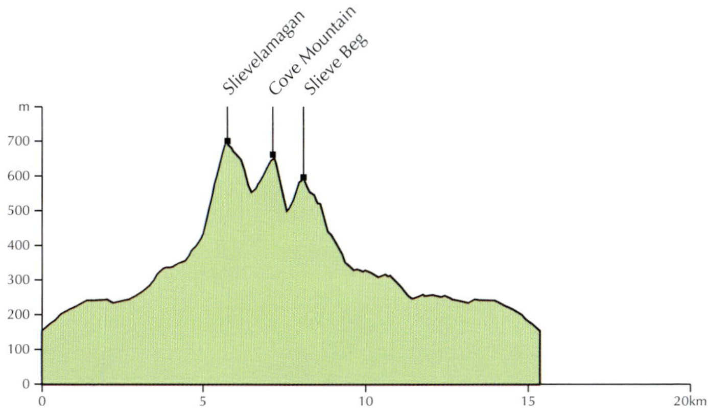

From Carrick Little car park, head north along the track just beside it. Follow the track for 1km to where it passes through the **Mourne Wall** at a gate. Continue through this and another gate a short distance directly ahead to enter open mountain land. Continue north-west for 200m to a junction. If combining with Slieve Binnian, divert to Route 8 here. Bear right along a path beside the fence. Stick to the path as it bends right with the fence to rejoin the track.

Beyond the fence lies Annalong Wood (see Route 6). Follow the track for 1.4km alongside the fence to meet a dry-stone wall at the north-west corner of the forest. Keep straight ahead through the gap in the wall and continue north-west along the path for 1.9km, past **Blue Lough**, ignoring all turn-offs to reach a junction at a **398m col**.

Turn right here along a path for a tough zigzagging ascent north-east for 1km to the summit cairn on **Slievelamagan** (702m). Continue straight over the summit, descend north-east for 780m to a 553m col, then ascend for 620m, past a cliff edge on the right, to the summit cairn on **Cove Mountain** (655m). Turn left past the summit cairn along a path and descend north-west for 450m to meet a stream to the right of a 507m col. Beware of the cliff edge and steep slope on the right along this descent.

Slieve Binnian (left) and Slievelamagan (right) from Carrick Little Track

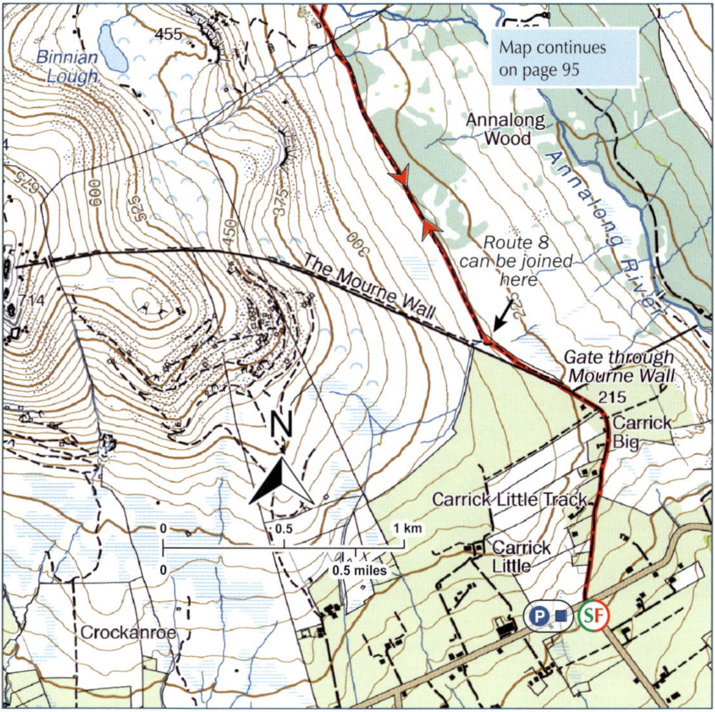

Cross the stream and turn right to ascend a clear path for 370m, passing the top of the Devil's Coachroad gully. Pause here for a look down this impressive gully. Continue straight to pass over the summit of **Slieve Beg** (596m), then descend north-east for 360m to meet the Brandy Pad (see Route 2). Turn right to follow the **Brandy Pad** east for 250m to locate a faint side path on the right descending steeply south into Annalong Valley.

The path may not be obvious among the tributary streams also descending across the Brandy Pad. Turn right onto the side path and proceed down it. Take care when stepping on exposed rock, loose gravel and peat to avoid slipping on this descent. The path becomes clearer as you descend the valley. Try not to stray too far right onto a higher path towards the Devil's Coachroad gully. Continue south, passing under the dramatic **crags of Cove Mountain** and ignore any side paths.

Looking down the Annalong Valley from the Brandy Pad

After 3km, the path bends sharply right for 90m to a junction. Turn left and follow the path south-west for 670m to meet a broader path. Bear left here for 110m to meet a dry-stone wall. Keep straight through a gap in the wall and follow the track alongside a fence for 1.4km to a **junction**. Bear left, south-east, along the path for 300m, with the fence on your left and the Mourne Wall on your right, passing through a couple of gates to access a track. Follow this for 1km to finish at **Carrick Little car park**.

Map finishes on page 93

ROUTE 10

Slieve Binnian from Silent Valley

Start/finish	Silent Valley car park
Time	4hr
Distance	11.4km
Ascent/descent	675m
Grade	Hard
Options	Combine with Route 11 (+9km/+470m/+3hr 30min)
Bus stop	The Mourne Rambler summer bus service stops 600m from Silent Valley car park

Starting from Silent Valley Mountain Park as a gentle, flat stroll alongside the lower reservoir on a surfaced access road, the route changes dramatically when you reach the wall of Ben Crom Dam. After this, a steepening ascent becomes a pleasant ridge traverse through rocky tors to the summit of Binnian, finishing with a steep descent requiring focused attention and precise foot placement. Route 8 describes a much easier option from Carrick Little in Annalong Valley.

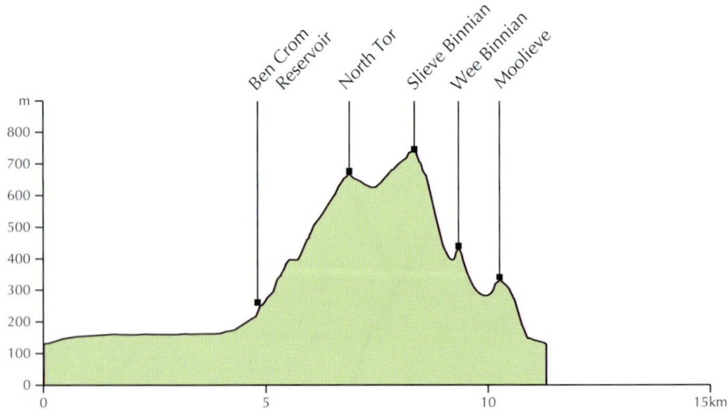

From the north end of Silent Valley car park, follow the access road for 100m north, curving right between a toilet block and a pond, to a junction beside *The Mourne Hand* sculpture. Turn left and walk 600m along any of the paths and access roads that head north to the top of the grassy embankment wall of Silent Valley Reservoir (see 'Silent Valley and Watertown' in Route 12). Aim for the right-hand (east) end of the wall where a large plughole-shaped overflow sits in the reservoir.

With the reservoir on your left, proceed north along the access road. After 1km, pass the outflow of the **Binnian Tunnel** on your right. Continue past the top end of Silent Valley Reservoir and onwards up the valley for 3km to **Ben Crom Reservoir** (see Route 11). From a turning circle at the base of the dam wall, climb a set of zigzagging steps to the right. You can take the short out-and-back detour along the top of the dam if you wish.

THE BINNIAN TUNNEL

After plans for the Annalong Valley Reservoir were cancelled due to difficulties encountered during the Silent Valley Reservoir project 20 years earlier, engineers had to come up with new ideas to fulfil Belfast's increasing water demands. Part of the solution came in the form of the 3.6km-long Binnian Tunnel. Starting just above the 160m contour, where the stream from Blue Lough meets Annalong River (Route 6), the tunnel passes almost directly beneath the 747m summit of Slieve Binnian before discharging into Silent Valley Reservoir at Ardley River (Routes 10, 11 and 12). The tunnel reaches its maximum depth of about 587m below the surface where it passes under the summit.

Construction of the Binnian Tunnel commenced in late 1947. Two teams of men, more than 150 in total, working from opposite ends, made their way towards each other, aiming to meet in the middle. This involved a repeated process of drilling, setting explosives, detonation, clearing out rock debris and checking the alignment of the tunnel's path. Conditions underground were harsh: workers had to endure long periods in the dusty tunnel, breathing smoky air and fumes. On 6 December 1950, the two teams met beneath Slieve Binnian, only a couple of inches off-centre. Binnian Tunnel was officially opened in August 1952.

Binnian Tunnel's catchment area covers approximately $9km^2$ of the upper Annalong Valley. From map contours, the tunnel appears to drop by no more than a metre or two along its length, resulting in a very shallow fall. Making the tunnel any steeper would have meant starting further upstream on Annalong River, thereby decreasing its catchment area. Starting it any further downstream would have compromised its ability to transport water using gravity alone.

Take a break on the ascent to enjoy the views across Silent Valley

Cross a stile near the top of the steps you ascended moments earlier. If combining with Slieve Beg, Cove Mountain and Slievelamagan, divert to Route 11 here. Facing north-east along the right-hand shore of Ben Crom Reservoir, bear right to ascend north-east along a clear path for 670m, away from the water, to a junction at a **398m col**. Turn right to ascend south-west on a constructed path curving south. Pause every now and then to take in the views behind you over Ben Crom Reservoir. After 1.4km, arrive at the right-hand side of **Slieve Binnian North Tor**. (Its 683m summit is accessible, but care is needed.)

Descend south along the path for 450m to cross a **627m col** – the highest col between two official mountain summits in the Mournes – to reach the first in a chain of interesting ridgeline rock formations. You can pass these on either side, but the best path stays close to their left-hand side. Be careful not to stray down a path forking left off the ridge. After 400m, go through a gap in a wall, then pass another rock formation – either side is fine. With the summit tor now in sight, continue 350m south across the grassy plateau, past a couple of smaller formations, including one where the top slab looks to be quite precariously balanced.

Ascend the summit tor of **Slieve Binnian** (747m) and take some time to admire the views in all directions. Descend south to a mini col. (The actual summit is marked by a metal post on the rocks above you directly ahead to the south. It is accessible, but care is needed.) Turn right at the mini col and descend west down the Silent Valley side, bearing left immediately and staying close to the tor's base on your left to where the Wall restarts. Brace yourself for a steep downhill section.

N
0
0.5
1 km
0
0.5 miles
526
Ben Crom River
Steps
215
398
Route 11
can be joined
here
Buzzard's
Roost
Blue
Lough
357
Blue
Lough
Buttress
Shannagh River
North Tor
683
677
627
455
Binnian
Lough
Miners Hole River
Miners Hole
Gap in wall
694
Interesting
rock formations
Silent Valley Reservoir
Access road
747
Slieve Binnian
746
Summit Tor
Very steep
descent
714
South Tor
Wall
Slievenaglogh
445
Binnian
Tunnel
outflow
459
Wee
Binnian
Plughole
overflow
Moolieve
332
Crockanroe
154
Mourne
Hand
Sculpture
Old Quarries
Scarden
Hill
Brackenagh
Cross Water
Bridge
Silent Valley

The approach to Slieve Binnian's summit

Bear right along the Wall and carefully descend alongside it. The worn zig-zagging path has short straights and some deep rock-and-earth steps to negotiate. If you are a confident user of walking poles on this type of descent, your legs will appreciate them here. After 500m, pass a stile at the next col and keep straight ahead to ascend south-west for 150m. Note the path bearing right from the stile and any others heading right on the ascent. You may need to follow one of these soon. Ascend to where the Wall stops. The summit of **Wee Binnian** (459m) is among the rocks just to your right.

If visiting the summit, return to where the Wall ended minutes earlier. You now have a few options. You could exit by passing just left of the summit rock to descend a path west. A safer option is to retrace your steps by descending north-east beside the Wall. If you spotted a path heading right when ascending this part minutes earlier, it will be on the left as you descend. If you cannot find it, continue to the one at the **stile** in the col. Whichever path you choose, follow it left, away from the Wall, to contour around the right-hand side (west) of Wee Binnian.

When the Wall reappears south-west of Wee Binnian, bear left and make your way to where it restarts. Turn right and follow the Wall south-west. After

600m, pass through a broken side wall where the Mourne Wall bends right to pass the subsidiary top of **Moolieve** (332m). Continue south-west beside the Wall for a steep descent towards Silent Valley Mountain Park. From here you can see some of the early 20th-century water-related buildings downstream of the reservoir embankment.

After 550m, arrive at a stile over a fence. Take care when crossing this stile because the flight you descend is considerably longer than the one you ascend. When safely across, continue down the path for 30m. You have now entered Silent Valley Mountain Park. Keep straight at a fork, then bear left after 40m onto a constructed path. Follow this south-south-west, keeping straight ahead across another path to enter a forest.

After 350m, bear right at a path junction to arrive immediately at an access road beside *The Mourne Hand* sculpture. Check for traffic then continue straight across along another access road, curving left past a pond and a toilet block, to finish in **Silent Valley car park**.

Stile bringing you back into Silent Valley Mountain Park

ROUTE 11

Beg, Cove and Lamagan from Silent Valley

Start/finish	Silent Valley car park
Time	6hr 30min
Distance	20.2km
Ascent/descent	770m
Grade	Hard
Options	Combine with Route 10 (+0.2km/+375m/+1hr)
Bus stop	The Mourne Rambler summer bus service stops 600m from Silent Valley car park

Starting from Silent Valley Mountain Park, this route brings you along the full length of two reservoirs and beyond to one of the range's finest cols, at Hare's Gap. After a section of the Brandy Pad smugglers' route, dare to look down the Devil's Coachroad gully from the top of Slieve Beg, then finish off by bagging two mountains. Route 9 describes a shorter option from Carrick Little in Annalong Valley.

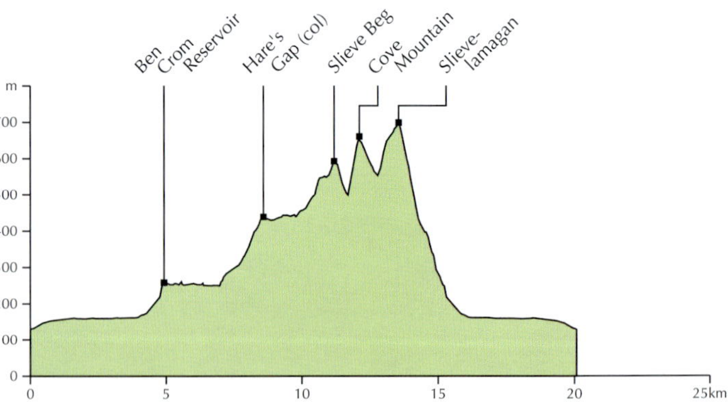

From the north end of Silent Valley car park, follow the access road north for 100m, curving right between a toilet block and a pond, to a junction beside *The*

Mourne Hand sculpture. Turn left along any of the paths and access roads heading north for 600m to the top of the grassy embankment wall of **Silent Valley Reservoir** (see Route 12). Aim for the right-hand (east) end of the wall where a large plughole-shaped overflow sits in the reservoir.

With the reservoir on your left, proceed north along the access road. After 1km, pass the outflow of the **Binnian Tunnel** (see Route 10) on your right. Continue past the top end of Silent Valley Reservoir and onwards up the valley for 3km to **Ben Crom Reservoir**. From a turning circle at the base of the dam wall, climb a set of zigzagging steps to the right. You can take the short out-and-back detour along the top of the dam if you wish.

BEN CROM RESERVOIR

Path beside Ben Crom Reservoir

After the Annalong Valley Reservoir project was cancelled, an alternative plan was drawn up. Part of this involved building a second reservoir in the upper Kilkeel River valley to capture the highest 8.4km^2 section of its catchment area. Spanning a relatively narrow and steep-sided section of the valley, Ben Crom Reservoir was designed as a mass gravity dam, constructed and faced with concrete. Work got underway in 1953, shortly after the Binnian Tunnel was completed.

It is very likely that some of the men who worked on the Binnian Tunnel were recruited again to construct Ben Crom Reservoir. The project also involved building a new access road from the Silent Valley Reservoir, using excavated rock from the tunnel. One workman died during the Ben Crom project. A plaque commemorating him can be seen near the waymarked Heritage Trail in Silent Valley Mountain Park. Ben Crom Reservoir was completed in 1957. Interestingly, Spelga Dam in neighbouring Bann Valley, just 5km to the west, was completed the same year.

Map continues on page 107
Shannagh River
Miners Hole River
Miners Hole
North Tor
683
677
627
694
282
The Mourne Wall
Silent Valley Reservoir
Access road
Slieve Binnian
747
746
714
Slievenaglogh
445
Binnian Tunnel outflow
292
N
459
Wee Binnian
0
0.5
1 km
0.5 miles
Plughole overflow
Moolieve
332
335
154
Mourne Hand Sculpture
Old Quarries
SF
P
Scarden Hill
Brackenagh Cross Water Bridge
225
300
375
450
525
600
675

Approaching Ben Crom Reservoir

Cross a stile near the top of the steps you ascended moments earlier. Proceed north-east, bearing left along a path beside Ben Crom Reservoir for 2km. At the far end, head left and jump over **Kilkeel River**. Continue west to where another stream tumbles down over rocky waterfalls. Choose a safe place to cross upstream, bearing in mind that the rocks could be very slippery. If in doubt, to avoid the rocky part, head further upstream to where the stream narrows. On the other side, ascend away from the stream to find a path.

View across Silent Valley from the summit of Slievelamagan

Follow this for 1.4km up the left-hand side of the valley to **Hare's Gap** (437m). Bear right past the start of some rock steps onto the **Brandy Pad** (see Route 2), a clear path contouring east. Follow this for 2.2km to a **553m col**. Turn right here to ascend south-west along a path for 360m to the summit of **Slieve Beg** (596m). A short distance past the summit, pause for a look down the gully.

Continue straight past the top of the Devil's Coachroad gully, then curve right to descend west on a path for 370m to meet a stream. Turn left across the stream and ascend south along a path for 450m, keeping away from the steep slope and cliffs on the left to reach the summit cairn on **Cove Mountain** (655m). Turn right to descend a path, heading west-south-west for 620m. Pass a cliff edge on the left, cross a 553m col and ascend south along the path for 780m to the summit cairn on **Slievelamagan** (702m).

Continue straight over the summit and descend a zigzagging path for 1km to a junction at a **398m col**. If combining with Slieve Binnian, divert to Route 10 here. Turn right and descend along a clear path, initially north-west then south-west, for 670m to a stile beside Ben Crom Reservoir. Cross the stile, continue straight for a few metres, then descend the steps beside the dam wall. Retrace your steps south-west for 4.8km along the access road beside Silent Valley Reservoir to finish in **Silent Valley car park**.

Descending the steps beside Ben Crom Reservoir

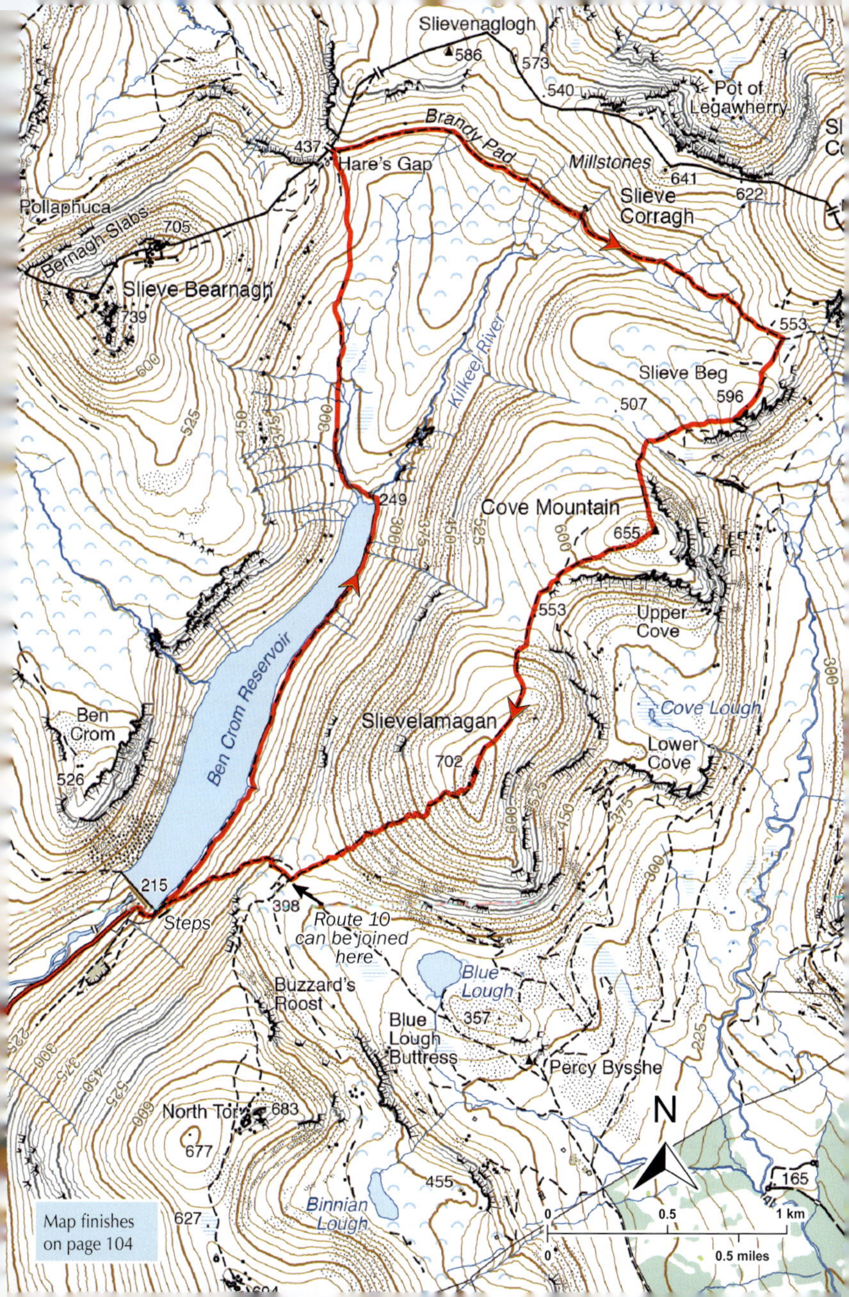

Map finishes on page 104

ROUTE 12

Silent Valley floor

Start/finish	Silent Valley car park
Time	5hr 30min
Distance	18.8km
Ascent/descent	420m
Grade	Moderate
Options	Turn back at south end of Ben Crom Reservoir (-9km/-290m/-2hr 45min); turn back at north end of Ben Crom Reservoir (-4km/-190m/-1hr 15min)
Bus stop	The Mourne Rambler summer bus service stops 600m from Silent Valley car park

In the late 19th century, city leaders in Belfast needed to find new sources of water to meet the rising demands of a growing population and expanding industries. Identifying the upper Kilkeel River valley in the Mournes as the potential site for a new reservoir marked the start of a massive multi-phase civil engineering project that would take decades to complete. This route takes you along the full length of Silent Valley, passing Watertown, two reservoirs, a tunnel and an eerie gorge along the way.

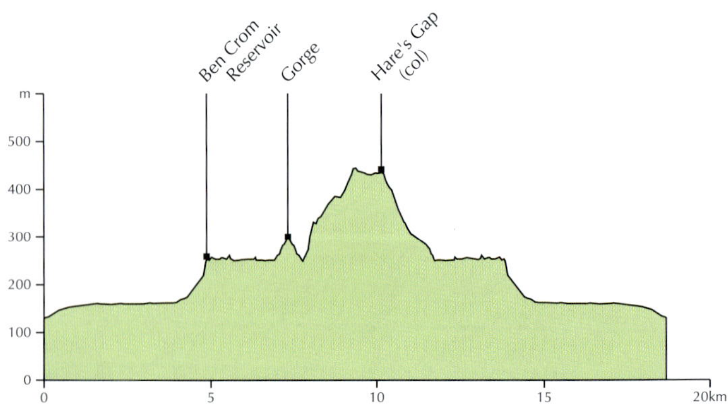

The Mourne Hand *sculpture in Silent Valley Mountain Park*

From the north end of Silent Valley car park, follow the access road north for 100m, curving right between a toilet block and a pond, to a junction beside *The Mourne Hand* sculpture.

Turn left along any of the paths and access roads heading north for 600m to the top of the grassy embankment wall of Silent Valley Reservoir. Aim for the right-hand (east) end of the wall where a large plughole-shaped overflow sits in the reservoir. With the reservoir on your left, proceed north along the access road.

SILENT VALLEY RESERVOIR AND WATERTOWN

Detailed design work on the reservoir envisaged by civil engineer Luke Livingstone Macassey for the Kilkeel River valley did not start until 1910, two years after his death. The project was further delayed by World War 1. At that time the area was known as Happy Valley, supposedly because of the merry Cornish miners who had previously searched the area for silver and lead.

Construction work on the dam's earth-and-rock embankment wall eventually got underway in 1923. But unexpectedly difficult ground conditions encountered during the works delayed progress significantly, and as a result of various accidents, eight workmen died. A plaque commemorating them can be seen near the waymarked Heritage Trail in the park. Silent Valley Reservoir and the landscaped parkland south of it were completed in 1933.

During construction, workers and their families were accommodated in a temporary on-site village called Watertown. As well as housing, the village also had a shop, a hospital and a police station. For entertainment, there was a cinema and a hall where dances and boxing competitions were held. Watertown also had the first electric street lighting in Ireland. A purpose-built 6km railway line was used to transport machinery, materials and workers and their families to and from the coastal village of Annalong. No record of the railway appears on historical maps.

Silent Valley Reservoir has a primary catchment area of approximately 22.6km^2; this includes the sub-catchment areas of Ben Crom Reservoir (8.4km^2) and Lough Shannagh (1.1km^2), both of which feed into it. Additional rainfall from a 9km^2 section of the neighbouring Annalong Valley can also be diverted into Silent Valley Reservoir via the Binnian Tunnel as and when required. Prior to flooding, the valley floor had a moraine landscape similar to that of Annalong Valley.

The gorge on Kilkeel River at the north end of Ben Crom Reservoir

After 1km, pass the outflow of the **Binnian Tunnel** (see Route 10) on your right. Continue past the top end of Silent Valley Reservoir and onwards up the valley for 3km to **Ben Crom Reservoir** (see Route 11). From a turning circle at the base of the dam wall, climb a set of zigzagging steps to the right. You can take the short out-and-back detour along the top of the dam if you wish. Walkers often choose this spot to turn around and retrace their steps to the start. During the summer months, it may also be possible to catch a shuttle bus back to the start from the turning circle at the base of the dam wall.

Cross a stile near the top of the steps you ascended moments earlier. Proceed north-east, bearing left along a path beside Ben Crom Reservoir for 2km. At the far end, head left and jump over **Kilkeel River** – just a stream here. Walkers also choose this spot to turn around and retrace their steps to the start. Head north-east, upstream, for 150m along the river into a **gorge**, following a faint path that crosses the stream and rocks several times.

This unique place has an otherworldly charm and is worth the short detour. Do not attempt to climb up the sides of the gorge. From a waterfall 250m into the gorge, retrace your steps to the reservoir. With your back to the reservoir, face north and survey the terrain ahead. To the immediate left of the gorge, a ridgeline begins. Choose your own route for 200m to

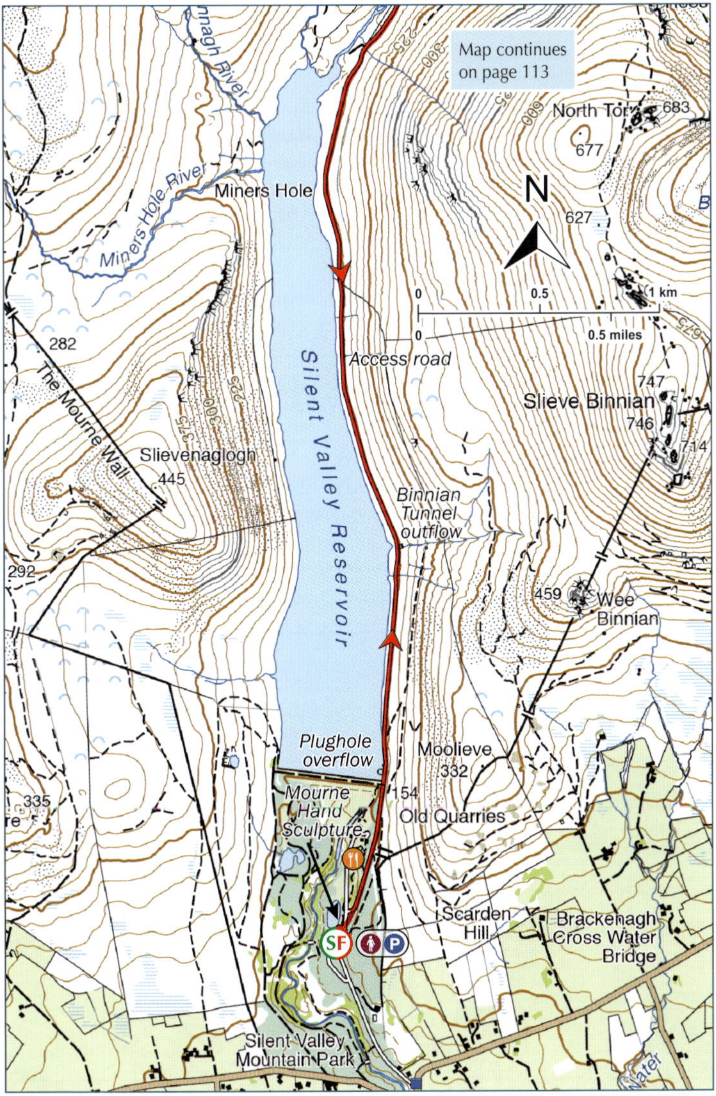

Map continues on page 113
Silent Valley Reservoir
Miners Hole
Miners Hole River
Access road
Binnian Tunnel outflow
Plughole overflow
Mourne Hand Sculpture
Silent Valley Mountain Park
Slievenaglogh
445
The Mourne Wall
282
292
335
North Tor
683
677
627
Slieve Binnian
747
746
714
459
Wee Binnian
Moolieve
332
154
Old Quarries
Scarden Hill
Brackenagh Cross Water Bridge
N
0
0.5
1 km
0.5 miles
SF

gain the high line, keeping well left of the gorge. Ascend north-north-east along the high line, crossing pathless heather for 1.2 km. Beware of holes among the heather. Walking poles would be useful here.

Aim between tributaries for a dry approach to the **Brandy Pad** (see Route 2). Turn left along this obvious path for 840m to **Hare's Gap** (437m). Bear left, away from the Wall, and head south along a path descending the right-hand side of the valley. As you lose height, Ben Crom Reservoir reveals itself directly ahead and the path comes alongside a stream on the left. After about 1.4km, as you approach the reservoir, you need to cross the stream.

Consider crossing while it is still jumpable, as it gets more treacherous closer to the reservoir due to rocky waterfalls. On the other side, with the stream now on your right, follow a faint path above it for 200m down to the reservoir. Head east across the top end of the reservoir and jump over Kilkeel River. Turn right and head south-west, retracing your steps for 7km along the path and access road beside the two reservoirs to finish in **Silent Valley car park**.

Other walks in Silent Valley Mountain Park

The main route described above starts and finishes in Silent Valley Mountain Park, where there is a selection of shorter waymarked trails. These are all marked on a free map that you can request from a staff member upon arrival. The trails are also displayed on an information panel close to the start point. A photo of this would be a handy reference along the waymarked trails.

Plug-hole overflow in Silent Valley Reservoir

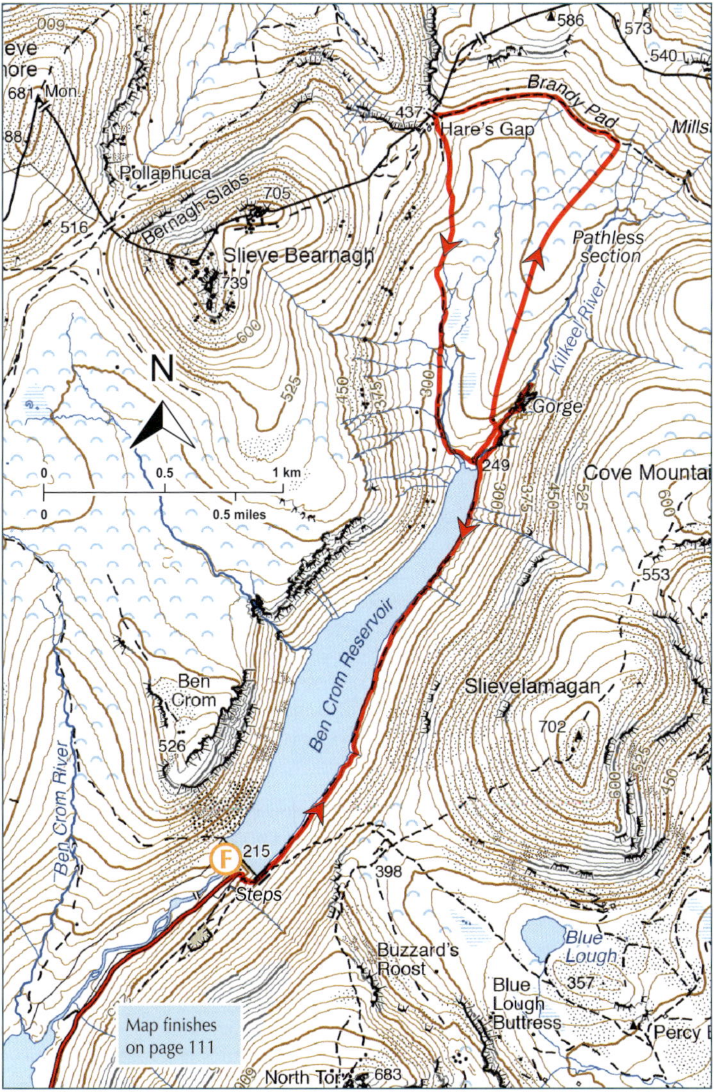
Brandy Pad
Hare's Gap
437
586
573
540
Pollaphuca
Bernagh Slabs
705
516
Slieve Bearnagh
739
Pathless section
Kilkeel River
Gorge
249
Cove Mountai
N
0
0.5
1 km
0
0.5 miles
553
Ben Crom Reservoir
Ben Crom
526
Slievelamagan
702
Ben Crom River
215
Steps
398
Blue Lough
357
Buzzard's Roost
Blue Lough Buttress
North Tor
683
Map finishes on page 111

ROUTE 13

Silent Valley Horseshoe

Start/finish	Silent Valley car park
Alt start/finish	Banns Road car park
Time	11hr
Distance	27.1km
Ascent/descent	2265m
Grade	Very hard
Options	West loop (-4.5km /-1005m/-3hr); east loop (-5.2km/-880m/-3hr); Banns Road car park (+3.2km/+100m/+45min); Slievenagore loop extension (+2.3km/+45m/+30min)
Bus stops	The Mourne Rambler summer bus service stops at Banns Road car park and 600m from Silent Valley car park

Walk one of Ireland's most challenging horseshoe routes. Following Silent Valley's enclosing ridgeline, you will pass over (or very close to) 16 summits, including 10 official mountain summits. Northern, western and southern sections of the route include some stretches of the Mourne Wall, deviating from it slightly in places to follow the valley's true catchment boundary. The eastern section is a south–north traverse of the Western Mournes central ridge. This route can be linked with the Annalong Valley Horseshoe (Route 7) as an alternative to the Mourne Wall Challenge (Route 25).

From the north end of Silent Valley car park, follow the access road north, curving right between a toilet block and a pond, to a junction beside *The Mourne Hand* sculpture. If walking the west loop, depart from the main route here (Variant 1). Check for traffic, then continue straight across onto a path heading into the trees. After a few paces, bear left immediately onto a side path. Follow this north-east through the trees for 310m. Keep straight ahead where another path crosses.

After a further 40m, bend sharply right to start a brief zigzagging ascent. Leave the constructed path as you round the second sharp bend (left) and ascend east for 80m along a worn path through heather to a **stile**. Cross this and bear right to ascend beside the Mourne Wall for 550m to the subsidiary top of **Moolieve** (332m). Bear left, away from the Wall, to descend north along the pathless

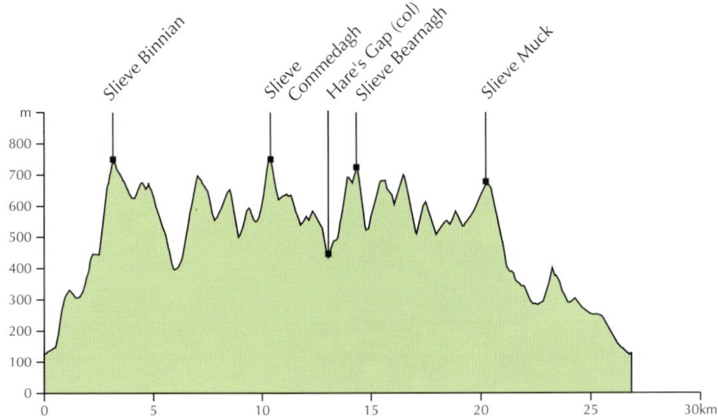

ridgeline. If visibility is poor or you're not strict about the route, just head north-east along the Wall to Wee Binnian and skirt left around its rocky tor.

Gradually curve right along the high line for 350m, passing through a gap in a broken wall to a broad col. The ground is good here, with lots of small boulders. You may notice a path crossing your route soon after the col. Turn left along this for a short distance to where it bends right to zigzag its way along the high line. When it bends left to contour north, bear right to follow the pathless steepening high line as closely as possible and curve towards the west side of Wee Binnian. After 550m, as you approach the rocky tor, meet a clear path.

Cross this stile to exit the east side of Silent Valley Mountain Park

From left to right: Lamagan, Binnian and Bearnagh from the summit of Slievenaglogh (586m)

Follow this left as it skirts around the tor. Look for a path forking off to the right. Follow this to arrive near the summit of **Wee Binnian** (459m). The summit is the rocks to your left. If you choose to visit, do so carefully and return to this point. A few metres south-east, you will find the Wall where it has been interrupted by Wee Binnian's tor. Turn left to descend north-east, with the Wall on your right, for 150m to a stile at the col. Continue straight ahead beside the Wall and brace yourself for the imminent steep ascent.

The worn zigzagging path beside the Wall comprises short straights and some high rock-and-earth steps. This is one of the toughest ascents in the Mournes. Take breaks along the way to enjoy the views behind you over Silent Valley Reservoir. After 500m, where the Wall meets the base of the summit tor, bear left to skirt around it to a mini col near the summit of **Slieve Binnian** (747m). (The actual summit is marked by a metal post on the rocks to your right. It is accessible, but care is needed.) Turn left at the mini col and ascend north over the rocks.

Continue north across the plateau for 900m, passing rock formations – one with a precariously balanced top slab – and bypassing a large granite outcrop (either side is fine). Go through a gap in a wall, skirt the last ridge rocks (best path is to their right) and head north across a 627m col – the highest col between two official mountain summits in the Mournes. Bear left off the path for 300m along the high line to **Slieve Binnian North Top** (677m), then turn right for 200m to rejoin the path beside **Slieve Binnian North Tor** (683m). (The unmarked summit is accessible, but care is needed.)

Map continues on page 119
215
Steps
Ben Crom River
Shannagh River
Miners Hole River
Miners Hole
398
Buzzard's Roost
Blue Lough
357
Blue Lough Buttress
North Tor
683
Slieve Binnian North Top
677
455
Binnian Lough
627
Access road
694
Gap in wall
Interesting rock formations
Silent Valley Reservoir
747
Slieve Binnian
746
Summit Tor
714
Very steep ascent
South Tor
Slievenaglogh
445
Binnian Tunnel outflow
459
Wee Binnian
Plughole overflow
Moolieve
332
154
Old Quarries
Mourne Hand sculpture
Delicate stone wall without stile/gate
Crockanroe
Scarden Hill
Brackenagh Cross Water Bridge
SF
P
N
0
0.5
1 km
0.5 miles
Silent Valley Mountain Park

Walking east beside the Mourne Wall towards Silent Valley Mountain Park

Turn left along the path and descend north for 1.4km. Pause every now and then to take in the views over Ben Crom Reservoir as you descend this constructed path to a junction at a **398m col**. Continue ahead for a tough zigzagging ascent north-east for 1km to a cairn at the summit of **Slievelamagan** (702m). Continue straight to descend north-east for 780m to a 553m col, then ascend for 620m, past a cliff edge on the right, to the summit cairn on **Cove Mountain** (655m).

Turn left past the cairn along a path, descending north-west for 450m to meet a stream to the right of a 507m col. Beware of the cliff edge and steep slope on the right along this descent. Strict horseshoe challenge walkers will bear left of the path along the high line to pass over the 507m col. Cross the stream and turn right to ascend a clear path for 370m, passing the top of the Devil's Coachroad gully. Continue straight over the summit of **Slieve Beg** (596m), then descend north-east for 350m to meet the **Brandy Pad** (see Route 2) at a 553m col.

Continue straight across the Brandy Pad and zigzag north up the steep pathless slope for 620m to meet the **Mourne Wall** at a stone shelter. (The summit cairn on Slieve Commedagh, 765m, is just 270m to the north-east of here if you fancy the short out-and-back detour.) Turn left to descend westwards for 2.6km, with the Wall on your right. Fresh water flows from an obvious pipe a few metres left of the Wall. Continue over the subsidiary top of **Slieve Corragh** (641m) and the summit of **Slievenaglogh** (586m) to reach **Hare's Gap** (437m). If walking the east loop, depart from the main route here (Variant 2).

Map continues on page 120
Slievenagloigh
586
573
540
Pot of Legawherry
Slieve Commedagh
683
765
Brandy Pad
437
Hare's Gap
Millstones
641
622
Slieve Corragh
Mon.
Slieve Bearnagh North Tor
705
Slieve Bearnagh
739
553
The Castl
Slieve Beg
596
507
Devil's Coachroad gully
Kilkeel River
249
Cove Mountain
655
553
Upper Cove
Cove Lough
Lower Cove
Ben Crom Reservoir
Slievelamagan
702
215
Steps
398
Buzzard's Roost
Blue Lough
Blue
357
Hare's Castle
N
0
0.5
1 km
0.5 miles

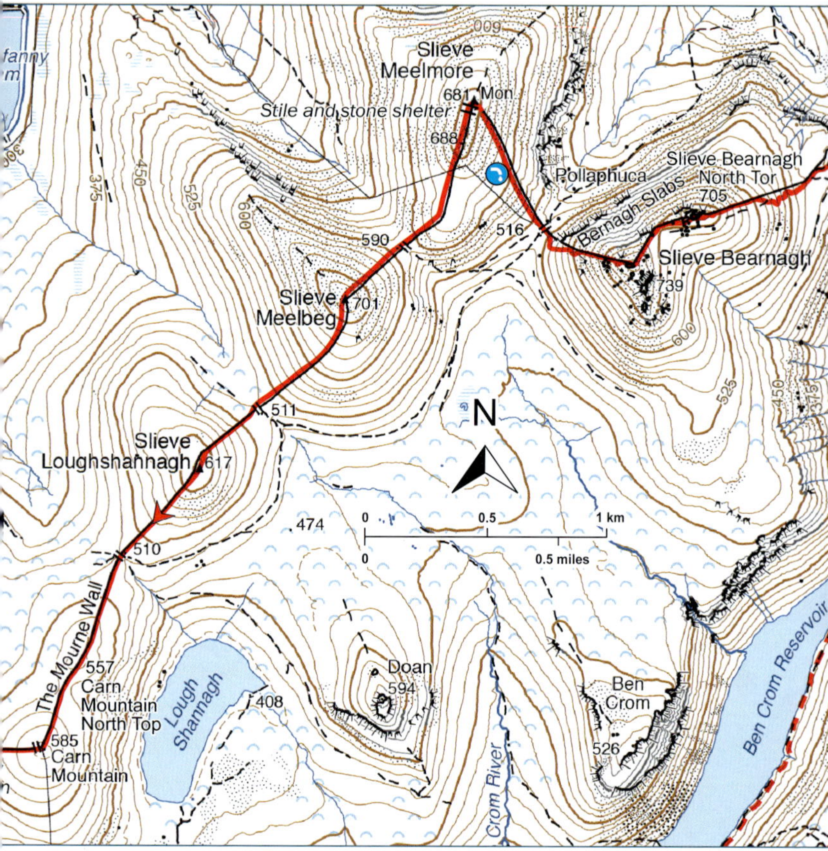

Bear slightly left of the Wall to ascend some stone steps, then head right to rejoin the Wall and ascend beside it for 850m to the base of **Slieve Bearnagh North Tor**. Skirt left around the rock to pick up the Wall where it restarts. Continue west-south-west beside the Wall for 280m to a sharp right-hand bend on a rocky subsidiary top near the summit of **Slieve Bearnagh** (739m). (The actual summit is located on a granite tor 100m south of here. It is accessible, but care is needed.) Work your way clockwise around the south side of the rocks on the subsidiary top to rejoin the Wall. Brace yourself for a steep descent.

Follow the Wall as it descends west. Take care on this section. Bear slightly left of the Wall as you approach the bottom along one of the worn paths. The ground is steep and quite eroded. Carefully zigzag your way down, always keeping the Wall in sight. Keep straight on through a 516m col. Two walls radiate north-west from here. Follow the right-hand one – the Mourne Wall – and ascend beside it for 620m. Fresh water flows from a pipe in the heather a few metres left of the Wall. Arrive at a stone shelter built into a sharp corner and cross the stile.

Turn left alongside the Wall for 110m to the summit cairn on **Slieve Meelmore** (688m). With the Wall on your left, descend south-west for 600m to a 590m col and continue straight through. Ascend south-west for 330m to the summit cairn on **Slieve Meelbeg** (701m). Follow the Wall as it bends left and descend south-west for 620m to a 511m col. Cross the stile here. With the Wall now on your right, ascend south-west for 360m to the summit cairn on **Slieve Loughshannagh** (617m).

Descend south-west for 500m to a 510m col and continue straight through. With the Wall still on your right, follow it for 880m over **Carn Mountain North Top** (557m) to a gap. The Mourne Wall bends right here. Turn right through the gap in the adjoining broken wall beside the summit cairn on **Carn Mountain** (585m). Ignore the stile and descend west, beside the Wall, for 300m to a 531m col, where it bends left. Bear left to ascend around a short rocky section. Rejoin the Wall and ascend south for 1km to a stile where the Wall bends left.

Turn right across the stile and walk a short distance south-west to the summit trig on **Slieve Muck** (674m). Return to the Wall. From this side, there are two stiles. Cross the one on the right, then turn right to follow the Wall south-west for 140m. Bear left to pass a small cliff face. If visibility is poor, or you're not strict about the route, head right after the ledge to descend beside the Wall to where it crosses Bann's Road. Along the way, you will have to bear left to bypass a steep rocky section that interrupts the Wall further down.

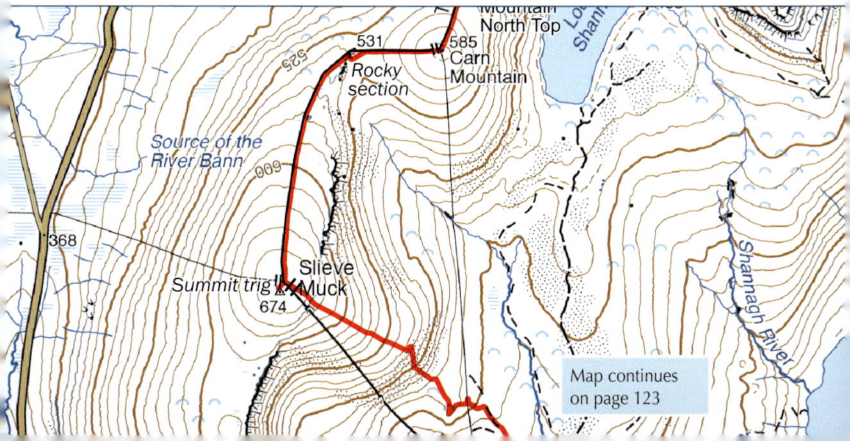

Map continues
on page 123

Head left, away from the Wall, to follow the ridgeline that separates the Kilkeel River catchment area from that of the White Water River catchment. It is unclear why the Wall deviates out of the catchment area for 1.9km between Slieve Muck summit and Banns Road. Descend south-east along the ridgeline, directly towards the summit of Slieve Binnian on the far side of Silent Valley. Zigzag on the steeper sections and maintain the high line. After a relatively flat section, you can follow a path for a bit before curving right to descend onto the Banns Road track. After 1.9km, come to a gate where the track passes through the Wall.

If visibility is poor, or you're not strict about the route, bear left at the gate to follow the Wall south-east over the **summit of Slievenaglogh** (445m), then head south-west to a corner of the Mourne Wall. It is interesting to note that the Wall deviates into the catchment area for 3.3km between Banns Road and Silent Valley Mountain Park. As a result, 0.8km^2 of the Silent Valley Reservoir catchment area is not enclosed by the Wall.

Cross the stile and head south for 200m along the track to where it bends right. Bear left off the track and ascend south-east through heather for 600m to Slievenaglogh's west shoulder. There is no need to visit the summit. Turn right and descend south-west along the ridge for 440m to join a track. Descend along this for 400m and continue south-west, across a broad **292m col**, for 210m to the high point on a wall. The alternate start/finish at Banns Road car park ties in here (Variant 3). Turn left and follow the wall east for 190m to a stile. From here, you can maximise the length of catchment perimeter walked by including a short loop over Slievenagore (Variant 4).

Continue straight past the stile and follow the wall east for 60m to where it meets **a corner of the Mourne Wall**. Keep straight through a low gap at the wall junction and continue east beside the Wall for 440m to another stile. Turn right and cross the stile. Follow a track south-south-east for 650m to where it comes close to the Wall on the left. Leave the track here and continue south beside the Wall for 620m to a stile. Turn left across the stile to enter **Silent Valley Mountain Park**.

Follow a constructed path east for 140m, ignoring two side paths on the left, until you reach a track. Turn right and follow the track south for 100m, then turn left onto a side path. Follow this north-east initially for the closing 390m beside a fence curving east. Bear right at a junction, then curve left to pass the bottom of a stepped side path ascending left. Cross a bridge over Kilkeel River, turn left at the final junction and ascend to finish at **Silent Valley car park**.

Slieve Muck
Summit trig
674
Shannagh River
Miners Hole River
Miners Hole
282
The Mourne Wall
Slievenaglogh
445
Silent Valley Reservoir
Yellow Water
Binnian Tunnel outflow
292
Banns Road
Plughole overflow
Mourne Hand sculpture
Slievenagore
335
Delicate stone wall without stile/gate
154
Old Quarr
Mooliev
332
194
193
217
N
0
0.5
1 km
0.5 miles
Silent Valley
225
300
375
600

Variant 1: west loop

From *The Mourne Hand* sculpture, follow Route 12 to the north-east end of Ben Crom Reservoir. Head left, jump over **Kilkeel River** and proceed west to where another stream tumbles down over rocky waterfalls. Choose a safe place to cross, bearing in mind that the rocks could be very slippery. If in doubt, head further upstream to get past the rocky part to where the stream narrows. On the other side, ascend away from the stream to find a path. Follow this north for 1.4km up the left-hand side of the valley to **Hare's Gap** (437m). With the Mourne Wall in front of you, take a sharp left up some stone steps and follow the main route.

Variant 2: east loop

At Hare's Gap (437m), bear left, away from the Wall, and follow Route 12 to the north-east end of Ben Crom Reservoir. Head east past the top end of the reservoir and jump over **Kilkeel River**. Turn right and proceed south-west for 7km along a path beside Ben Crom Reservoir and an access road beside Silent Valley Reservoir to finish in **Silent Valley car park**.

Variant 3: alternate start/finish at Banns Road car park

Starting from the north-east end of Banns Road car park, follow the **Banns Road** track north-east for 1.1km to a gate where it enters open mountain land. Pass

Take the access road beside Silent Valley Reservoir to start the west loop

through the gate and turn right immediately to ascend for 400m alongside a dry-stone wall. Keep straight on at a high point on the wall to tie into the main route.

When you return to this point later, turn right and descend alongside the wall to meet the Banns Road track. Turn left along the track and retrace your steps to finish at **Banns Road car park**.

Variant 4: Slievenagore loop extension

Cross the stile. Turn right along the wall for 190m to its high point. Turn left here and follow the ridgeline south. After 300m, in a shallow col, you may or may not find a track to follow. Either way, continue south along the ridgeline for 480m to the summit of **Slievenagore** (335m). Descend south-east off the summit, carefully negotiating a small quarry. Head east to pick up a track and follow to a junction. Continue straight on for a few metres to meet a dry-stone wall directly ahead where it passes over the high point of a small col. Do not attempt to cross this delicate wall if there is no stile or gate in place. At the time of writing, the absence of a stile or gate at this location prevented a section of the horseshoe from being completed. If a stile or gate has been installed by the time you reach here, you could continue straight along the ridgeline east to meet the Mourne Wall. Retrace your steps a few metres to the track junction. Turn right along the track and follow it north for 740m to the **stile** you crossed earlier. Cross the stile and turn right, east, along the wall to join the main route.

ROUTE 14

Slieve Muck, Carn Mountain and Slievenaglogh

Start/finish	Banns Road car park
Time	5hr
Distance	14.9km
Ascent/descent	685m
Grade	Hard
Options	Slievenaglogh only (-8.1km/-430m/-2hr 45min); Slievenaglogh omitted (-1.6km/-160m/-45min); alternate Slievenaglogh descent (-0.5km/+15m)
Bus stop	The Mourne Rambler summer bus service stops at Banns Road car park

Explore the quiet south-west corner of the stunning Silent Valley. Starting along Banns Road, one loop on this figure-of-eight route includes the eighth highest mountain in the range and a circuit of the Mournes' largest natural lake. The other loop features a lower neighbouring summit overlooking the two reservoirs in the valley. Either loop can be omitted if you prefer a shorter walk.

From the north-east end of Banns Road car park, follow the **Banns Road** track north-east for 1.1km to a gate where it enters open mountain land. Pass through the gate. With Slieve Muck dominating the skyline on your left, continue north along the track for 1.4km to a stile over the **Mourne Wall** where the track passes through a gate. Cross the stile. If walking Slievenaglogh only, turn right and follow the Wall south-east.

Turn left and ascend north-west, with the Wall on your left. Slieve Muck is now directly ahead. At a couple of short rocky sections, bear right from the Wall to bypass these before returning to the Wall above them. After 1.8km, come to a stile where the Wall turns right. Cross the stile and walk 40m south-west to the summit trig on **Slieve Muck** (674m). Return to the Wall. From this side, there are two stiles. Cross the one on the right, then turn left to follow the Wall north for 1km.

Just before the Wall bends right, negotiate a short rocky section. Bear right to descend around this to a 531m col. Ascend east for 300m to a wall junction

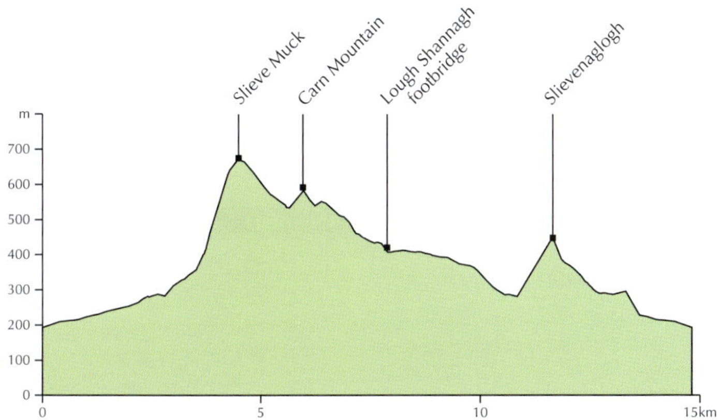

beside the summit cairn on **Carn Mountain** (585m). Ignore the stile, pass through a gap in the adjoining wall and turn left to follow the Wall north-east. Keeping the Wall on your left, pass over Carn Mountain North Top (557m). After 880m, arrive at a **510m col**.

Walker leaving the summit of Slieve Muck

Turn right here to see three paths heading off between east and south-east. Take the one on the left to descend south-east along a green path. This becomes boggy after 150m. Look for a faint path on the left. Follow this east as it contours above Lough Shannagh. Curve south-east with the path. Look across the water for a small metal bridge at the north-east corner of the lake. This is where you are aiming for. After 600m, locate a side path on the right which clearly descends to the footbridge. Turn right and descend for 160m.

LOUGH SHANNAGH

Lough Shannagh from the north

As the largest natural lake in the Mourne Mountains, Lough Shannagh covers an area of $0.15km^2$ and has a catchment area of approximately $1.1km^2$. The enclosing ridge includes the summits of Slieve Loughshannagh and Carn Mountain. At some point during or after the construction of Silent Valley Reservoir, the surface level of Lough Shannagh was artificially raised by about 1m; this was achieved by building a low dam across the lough's north-eastern corner, where Shannagh River outflows towards Silent Valley Reservoir. A sluice in the dam wall allows the additional water stored in Lough Shannagh to be released into the main reservoir below when required. At maximum capacity, with the sluice fully closed, Lough Shannagh covers an area of $0.17km^2$. As a feeder reservoir, it can hold about $160{,}000m^3$ of water to help top up Silent Valley Reservoir.

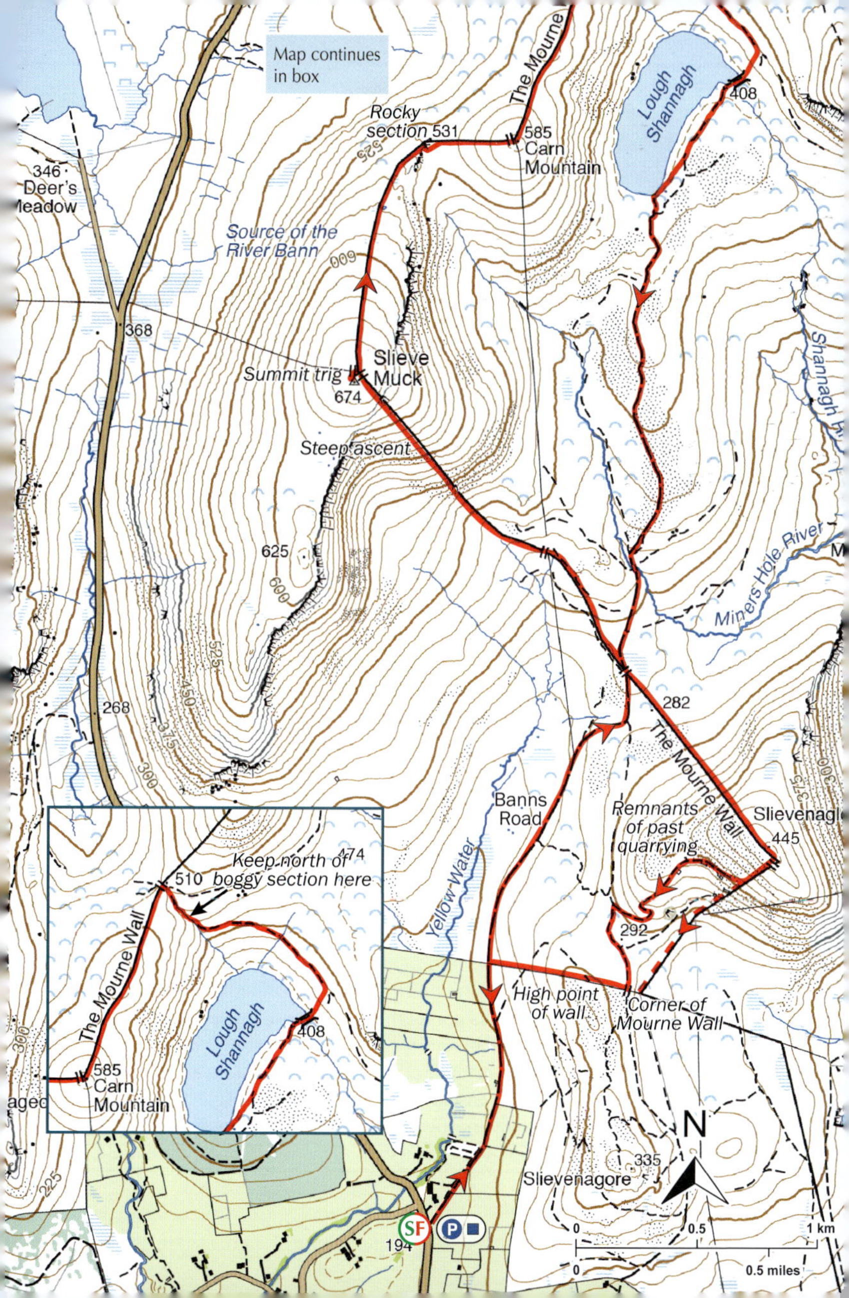

Map continues in box
The Mourne Wall
Rocky section 531
585 Carn Mountain
Lough Shannagh
408
346 Deer's Meadow
Source of the River Bann
368
Summit trig
Slieve Muck
674
Steep ascent
625
Shannagh River
Miners Hole River
282
268
The Mourne Wall
Banns Road
Remnants of past quarrying
Slievenagle
445
Yellow Water
292
High point of wall
Corner of Mourne Wall
Keep north of boggy section here
474
510
The Mourne Wall
Lough Shannagh
408
585 Carn Mountain
N
335
Slievenagore
SF
194
0
0.5
1 km
0
0.5 miles

Crossing the Lough Shannagh outflow stream with Doan in the background

Walk along the small dam wall at the north-east corner of **Lough Shannagh**, crossing the metal footbridge at its midpoint. With the lake on your right, pass a small square building and pick up a stony path heading south-west. You can walk closer to the lake shore if you prefer. After 650m, all paths converge to become the Banns Road track at the south end of the lake. Follow this south for 2km to the stile where you crossed the **Mourne Wall**. If omitting Slievenaglogh, cross the stile and continue straight on to retrace your steps south along the Banns Road track to finish at Banns Road car park.

Turn left to ascend south-east for 1km with the Wall on your right. When it comes into view, bear left from the Wall to the summit cairn on **Slievenaglogh** (445m). Rejoin the Wall for a few metres south-east to where it bends sharply right. Turn this corner and cross the stile there. Turn left to descend south-west beside the Wall. Tread carefully on this descent as it gets rocky in places. After about 150m, look for a couple of tracks heading off to the right. When you spot one, make your way towards it. If you have any difficulty finding the tracks, continue south-west beside the Wall to a wall junction. Turn right, west, along the adjoining wall to a nearby stile. Continue straight past the stile to rejoin the main route.

Pick up either of the two tracks contouring south-west. Evidence of past quarrying visible along these tracks includes rock faces, rubble piles and the ruins of stone buildings. Continue south-west for 750m along the track to a junction. Turn left to follow another track south-east for 390m to a stile. Turn right at the stile and follow the wall west for 590m over a low ridge to meet the **Banns Road** track. Turn left, pass through the gate and retrace your steps along the track to finish at **Banns Road car park**.

ROUTE 15

Doan, Ben Crom, Slieve Loughshannagh and Carn Mountain

Start/finish	Ott car park
Time	4hr 30min
Distance	14.2km
Ascent/descent	575m
Grade	Moderate
Options	Carn only (-9.1km/-350m/-3hr); Doan omitted (-2.3km/-105m/-1hr); Doan only (-7.3km/-305m/-2hr 30min); Ben Crom omitted (-4.8km/-135m/-1hr 30min); Ben Crom only (-3.7km/-260m/-1hr 30min); Carn omitted (-1.7km/-75m/-45min); Slieve Loughshannagh only (-8.5km/-315m/-2hr 45min)
Bus stop	The Mourne Rambler summer bus service stops at Ott car park

Journey to the very centre of the high Mournes on a route that allows you to pick and choose from four different summits along the way. One, two, three or all four – it's up to you. Options include the best big hill and the best small mountain in the range. Depending on your chosen route, you will enjoy views of the Mournes' largest natural lake, two beautiful reservoirs and mountain summits in almost every direction.

Group of walkers ascending Doan

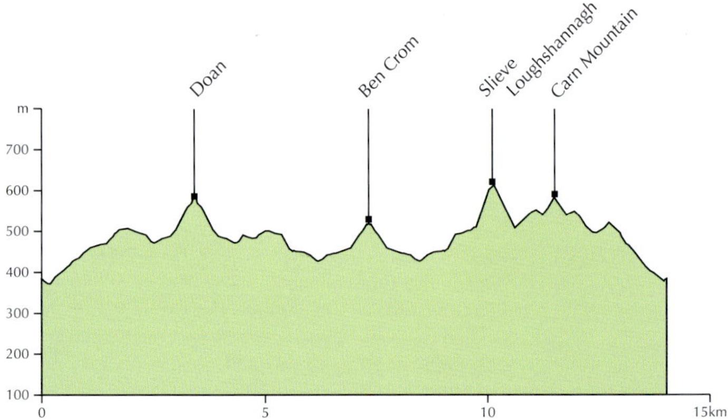

From the entrance of Ott car park, bear left across the road carefully to a stile. Cross the stile and follow **Ott Track** south-east for 160m to a fork. Turn right and follow the track for 1.2km to its end, where a path continues east for 400m through peat hags to meet the Mourne Wall at a **510m col**. Cross the stile. If walking Carn Mountain only, turn right here and ascend south-west beside the Wall. In front of you, three paths head away from the Wall between east and south-east. Take the highest and most obvious one on the left.

Follow this path for 550m as it contours around the base of Slieve Loughshannagh, curving left, north-east, to a fork in the path. If omitting Doan, bear left here. Bear right onto a much more obvious path heading south-east along the high line towards Doan. After 900m, pass a false summit along the way – the left or right side is fine. For the final 180m approach to the rocky summit, bear right to find an ascent route heading left – take care here – to arrive at the summit of **Doan** (594m). It is easy to see why this is one of the most popular viewpoints in the Mournes.

Return the way you came. Do not attempt to descend the south, east or west sides. Just north of the actual summit, descend west initially – take care here – and you will soon find a path. Turn right along this and follow it north. Bypass the false summit you saw earlier. If you find yourself looking down its north face, retrace your steps and descend onto a lower path around it. Follow the obvious path back to the fork in the path. If you are not visiting any more summits after Doan, bear left here and retrace your steps to Ott car park.

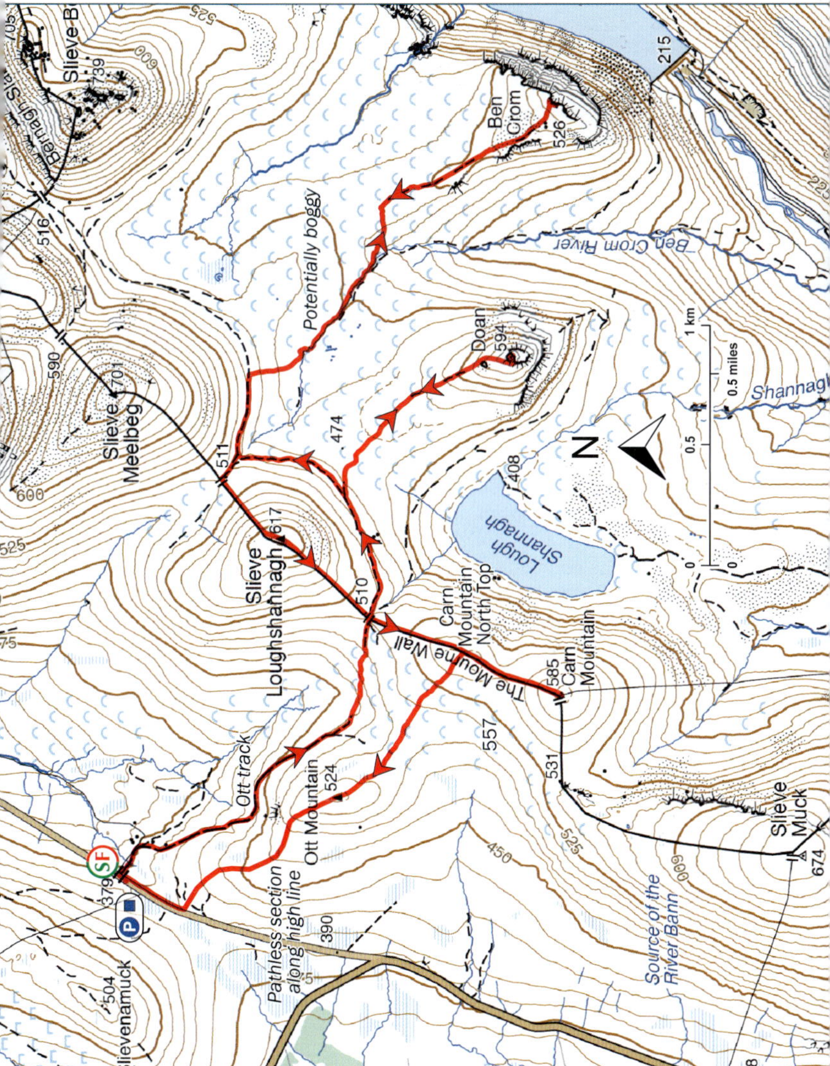
Ben Crom
526
215
Ben Crom River
Potentially boggy
Doan
594
474
Slieve Meelbeg
701
511
Slieve Loughshannagh
617
510
Lough Shannagh
408
Carn Mountain North Top
Carn Mountain
585
The Mourne Wall
557
531
Slieve Muck
674
Ott track
Ott Mountain
524
Pathless section along high line
390
379
Slievenamuck
504
Source of the River Bann
Slieve Bearnagh
739
516
590
368
Shannagh
0
0.5
1 km
0.5 miles
N

Looking down Silent Valley from the summit of Doan

The fork may not be obvious from this direction. With the ground now rising towards Slieve Loughshannagh in front of you, bear right onto the contouring path. You may need to ascend slightly to find this path. Proceed north-east, curving left towards the north. After 500m, with a 511m col coming into view on the left, come to another fork in the path. If omitting Ben Crom, bear left here. Bear right here and right again a few metres further to contour east around the base of Slieve Meelbeg for 340m. Look for a perpendicular path descending south on the right.

Turn right along this path. After 70m, continue straight ahead where a faint path crosses. Keep a mental note of this and remember to keep straight ahead here on the return leg later. Continue for 180m to arrive at a bend on **Ben Crom River**. Bear left to follow the river south-east, downstream. You can walk on either side of the river, but you will locate an upcoming turn-off more easily if you are on the left-hand side. Move away from the river if you need to avoid soft spots where boggy tributaries join. Look for where the path forks when the river starts to bend right 550m downstream. This may not be immediately obvious.

Bear left at the fork, south-east, along a path through peat hags, keeping an eye out for soft spots. This path follows a worn channel and has a few small cairns dotted along its banks. After 240m, arrive on the high line of Ben Crom's ridge where a cairn sits in the middle of the path at a junction. Turn right here and follow the high line south-east for 880m to the summit of **Ben Crom** (526m). There is a sheer drop of 150m to Ben Crom Reservoir on the far side (south-east), so be extremely careful on this summit.

Retrace your steps north-west along the clear high-line path into the peat hags to the junction cairn. Turn left towards the river, then bear right alongside it, keeping straight ahead when the river bends left, and contour left to the fork near the 511m col. If you are not visiting any more summits after Ben Crom, bear left here and retrace your steps to Ott car park. Bear right for 120m to meet the Wall at the **511m col**. Turn left and ascend south-west for 360m, with the Wall on your right, to the summit cairn on **Slieve Loughshannagh** (617m).

Descend south-west for 500m to a **510m col**. If omitting Carn Mountain, turn right here, cross the stile and retrace your steps along Ott Track to Ott car park. Continue straight through the col. With the Wall still on your right, follow it south-west for 880m, passing over Carn Mountain North Top (557m) along the way to a gap. Turn right through the gap beside the summit cairn on **Carn Mountain** (585m).

Turn right again immediately to cross a stile here and follow the other side of the Wall north-east for 450m. Arrive back at **Carn Mountain North Top**, turn left, away from the Wall, and descend north-west for 500m into a peat haggy col. Stick to the high line as best you can through here. Ascend for 300m to a cairn marking the subsidiary top of **Ott Mountain** (524m). Descend north-west for 880m along the high line to meet a fence at the high point of Slievenaman Road. Turn right along the fence for 300m to reach a stile. Cross this and the road, then turn left uphill for 30m to finish at **Ott car park**.

Lough Shannagh and Silent Valley Reservoir from the descent off Slieve Loughshannagh

ROUTE 16

Slieve Meelbeg and Slieve Loughshannagh

Start/finish	Happy Valley car park
Alt start/finish	Ott car park
Time	3hr
Distance	8.3km
Ascent/descent	540m
Grade	Moderate
Options	Valley ascent (-0.1km); Ott car park (-0.6km/-35m/-15min); combine with Route 17 (+6km/+350m/+2hr 15min)
Bus stops	The Mourne Rambler summer bus service stops at Ott car park and 650m from Happy Valley car park

This route visits two official mountain summits, including the lowest in the Mournes. After you have made the initial ascent via either the ridge or the valley, the high-level section of the route follows the impressive Mourne Wall. It finishes with a short stretch of the Mourne Way, passing the oldest open reservoir in the range and the largest buried water treatment works in Ireland. The walk can be extended by combining it with Route 17.

From the south end of Happy Valley car park, take the path ascending south, crossing a stile along the way. After 300m, meet the Mourne Way close to a stream and **stile**. Turn left here for the valley ascent (see Variant). If combining with Slieve Bearnagh and Slieve Meelmore, divert to Route 17 here. Continue straight past the Mourne Way marker post and ascend south for 50m to a junction. Keep straight ahead for a further 50m to another junction. You are aiming for the rocks up on your right marking the start of the Meelbeg north-west spur. Turn right along a stony path ascending west for 120m, then turn left when you see a grassy path ascending towards the rocks.

After 200m, pass the rocks and follow a worn path ascending south along the high line of the spur. If you should happen to lose the path, just keep to the high line as it curves left towards the south-east. As you gain height, the ground becomes bouldery but manageable. After 1.6km, arrive at a corner of the Mourne

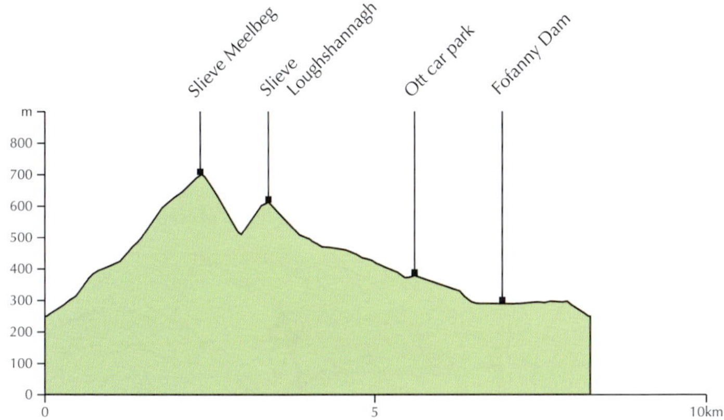

Wall beside the summit cairn on **Slieve Meelbeg** (701m). Bear right and descend south-west for 620m beside the Wall to a 511m col.

Cross the stile here. With the Wall now on your right, ascend south-west for 360m to the summit cairn on **Slieve Loughshannagh** (617m). Descend south-west for 500m beside the Wall to a 510m col. Turn right, cross the stile and proceed away from the Wall to descend along a path through peat hags for 400m to meet

Meet the Mourne Wall at Meelbeg's summit cairn

the top of **Ott Track**. Follow this for 1.3km to a stile beside Slievenaman Road near **Ott car park**. This can be used as an alternate start/finish. Cross the stile and turn right to descend north-east along the road.

This is the Mourne Way. After 690m, cross a stile on the right. Continue along the Mourne Way for 900m as it descends east, curving north past **Fofanny Dam**. At the north end of the dam, turn right across a footbridge and stile. Follow the Mourne Way north-east, curving east for 740m. Arrive at a path junction near the stream and stile you passed earlier. If using an alternate start/finish, turn right here. Turn left and retrace your steps north for 300m to finish at **Happy Valley car park**.

Follow the Mourne Way past Fofanny Dam

FOFANNY DAM

In 1902, the decision-makers in Banbridge and Portadown came together to investigate ways to meet the increasing demand for water in their towns. After ruling out the possibility of using the River Bann, which flows through both towns, officials identified the upper Shimna Valley in the Mournes as the site for a new reservoir. Built between 1904 and 1906, Fofanny Dam has a catchment area of approximately $4km^2$. Its enclosing ridge includes the mountain summits of Slieve Meelbeg and Slieve Loughshannagh.

In 1946, the Portadown and Banbridge Waterworks Joint Board decided that an additional water source was required for the towns. As part of their solution, Deer's Meadow in the uppermost section of the Bann Valley, just 2km south-west of Fofanny, was chosen as the site for another reservoir. Spelga Dam was constructed there between 1953 and 1957.

Just north of Fofanny Dam sits the Fofanny Water Treatment Works. Completed in 2007, this multi-award-winning plant is the largest underground water treatment facility in Ireland, although there is not much to see as it is so well hidden.

Variant route to Slieve Meelbeg via valley ascent

Turn left to cross the stream and stile. Once across, bear slightly right. Cross a ditch to pick up a rough track ascending south-east along the left-hand side of the valley. Pass through a wall as you approach the top of the valley and continue along a worn path to meet the **Mourne Wall** at a 590m col. Turn right and ascend south-west for 330m beside the Wall to the summit cairn on **Slieve Meelbeg** (701m).

ROUTE 17

Bearnagh, Meelmore and Meelbeg

Start/finish	Meelmore Lodge car park
Alt starts/finishes	Trassey car park and Happy Valley car park
Time	4hr 15min
Distance	11.4km
Ascent/descent	780m
Grade	Hard
Options	Trassey car park (+1.2km/+25m/+15min); Bearnagh omitted (-1.2km/-190m/-30min); Bearnagh only (-1.9km/-225m/-45min); Meelbeg omitted (-0.9km/-90m/-30min); Happy Valley car park (-0.6km/+10m); combine with Route 18 (+8.4km/+650m/+3hr 15min); combine with Route 16 (+3.5km/+105m/+1hr)
Bus stops	The Mourne Rambler summer bus service stops 650m from Happy Valley car park and 1.4km from Trassey car park

Visit three of the seven highest mountain summits in the Mournes from a well-equipped start/finish point. The three summits are linked by a fine section of the Mourne Wall, and all offer great views of each other, the whole range and the surrounding lowlands. Steep-sided Slieve Bearnagh, crowned by impressive granite tors, requires effort on ascent and concentration on descent. Join the Mourne Way to finish. Options allow you to easily omit summits if you want a shorter walk. The walk can also be extended by combining with Routes 16 and/or 18.

From Meelmore Lodge, proceed south through the car park behind Hare's Gap Bistro. At the lower end of the car park, access a track and follow it south-south-east for 500m to a dry-stone wall. Cross using the stile and turn left. Follow the Mourne Way east-north-east for 500m, alongside the wall and across a couple of streams, to a gated track entering open ground near a stone sheep pen. Trassey car park start/finish ties in here (Variant 1).

Turn right along **Trassey Track** to leave the Mourne Way. Pass the **sheep pen** on your left and proceed south-east. After a few initial zigzags, the track bends right

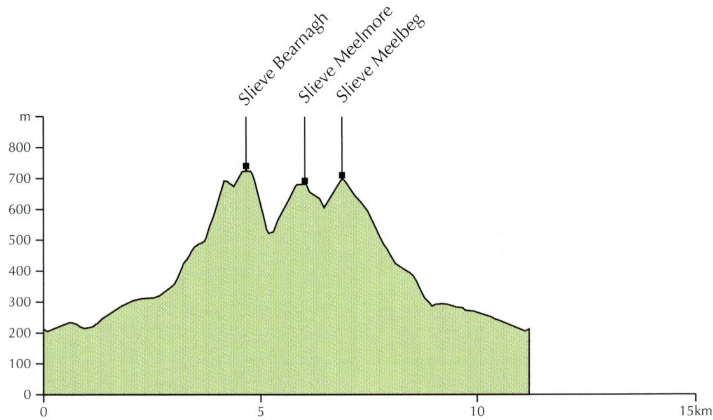

MEELMORE LODGE

Developed around an original farmhouse by the Patterson family, Meelmore Lodge has become a hub for hillwalking in the northern Mournes. The family home became a holiday house in 2001 before evolving into a hostel in 2007. In 2016, a new building was added to include a reception area and amenity block with toilets and showers. To the rear of the building, Hare's Gap Bistro is a great place to grab breakfast, lunch, coffees and treats. Facilities also include secure CCTV-monitored parking, direct access to the mountains via private lane, a self-catering cottage and a campsite.

Meelmore Lodge is a perfect example of how farming and outdoor tourism can work together as a business in the Mournes. The site can be used as a start/finish point or refreshment stop on a variety of local hillwalking routes, including five described in this book. Its location is also convenient for walkers passing along the nearby Mourne Way. For those planning their own bespoke A-B linear routes across the range from places like Carrick Little, Silent Valley and Banns Road, Meelmore Lodge would be an ideal finish point.

to ascend south before bending left to follow Trassey River upstream. Look for a sidetrack fording the river on your right about 880m further on. Ignore this and continue straight ahead for about 30m to where a grassy path departs on the left.

Start along the track behind Meelmore Lodge

If combining with Slieve Commedagh and Slieve Donard, divert to Route 18 here. Keep straight on past this turn-off. With **Spellack's cliffs** on your right, continue south-east along the main track towards the dramatic Hare's Gap col directly ahead.

After 600m, ford a shallow stream, to arrive immediately where a sidetrack departs to the right. If omitting Slieve Bearnagh, turn right here and follow the track, which becomes a path heading south-west to a 516m col. Ignore this turn-off, continue straight along the track for 60m, then bear left at a fork. As the valley narrows, the track splits into faint paths that all lead steeply through rough ground. Take care along this 500m section, especially if the ground is wet. Choose your own path heading south-east here, keeping close to the centreline, to meet the Mourne Wall at **Hare's Gap** (437m).

Cross the stile and turn right. Bear slightly left of the Wall to ascend some stone steps. Make your way right to rejoin the Wall and ascend beside it for 850m to the base of Slieve Bearnagh North Tor. Skirt left around the rock to pick up the Wall where it restarts. Continue west beside the Wall for 280m to a sharp right-hand bend on a rocky subsidiary top near the summit of **Slieve Bearnagh** (739m). (The actual summit is located on a granite tor 100m south of here. It is accessible, but care is needed.) Work your way clockwise around the south side of the rocks on the subsidiary top to rejoin the Wall. Brace yourself for a steep descent.

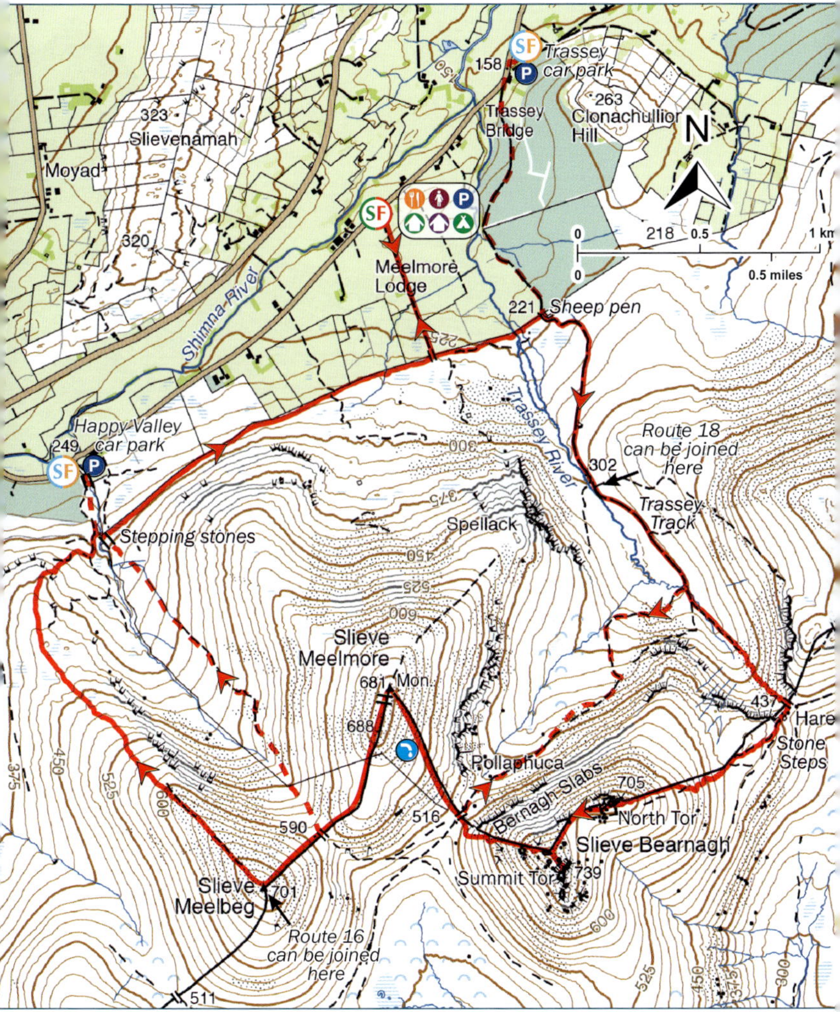

Follow the Wall and descend west for 470m – taking care on this section. Bear slightly left of the Wall as you approach the bottom along one of the worn

Skirt around Slieve Bearnagh's North Tor towards the summit

paths. The ground here is steep and quite eroded. Carefully zigzag your way down through this, always keeping the Wall in sight, to a **516m col**.

Alternative route

If visiting no further summits, turn right across the stile here and head north-east along a path that becomes a track to meet Trassey Track, then turn left to retrace your steps down the valley.

Main route continues

Two walls radiate north-west from here. Follow the right-hand one – the Mourne Wall. Ascend beside it for 620m. Fresh water flows from a pipe in the heather a few metres left of the Wall. Arrive at to a stone shelter built into a sharp corner. Cross the nearby stile and turn left alongside the Wall for 110m to the summit cairn on **Slieve Meelmore** (688m). Descend south-west for 600m to a 590m col.

Variant omitting Slieve Meelbeg

If omitting Slieve Meelbeg, turn right at the stile, away from the Wall, and descend north-west along a path that soon becomes a rough track down the right-hand side of the valley to meet a wall near a stile. Ignore the stile and turn right to follow the Mourne Way north-east.

Main route continues

Continue straight on alongside the Wall and ascend south-west for 330m to the summit cairn on **Slieve Meelbeg** (701m). If combining with Slieve Loughshannagh, divert to Route 16 here. Turn right, away from the Wall, along a worn path heading north-west. Follow this down the high line of Meelbeg's north-west spur. The ground becomes bouldery but manageable. Do not stray right towards the cliffs. Curve right with the path from north-west to north at the end of the spur. After 1.6km, bear right past rocks towards the valley floor.

Descend north-east then north along clear paths for 500m to meet the Mourne Way near a **stream and stile**. The Happy Valley car park start/finish ties in here (Variant 2). Turn right across these, then bear left to follow the Mourne Way north-east. Arrive at a stile you crossed earlier. If using an alternate start/finish continue straight here. Turn left, cross the stile and follow the track north-north-west to finish at **Meelmore Lodge**.

Variant 1: start/finish at Trassey car park

Starting from the entrance of Trassey car park, turn left to follow Trassey Road uphill for 100m to where it bends right. Follow the Mourne Way through the gate on the left at this bend. There is also an option to cross the wall to the left of the gate using built-in stone steps. You are now on **Trassey Track**. Continue south for 1.1km along the track, passing through a couple of pedestrian gates to enter open mountain land beside a stone **sheep pen**. Stay on the track here to join the main route. When you return to this point later, pass through the gate and retrace your steps north to finish at **Trassey car park**.

Variant 2: start/finish at Happy Valley car park

Starting from the south end of Happy Valley car park, take the path ascending south, crossing a stile along the way. After 300m, meet the Mourne Way at a junction near a **stream and stile**. Turn left across these to join the main route. When you return to this point later, keep straight and retrace your steps north to finish at **Happy Valley car park**.

ROUTE 18

Commedagh and Donard from Meelmore Lodge

Start/finish	Meelmore Lodge car park
Alt start/finish	Trassey car park
Time	5hr 30min
Distance	15.1km
Ascent/descent	925m
Grade	Hard
Options	Trassey car park (+0.3km/+5m); Donard omitted (-1.7km/-250m/-1hr); combine with Route 17 (+4.7km/+505m/+2hr)
Bus stop	The Mourne Rambler summer bus service stops 1.4km from Trassey car park

This alternative approach to the two highest summits in the Mourne Mountains starts and finishes at well-equipped trailhead facilities and includes a beautiful section of the Mourne Wall and two spectacular cols before returning along part of an old smugglers' route. The walk can be extended by combining with Route 17.

From Meelmore Lodge (see Route 17), proceed south through the car park behind Hare's Gap Bistro. At the lower end of the car park, access a track and follow it south-south-east for 500m to a dry-stone wall. Cross using the stile and turn left. Follow the Mourne Way east-north-east for 500m, alongside the wall and across a couple of streams, to meet a gated track, entering open ground near a stone sheep pen. The alternate start/finish at Trassey car park ties in here (Variant 1).

Turn right along **Trassey Track** to leave the Mourne Way. Pass the **sheep pen** on your left and proceed south-east. After a few initial zigzags, the track bends right to ascend south before bending left to follow Trassey River upstream. Look for a sidetrack fording the river on your right about 880m further on. Ignore this and continue straight on for about 30m to where a grassy path departs on the left.

Turn left and head east-north-east up the grassy path. After 340m, take a path on the right as it ascends south-east up the left-hand side of the valley. This becomes muddy and less obvious in places as it progresses beneath Slievenaglogh. Pay attention to the path ahead, maintaining a south-east course for 950m to a

A stile over the Mourne Wall on the way to Slievenaglogh

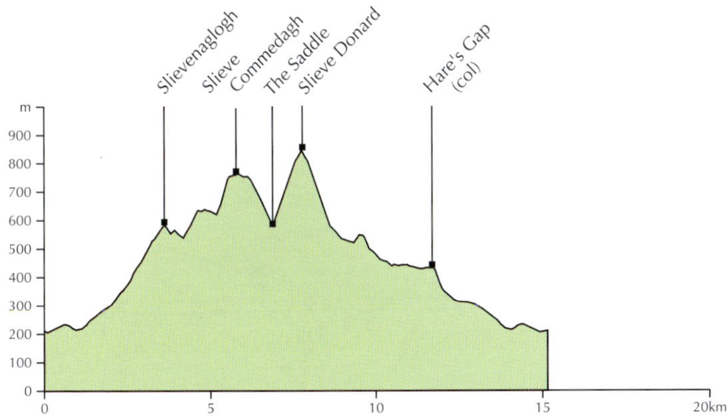

stile crossing the Mourne Wall. Cross here and turn left to follow the Wall east for 310m to the summit cairn on **Slievenaglogh** (586m).

Continue along the Wall for 1.9km, over the subsidiary top of **Slieve Corragh** (641m). Note an obvious freshwater pipe a few metres right of the Wall. Arrive at a stone shelter and cross the stile beside it, then follow a worn path north-east

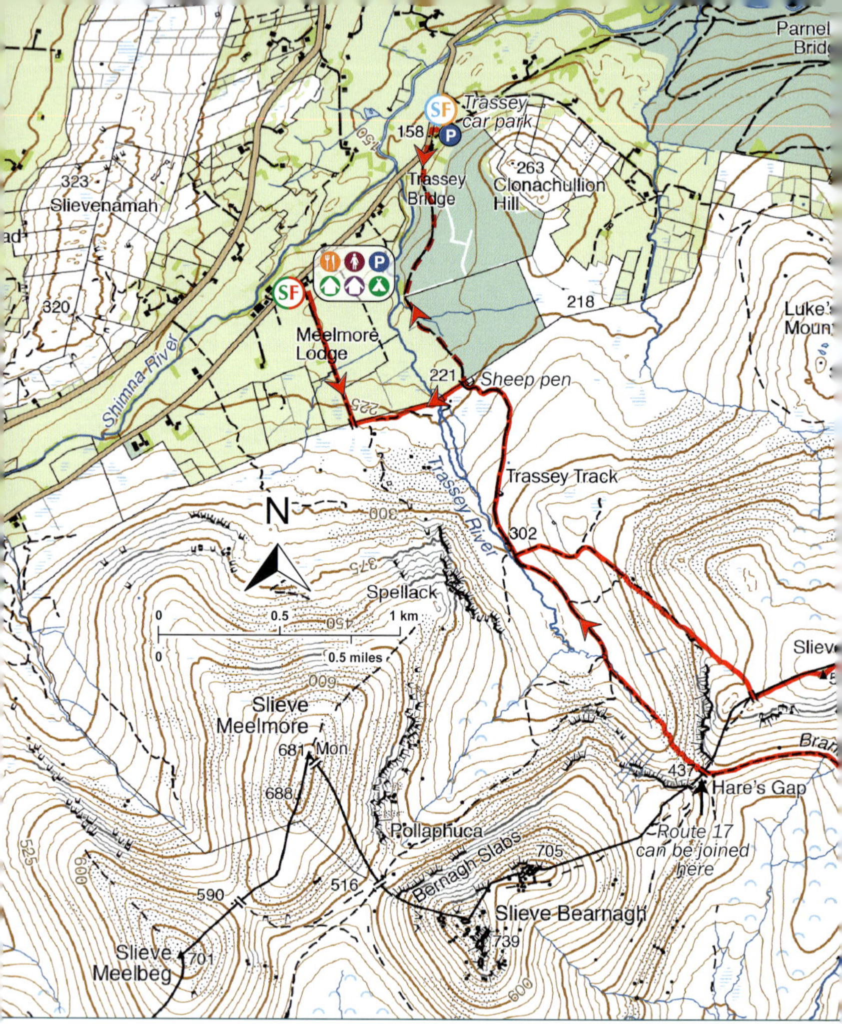

across a grassy plateau to the summit cairn on **Slieve Commedagh** (765m). Retrace your steps to the Wall at the stone shelter. Turn left to follow the Wall for 780m to the **Saddle** (583m). If omitting Slieve Donard, turn right across the stile here.

Continue straight across the Saddle and ascend east for 850m alongside the Wall, keeping it on your right to benefit from the constructed path. Climb steeply to the trig-adorned stone shelter and large summit cairn on **Slieve Donard** (850m) – the highest point in the Mourne Mountains and County Down (see Route 3).

Retrace your steps west down to the Saddle. Turn left, cross the stile and head south-west, away from the Wall. Several paths radiate away from the stile on the south side of the wall. Aim slightly right of centre before descending. If you can see the tor-studded profile of Slieve Binnian ahead, use that as your initial line. After 350m, meet a clear path contouring left to right. Turn right here to follow it west-north-west. This is the **Brandy Pad** (see Route 2). Proceed along the Brandy Pad for 590m, passing **The Castles** rock formations on your right, to a 553m col where the view ahead becomes dominated by the rugged granite tors of Slieve Bearnagh.

Continue along the obvious path for 2.2km until you meet the Wall at **Hare's Gap** (437m). If combining with Bearnagh, Meelmore and Meelbeg, divert to Route 17 here. Cross the stile and descend north-west along an initial rough

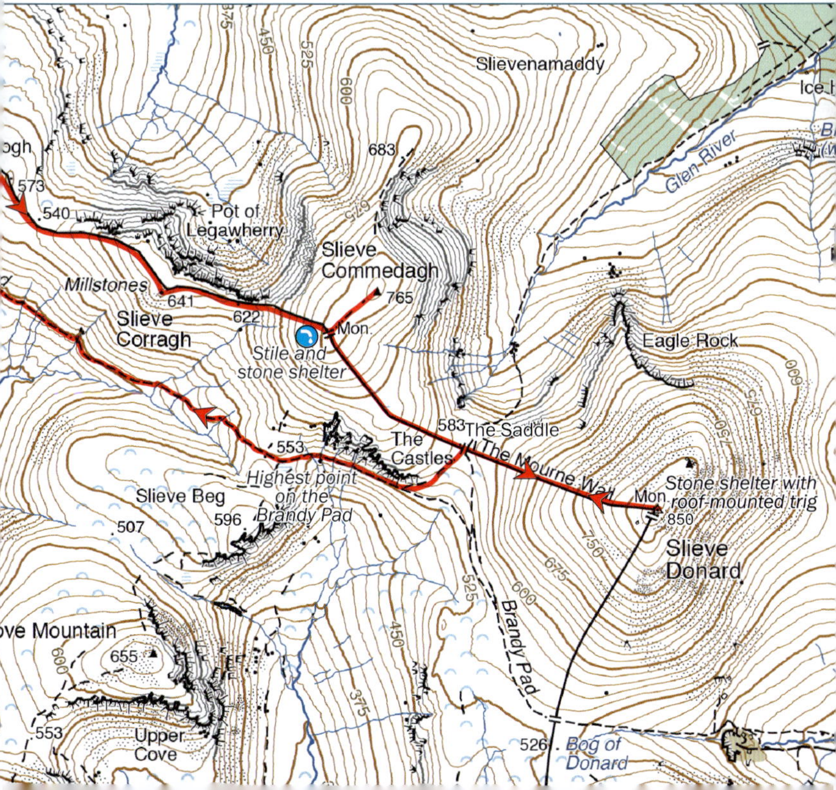

Following the Brandy Pad to Hare's Gap with Slieve Bearnagh directly ahead

section of the valley. Choose your own path, keeping close to the centreline. After 500m, pick up a track at the bottom of the slope. Follow this north-west for 1.6km down the Trassey River valley to a gate beside a stone **sheep pen**. If finishing at Trassey car park, follow the track through the gate (Variant 1). Turn left to follow the Mourne Way west-south-west alongside a wall for 500m over a couple of streams to a stile you crossed earlier. Turn right, cross the stile and retrace your steps north-north-west along the track to finish at **Meelmore Lodge**.

Variant 1: start/finish at Trassey car park

Starting from the entrance of Trassey car park, turn left to follow Trassey Road uphill for 100m to where it bends right. Follow the Mourne Way through the gate on the left at this bend. There is also an option to cross the wall to the left of the gate using built-in stone steps. You are now on **Trassey Track**. Continue south along the track for 1.1km, passing through a couple of pedestrian gates to enter open mountain land beside a stone **sheep pen**. Stay on the track here to join the main route. When you return to this point later, pass through the gate and retrace your steps north to finish at **Trassey car park**.

WESTERN MOURNES

The view back to Eagle Mountain and Windy Gap on the descent of Route 20

Stretching from the Carlingford Lough coast, just east of Rostrevor, to the main north–south B27 Moyad Road, the lesser-walked Western Mournes have a distinctly wild feel compared with their Eastern neighbours. Apart from the sprawling, predominately coniferous, woodlands of Rostrevor Forest, the adjoining Kilbroney Park and a couple of reservoirs, this quieter half of the Mournes is privately owned and managed by landowners and trustees of historical estates. Thanks to their ongoing goodwill, there is a long-established and widely accepted tradition for recreational walking in the area.

Two of the Mourne Mountains' 14 official mountain summits lie in the Western Mournes, and its most popular attractions include Rostrevor Forest, Kilbroney Park and the summits of Slievemartin and Hen Mountain. Outside of these, you can expect to encounter few, if any, other people. If you are looking for a wilder walk without the crowds, west is best. The six routes presented in this section lie entirely, or predominantly, within the Western Mournes.

In addition to these, TMU4, TMU5 and part of TMU3 (Routes 29, 30 and 28) of the Mourne Ultra are also in the Western Mournes.

Most of Route 23 can be seen from Rocky Mountain summit

ROUTE 19

Spelga Horseshoe

Start/finish	Spelga Dam car park
Alt starts/finishes	Deer's Meadow parking spot and Ott car park
Time	5hr 30min
Distance	15.6km
Ascent/descent	955m
Grade	Hard
Options	Butter Mountain Loop only (-11km/-730m/-4hr); road return from Deer's Meadow (-6.4km/-485m/-2hr 30min); Butter Mountain Loop omitted (-2.5km/-120m/-1hr)
Bus stops	The Mourne Rambler summer bus service stops at Ott car park and 1.2km from the Spelga Dam car park

An almost mandatory challenge among experienced local hillwalkers, this route takes in the skyline ridge enclosing Spelga Dam and the nearby source of the mighty River Bann – one of Ireland's major rivers. You will pass over six summits, including one official mountain and five subsidiary tops along the way. Shorter options are also available, the most popular being the Butter Mountain Loop.

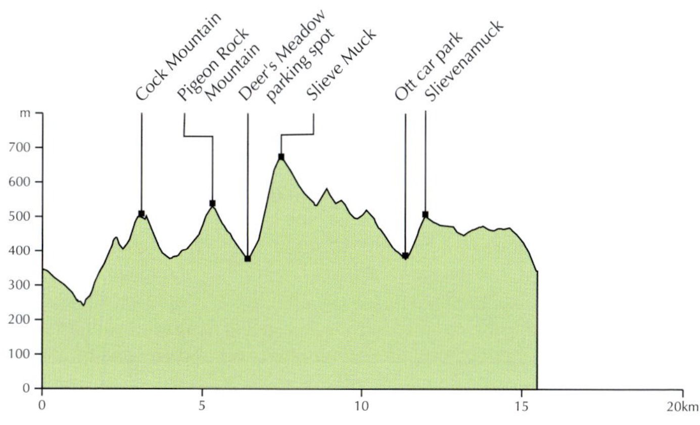

From the entrance of Spelga car park, turn left along the **B27 Kilkeel Road** for a short distance to the western end (left) of the toilet block opposite. Carefully cross the road and locate a small stile at a fence corner. Cross the stile. If walking the Butter Mountain Loop only, turn right along the fence here (Variant 1). Turn left to descend west for 1km along a worn path parallel to the road below on the left. Meet the Mourne Way at a stile beside the road. Cross the stile and carefully cross the road. Turn left up the road about 20m to where a stone wall begins. Turn right here and pass through a small gate, then turn left for 150m along a grassy path descending south-east to a footbridge over the **River Bann**.

SPELGA DAM AND THE RIVER BANN

Historical maps from the early 19th century show a road from Kilkeel to Hilltown passing straight through the middle of the present-day Spelga Dam, crossing an infant version of the River Bann. At that time, the site was known as Deer's Meadow (sometimes with no apostrophe), when local farmers would have brought their livestock to graze this upland area during the summer months. By the middle of the 19th century, another road had been added: branching north over the rim of the Bann catchment and down the Shimna Valley, past the present-day Ott car park and on towards the villages of Kilcoo and Bryansford. Deer's Meadow remained like this for the next century.

In the mid-20th century, the road to Hilltown was realigned to make way for the proposed Spelga Dam, linking up with the road to Kilcoo and Bryansford at a new junction 1.6km north of the old one. These are the roads we use today when driving across the Mournes. Construction of the dam itself got underway in 1953. Based on the larger-scale project undertaken in neighbouring Silent Valley to the east, Spelga Dam was to supply additional water to the towns of Banbridge and Portadown, which had outgrown the capacity of the nearby Fofanny Dam. Spelga Dam was completed in 1957. Interestingly, Ben Crom Reservoir in neighbouring Silent Valley, just 5km to the east, was completed the same year.

Part of the abandoned road to Hilltown remains above water today, running from the old junction (now used as the Deer's Meadow parking spot) to where it disappears into the dam. During prolonged periods of hot, dry weather, water levels in the dam occasionally drop low enough to reveal the old road to Hilltown and its bridge across the Bann. People use these rare events to walk along the old road, although it should be noted that the structural integrity of its bridge may have diminished after decades underwater.

Spelga Dam has a catchment area of approximately 7.4km^2. Raindrops landing here, which are destined to reach the open sea, have a 157km river and lake journey ahead of them after they escape the dam. Along the way they will travel the full length of one of Ireland's longest rivers (the Bann) and through the largest lake in the UK and Ireland (Lough Neagh) before entering the Atlantic Ocean at the Barmouth on the Causeway Coast between Portstewart Strand and Castlerock Beach. As the crow flies north-north-west, this is a distance of 120km.

More than a dozen tributaries have their sources within the Spelga Dam catchment area. Of these, the one generally regarded to be the infant River Bann is located on the western slopes of Slieve Muck at an elevation close to the 440m contour. However, another tributary rising a short distance away on the slopes of Carn Mountain, near the 500m contour, would add almost a full kilometre to the length. If maximum length and elevation are factors considered when identifying the source of a major river, the Bann deserves a revisit.

Switchback to cross the bridge, then bear right. Cross over some rocks to pick up a worn path heading north-west. Follow this for about 20m to where a side path forks off to ascend left. Turn left here, leaving the Mourne Way, and ascend west for 300m onto the north-north-west shoulder of Slievenamiskan. Follow the high line south-south-east for 600m. As you approach the top, keep left of a small rock face then bear right for 50m to the unmarked summit of **Slievenamiskan** (443m).

Some hillwalkers take a more direct route from Spelga car park to Slievenamiskan by passing close to the base of the **Spelga Dam wall**. Please note that Northern Ireland Water does not permit public access through this section of its property.

Cross the River Bann using this footbridge before ascending Slievenamiskin

271
Kinnahalla Plantations
B27
River Bann
Spelga
472
477
450
375
300
Gate
Hen Mountain
361
357
337
Millstones
225
272
Slievenamiskan
443
Sheep pen
345
Cock Mountain
505
505
Spelga Dam (Reservoir)
Rocky River
379
346
Deer's Meadow
N
233
Deer's Meadow parking spot
Pigeon Rock Mountain
534
Batt's Wall
0
0.5
1 km
0
0.5 miles
Rocky Water
Wee Slievemoughan
428
Rowan Tree

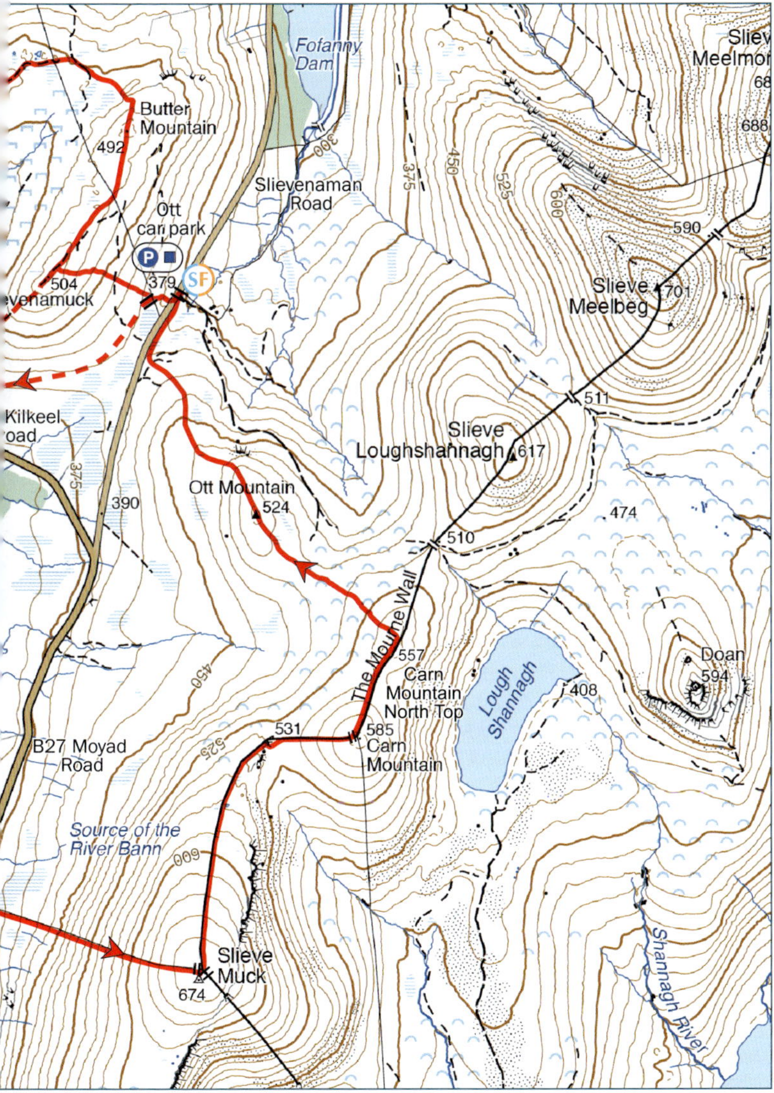
Fofanny Dam
Butter Mountain
492
Slievenaman Road
Ott car park
P
379
SF
504
Kilkeel road
375
390
Ott Mountain
524
The Mourne Wall
557
Carn Mountain North Top
585
Carn Mountain
531
Slieve Loughshannagh
617
510
511
Slieve Meelbeg
701
590
474
Lough Shannagh
408
Doan
594
B27 Moyad Road
Source of the River Bann
Slieve Muck
674
Shannagh River
450
525
600
300
688

Looking across Spelga Dam to Cock Mountain and Slievenamiskan from Ott Mountain

From Slievenamiskan summit onwards, Spelga Dam will be on your left for much of the walk. Descend west-south-west for 200m to a col, then ascend for 500m to the twin summits of **Cock Mountain** (505m). From the south-west summit, turn left to begin your descent south-east. With Pigeon Rock Mountain ahead of you, take a moment to survey the ridgeline and boggy col you need to cross to get there. The strict horseshoe challenger will tackle this in a mirrored S-shape to pass through the 379m col. If you want the driest possible route, stick to the one described here.

As you descend Cock Mountain, bear left to pick up a faint path heading south towards the col. After 740m, come to the midpoint of a raised straight section of bog track. Turn right, south-west, along this for 60m to where it bends left. Ascend the track in a general south-east direction. Expect some wetness underfoot. The ground improves when the track becomes a path further up.

After 1.2km, arrive at a corner of Batt's Wall (see Route 23) beside a cairn. The unmarked north summit of **Pigeon Rock Mountain** (534m) is about 50m south of here.

Descend north-east for 1km with Batt's Wall on your right. Cross a stile at the **Deer's Meadow parking spot**. This can be used as an alternate start/finish.

Road shortcut back to the start/finish

Turn left along the B27 Moyad Road and follow it north, taking care, to a junction. Bear left along the B27 Kilkeel Road to finish at Spelga car park.

Main route continues

Carefully cross the B27 Moyad Road, cross the stile and ascend east-south-east for 1km beside the wall to the summit trig on **Slieve Muck** (674m).

Head 40m north-east from the trig pillar, cross the right-hand stile, then turn left to follow the Mourne Wall north for 1km. Just before a bend to the right, negotiate a short rocky section. Bear right of the Wall to descend this to a 531m col. Ascend east for 300m to a wall junction beside the summit cairn on **Carn Mountain** (585m). Turn left across the stile and follow the Wall north-east for 450m to the subsidiary top of **Carn Mountain North Top** (557m).

Turn left, away from the Wall, and descend north-west for 500m into a peat haggy col, sticking to the high line as best you can. Ascend for 300m to a cairn marking the subsidiary top of **Ott Mountain** (524m).

Descend north-west for 880m along the high line to meet a fence at the high point of **Slievenaman Road**. Turn right along the fence for 300m to a stile. Cross this and the road, then turn left uphill for 30m to **Ott car park**. This can be used as an alternate start/finish.

Continue through Ott car park, away from the road. At the rear of the car park, locate a path departing through the trees. This is the Mourne Way. Follow the path uphill for 60m and cross a **stile** behind the car park. You can also take a shortcut back to Spelga car park from here (Variant 2). Bear right to ascend a grassy path north-west for 450m onto a ridgeline, then keep left for 40m to the unmarked summit of **Slievenamuck** (504m). Turnaround and follow a grassy path north-east for 450m, keeping slightly right of the ridge high line to meet a fence.

Approach the fence where another fence intercepts it from the far side. Locate some small boulders next to the fence that serve as a stile. Cross the fence here and continue north-north-east for 270m with the fence on your right. Pass over the subsidiary top of **Butter Mountain** (492m) and continue beside the fence for 150m. Negotiate two short, steep sections along the way. As you approach a third, bear left, away from the fence, down a grassy path. Follow a worn path north-west for 200m to join a grassy track.

Keep north-west along this for 100m to where another grassy track joins from the left. Turn left here and proceed west for 80m to meet a fence. Locate some small boulders next to the fence that serve as a stile. Cross the fence here and

The direct route up Slievenamuck from Spelga Dam

head south-west along a grassy path left of a mound with exposed rocks. After 300m, bear right off the path to follow the high line of the ridge for 150m to the subsidiary top of **Spaltha** (477m).

Follow a grassy path south-west for 800m along the high line to the subsidiary top of **Spelga** (472m). Turn left and descend south-east for 800m. Aim initially for the forest to the left of Spelga Dam. Curve with the high line towards the centre of the reservoir itself. When the toilet block comes into view, aim for it. Make your way to the building's right-hand side to the stile. If using an alternate start/finish, turn right here. Cross the stile and carefully cross the road to finish at **Spelga car park**.

Variant 1: Butter Mountain Loop only

Having just started from Spelga car park and crossed the stile beside the toilet block, follow the fence away from the road then turn right with it and head east to meet a **stream**. Step over this and ascend the opposite bank onto a grassy track. Turn left to ascend north along this. Just before a livestock pen, bear right and follow the grassy path north-east to the summit of **Slievenamuck** (504m). Continue north-east to join the main route to Butter Mountain.

Variant 2: Butter Mountain Loop omitted

After crossing the stile behind Ott car park, bear left along a faint path towards an electricity pole. Bear left again to follow the powerlines south-west. When the lines bend left, continue along the faint path as it contours right to meet another set of powerlines. Follow these to where they cross a track. Turn left down the track, then turn right to cross the **stream**. Walk west, parallel to the B27 road and around the back of the toilet block. Cross the fence using the stile and carefully cross the road to finish at **Spelga car park**.

ROUTE 20

Eagle Mountain and Shanlieve

Start/finish	Sandy Brae parking spot
Time	3hr 30min
Distance	9.6km (6 miles)
Ascent/descent	525m (1720ft)
Grade	Hard

Get 2 of the Mournes' 14 official mountain summits for the price of one! And with just 500m distance and less than a 50m drop between them, why do one without the other? Eagle Mountain and Shanlieve are the only two mountains in the western half of the range, but their separation from the more-accessible higher summits in the east tends to park them firmly at the back of hillwalkers' minds. As a result, there is a good chance you will have both of these lesser-visited summits to yourself, even on a weekend day at the height of summer. This route includes an ascent along a valley track, followed by a dramatic clifftop descent.

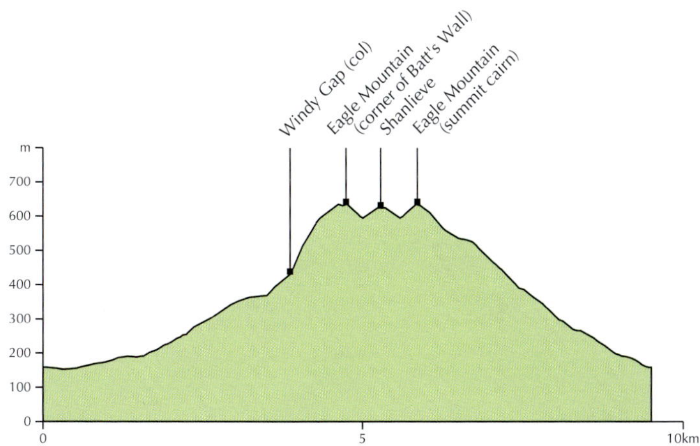

Head north from the Sandy Brae parking spot and cross **Red Moss River**. Depending on the flow, you can either ford the river or use the footbridge. Once across, proceed north along a track which bends right then left. After 360m, come to a gate. Pass through this and continue along the track through open mountain land with **Pigeon Rock River** initially on your right. A parallel stone wall appears after 450m. The track gets rougher as it ascends the valley beneath dramatic cliffs on the left. Later in the walk, you will descend along the clifftop.

After 3km, the track becomes a path to meet Batt's Wall (see Route 23) not far from **Windy Gap** (407m). Turn left and ascend steeply south-west, with the wall on your right, for 460m to where it bends left. Continue south-south-east beside the wall for 310m to where it bends right at a stile. Turn right here and follow the wall south-west for 500m, passing over a shallow col along the way to another right-hand bend. Turn left here, away from the wall, and head south for 60m to the summit cairn on **Shanlieve** (626m).

Retrace your steps to the corner on the wall and follow it north-east to the stile you passed earlier. Turn right, away from the wall, and head south-east for 60m to the summit cairn on **Eagle Mountain** (637m). Continue straight over the summit and descend south-south-east, curving south along a faint path and keeping in mind the dangerous cliffs on your left. The path curves left slightly, placing the masts on Aughrim Hill directly ahead in the distance. As you descend, the path becomes more obvious and occasionally lies close to the cliff edge on the left.

Following the track/path up the valley to meet Batt's Wall at Windy Gap col

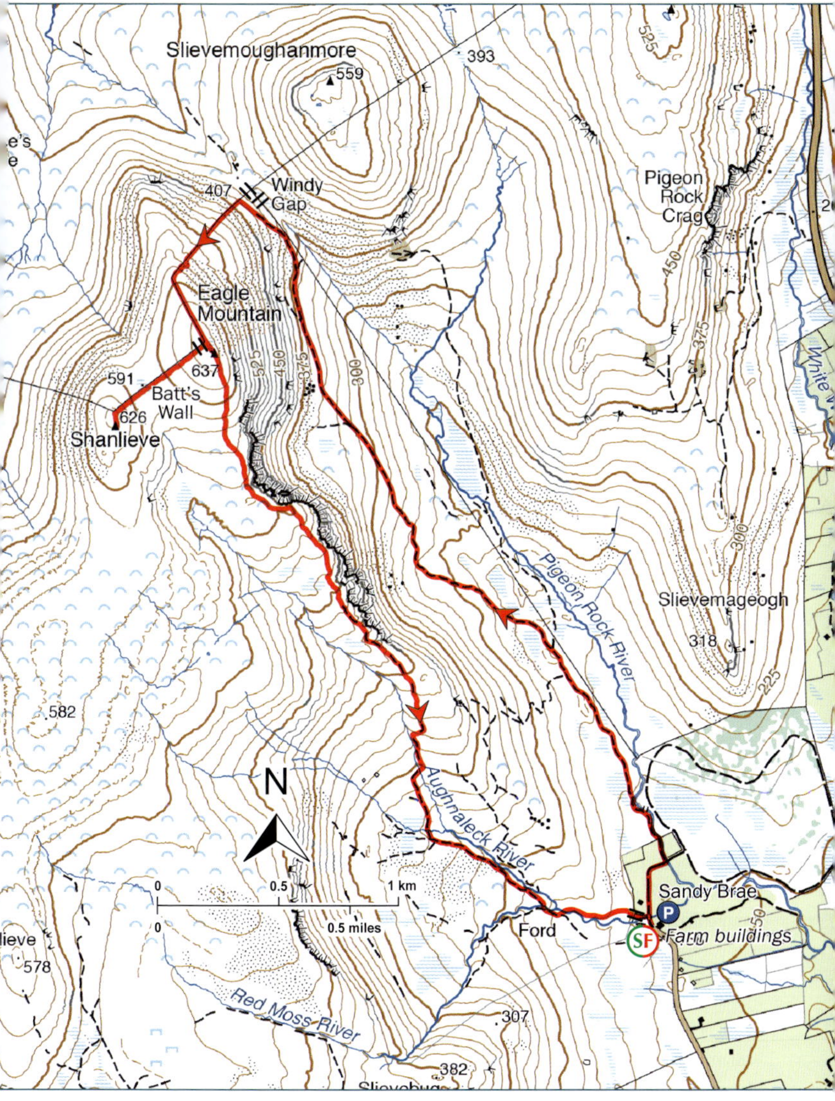
Slievemoughanmore
559
393
525
Windy Gap
407
Pigeon Rock Crag
450
Eagle Mountain
637
591
Batt's Wall
626
Shanlieve
525
450
375
300
375
White
Pigeon Rock River
Slievemageogh
318
300
225
582
N
0
0.5
1 km
0
0.5 miles
Aughnaleck River
Sandy Brae
P
Ford
SF
Farm buildings
lieve
578
Red Moss River
307
382

Taking in the views across Pigeon Rock River Valley towards the Eastern Mournes

Take a few moments to stop every now and then and enjoy the views from this platform over the **Pigeon Rock River Valley** and across to the higher Eastern Mourne summits. Take care along here, especially in strong crosswinds.

After 1.5km, depart from the clifftop to head slightly right of the ridgeline into the Aughnaleck River valley where the path gradually evolves into a broad, stony path. Stick to this, avoiding all lesser turn-offs. Bend sharp right then left a couple of times and cross **Aughnaleck River**. After 1km, cross an unnamed tributary to a junction.

Turn left along a broad grassy path heading south-east. This starts off good but becomes wet and rocky further down. When it does, you can find drier options just left of the path. After 600m, cross **Red Moss River** to another junction. Turn left along a grassy track heading east-south-east beside the river. A further 90m downstream, find a safe spot to cross Red Moss River just after Aughnaleck River flows into it. Take care as the rocks could be slippery. Once on the north side of the river, turn right and follow it east, downstream.

Follow the top of the riverbank along a worn path. Keep to the high path when the falling river takes a meandering course. With the farm sheds beside the Sandy Brae parking spot now directly in front of you, look for a stile up ahead. The line to it is between the sheds and a house to the left of them. Stick to the path as far as it brings you, then continue east across grass to the stile. Cross this and follow a grassy path east to meet a track. Turn right and cross Red Moss River to finish at **Sandy Brae parking spot**.

ROUTE 21

Slievemeen, Slievemartin and Crenville

Start/finish	Rostrevor Forest car park
Alt start/finish	Kilbroney car park
Time	3hr 30min
Distance	10.5km
Ascent/descent	405m
Grade	Moderate
Options	Kilbroney car park (+2.6km/+175m/+1hr); zigzag off Slievemartin (-5.7km/-115m/-1hr 45min); Crenville omitted (-0.9km/-35m/-30min)
Bus stops	Year-round local Ulsterbus services stop in Rostrevor village and along the A2 Shore Road
Notes	Rostrevor Forest is a popular mountain biking destination with a large network of bike-only trails (all clearly signposted) – walkers must not stray onto them. Consider gaiters for the boggy section before Crenville.

The hills towering above the village of Rostrevor on the shores of Carlingford Lough dominate the skyline, just as Donard and Commedagh do above Newcastle at the far side of the range. Bringing you to their summits from an elevated forest car park, this route is a must-do for every hillwalker visiting the Rostrevor area. Along the way, it is worth stopping for breaks at the Cloughmore (aka the 'Big Stone'), Ballynagelty and the trig-pillared summit of Slievemartin. Take your pick: they all offer stunning views across Carlingford Lough to the Cooley Mountains.

Locate an information panel at the top end (south-east) of Rostrevor Forest car park. Proceed south-east along a short path for 20m, then turn right at a junction to follow the Cloughmore Trail (pink arrows) and the Fallows Trail (purple arrows). Ascend for 460m, ignoring all turn-offs on the right, to a junction of broad paths where the Cloughmore Trail heads right and the Fallows Trail takes a sharp left. Bear left to ascend south-east on a grassy path for 40m to the **Cloughmore** (aka the 'Big Stone' – see Route 30).

Retrace your steps north-west to the junction. Turn right here along a good path marked as the Fallows Trail. Ascend south-east along this path for 480m, ignoring the well-marked bike trails crossing it. Do not loiter at the bike crossings.

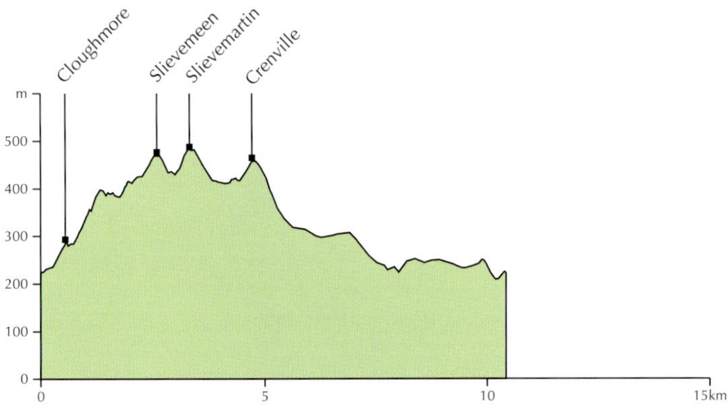

Turn right onto a side path and continue along a stepped section of the Fallows Trail to emerge above the treeline after 120m. With a small grassy top ahead, continue for 250m to a junction. Continue straight through a gap in a broken stone wall and ascend south for 70m along a clear path to the **Ballynagelty viewpoint**. From here you can see the full length of Carlingford Lough.

Retrace your steps to the junction and turn right. Continue along the path as it zigzags up and then follows a boundary fence and wall east. After 890m, keep an eye out for a grassy path on the left to the nearby summit cairn on **Slievemeen** (471m). Return to the main path and turn left along it. Descend north beside the fence, with Slievemartin and a mast directly ahead. After 400m, reach a col where several paths meet beside a stile.

Shortcut back to start/finish

A shortcut back to the car park starts from here. You can use this now or return to it after visiting the summit of Slievemartin. In either case, take the path heading north-west into the forest. This path immediately splits into two. Ignore the one bearing right – a mountain bike trail which you must not walk on – and follow the left path for a zigzagging descent through trees to finish at **Rostrevor Forest car park**.

Main route continues

Keep straight and ascend for 320m beside the fence and up some stone steps to the summit trig on **Slievemartin** (485m). A bench is located 20m beyond the trig if

Leckan Beg
Kilbroney River
Kilbroney House
Rostrevor Forest
308
Mountain bike trail crossing
Mountain bike trail crossing
Fallows Trail
439
Slievedermot
Crenville
460
Old fence posts
No path
40
75
150
225
300
375
450
Kilbroney Park
Cloughmore Trail and Fallows Trail
Rostrevor Quay
Mast
Slievemartin
485
Mast
N
0
0.5
1 km
0
0.5 miles
Watergap River
Rostrevor Forest car park
Cloughmore (Big Stone)
404
Ballynagelty
471
Slievemeen
Slievefadda
425
The Clasha
The Point Park
Spelga
Ballincurry River
12
241
Killowen
Bullinran
Cloghgarran
A2

Carlingford Lough from the Cloughmore

you want to spend a few minutes taking in the views over Rostrevor, Warrenpoint and the lough. Return to the main path and bear left to follow it north. Descend for 540m to the edge of the forest.

Bypassing Crenville

Continue north into the forest along the Fallows Trail (purple arrows) for 2.2km to meet a forest track near a **308m spot height**.

Main route continues

Bear right off the track to follow the forest's boundary fence east-north-east. Keep the fence close on your right. An overgrown ditch comes in tight on the left, leaving just enough width. After 90m, turn left at a gap into the trees. Cross the ditch and a parallel stream 5m further on. Turn right to zigzag east-north-east through the trees, keeping parallel to the fence and watercourses for about 160m. The ground is good here but be aware of pointy tree branches at eye level. The trees have been planted in diagonal lines with parallel soft channels in every second gap.

Emerge from the trees at a corner of the forest into an open area beside the fence on your right. Turn left along a faint path heading north-east. You may see the occasional post along here. These are the remnants of an old fenceline and can be used as an intermittent guide. After 120m, bear left uphill to avoid a rough section, then turn right to contour north-east for 100m. Bear right and descend to a short boggy gap between two blocks of forest. Find the driest route you can through this. Gaiters would be useful here.

A couple of posts among the rushes indicate that you are on course. Ascend north-east for 70m to where the posts resume. Follow a faint grassy path north-east, keeping left of and parallel to the line of posts. After 60m, arrive beside a small peaty mound on your right. Turn left here and ascend north-north-west, away from the line of posts, through an area of grass. Crenville summit is directly ahead but not yet in view. As you ascend, bear slightly left through heather, where you may find a faint path to follow. After about 200m, arrive at a post marking the summit of **Crenville** (460m).

Crenville is one of the least visited summits in the Mournes, and one of the eeriest. Due to the surrounding dense forestry and rough ground, most hill-walkers tend to avoid it. Those who do make the effort to visit are likely to have the place to themselves.

Head north-west initially from the summit then curve right towards north-north-west to find a grassy path. After 100m, walk through a grassy strip, past a couple of small rocky outcrops close on the left. Continue descending north-north-west for 200m through a dry grassy channel. When the forest comes into view ahead, aim for an obvious entry point about 30m left of its right-hand corner. Bear slightly right and descend into a wider grassy area to the forest entry point.

Looking back at Slievemeen from the summit of Slievemartin

Enter the forest and bear left along what appears to be a firebreak. Follow a path north-west along the left-hand side. Cross a stream flowing along the firebreak when required to avoid any soft spots and protruding branches. Walking poles are useful to identify firm footholds in the stream. About 50m into the forest, turn right along a faint path departing from the firebreak to descend north through the trees. The path, now very clear, drops to where a constructed mountain bike trail crosses it 50m further. You must not turn left or right along the bike trail or loiter at the junction.

Look both ways to check for passing bikers and continue straight across when safe to do so to the path opposite. Descend north for 80m to meet a forest track. Turn right to follow the track north-east, curving left towards north-north-west for 340m to a track junction. Turn right to follow a forest track north-east for 760m to a track junction at the north edge of the forest. Turn left here to follow the forest boundary track west for 620m to where the waymarked Fallows Trail crosses just after a **308m spot height**.

Continue straight along the track, heading north-west. After 50m bend left with it to head south-west. Follow this forest track for 3.1km to the north-west end of Rostrevor Forest car park. Along the way, keep left at a fork, ignore all other turn-offs and pass two arched mountain bike trailheads. Finish wherever you started from in the **car park**.

KILBRONEY PARK AND ROSTREVOR FOREST

In the early 18th century, Kilbroney Park was known as The Meadow. At that time, it was part of a large estate owned by the Ross family, who lived in The Lodge, which stood close to the present-day Narnia Trail walk. The house was built in 1716 and demolished in 1980, three years after it was sold to Newry and Mourne District Council (renamed Newry, Mourne and Down District Council in 2015). Today, Kilbroney Park offers parking, a café, a campsite and a selection of walking trails; two of these, the Cloughmore Trail and the Fallows Trail, extend into neighbouring Rostrevor Forest.

Rostrevor Forest covers an area of 2500 acres and extends the full length of Kilbroney River on the valley's steep eastern side. A forest drive allows motorised access from Kilbroney to a large car park at 220m above sea level, making it easier to reach the numerous viewpoints higher up, including the Cloughmore (the 'Big Stone'): a glacial erratic deposited here from Scotland 10 millennia ago. The Mourne HRT challenge walk also passes through the forest to meet the sea at Rostrevor. The forest is home to one of Ireland's largest mountain biking centres, with many kilometres of dedicated bike-only trails available.

Rostrevor Forest, Kilbroney Park and Rostrevor village from Slievemartin

The facilities at Kilbroney Park and Rostrevor Forest surpass those offered by many of Ireland's forest parks. At the time of writing, their combined area had not been officially elevated to the forest park status it deserves. This development seems inevitable and may even have happened by the time you read this.

Alternate start/finish at Kilbroney car park

From the entrance of Kilbroney car park, turn left and follow the waymarked Cloughmore Trail (pink arrows) and Fallows Trail (purple arrows) to tie into the main route at the top end of **Rostrevor car park**. When you return to this point later, descend north-west along the left-hand side of the car park and retrace your steps to finish at **Kilbroney car park**. At the time of writing, this section of the Cloughmore Trail and Fallows Trail was waymarked in the uphill direction only.

Other walks in Rostrevor Forest and Kilbroney Park

Parts of the main route described above follow sections of various looped waymarked trails through Rostrevor Forest and neighbouring Kilbroney Park. You can stick to one of the waymarked trails if you prefer. These are all marked on a free map that you can request from a staff member as you drive into Kilbroney Park. The trails are also displayed on an information panel close to the walk's start point at Rostrevor Forest car park and at the lower-level Kilbroney car park. A photo of this would be a handy reference along the waymarked trails.

ROUTE 22

Tievedockaragh, Tornamrock and Rocky Mountain

Start/finish	Leitrim Lodge car park
Alt start/finish	Yellow Water car park
Time	4hr
Distance	11.8km
Ascent/descent	485m
Grade	Moderate
Options	North-east loop (-5.3km/-95m/-1hr 30min); Yellow Water car park (same stats); alternate Yellow Water River ascent (+0.3km); south-west loop (-1.4km/-115m/-45min); Pierce's Castle only (-5.6km/-195m/-1hr 45min)

This route takes in a quiet section of the Mourne Way, a river ascent through a Narnia-like forest, the boundary wall of a historic estate, dry elevated tracks across cut bog, a stunning natural rock castle and finishes with a surprisingly straightforward ridgeline – with three relatively easy summits along the way. What this route lacks in height it makes up for in variety. Shorter options are also available via the popular Pierce's Castle track.

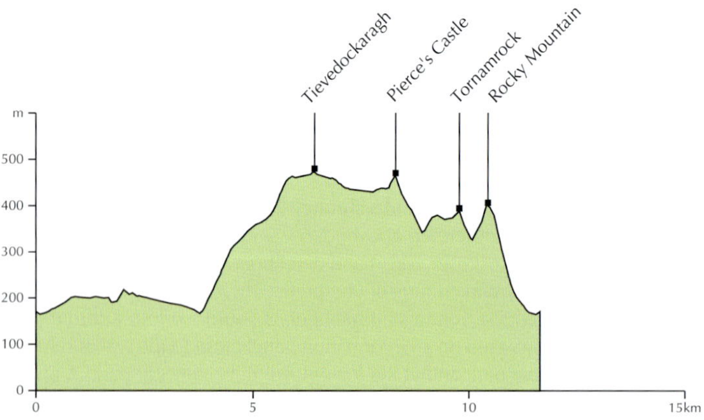

Heading up the Yellow Water River valley

From the south end of Leitrim Lodge car park, follow a path south-east through a gate. Continue along a track across **Shankys River**. After 270m, arrive at the first junction on the route. If walking the north-east loop or Pierce's Castle only, bear left here (Variant 1). Turn right here to follow the **Mourne Way** south. About 1.3km further along, the track narrows to a path, which can become quite rough and overgrown by ferns in places. Pay attention to waymarkers along this 800m section. Come to a stile crossing **Batt's Wall** (see Route 23).

Cross the stile to enter Rostrevor Forest and continue south-west along the track for 1.4km to a junction. Turn left along a forest track for 40m, then head right a few metres towards where the Mourne Way crosses a footbridge. Just before you reach the footbridge, locate a side path on the left heading uphill. The Yellow Water car park start/finish ties in here (see Variant 2).

Potential diversion

If the side path heading uphill is closed for any reason, turn around and retrace your steps north a few metres, then turn right to ascend the forest track north-east. At a track junction, take a sharp right and continue uphill to rejoin the main route.

Main route continues

Turn left to ascend the path east for 680m. This is a section of the Fallows Trail, which, at the time of writing, was waymarked for walking in the opposite direction only. Take care when walking over the exposed tree roots and rocks along this section, especially in wet conditions. To your right, Yellow Water River can be heard cascading its way down this steep-sided valley. After a long flight of **steps**, you will soon emerge from the path onto a forest track.

Turn right here along the track for 70m, then bear left at a fork to continue east along the main track. After 200m, look for a grassy path on the left. (If you reach a bridge where the track bends right, you have gone 40m too far.) Turn left to ascend along the grassy path north-east beside a stream flowing through coniferous forest. This path gets muddy in places and there are a few hidden holes to watch out for. After 650m, exit the forest through a pedestrian gate into open mountain land.

Ascending east initially, follow an obvious worn path, curving north-east for 570m to meet **Batt's Wall**. Turn left to follow the wall west-north-west. After a section of wire fence, the wall resumes again. After 390m turn left, away from the wall, to reach the summit cairn on **Tievedockaragh** (473m). Retrace your steps north-east to the wall, then turn right to follow it east-south-east. Just before the wall resumes after the fence section, turn left to cross at some placed boulders, where posts and a timber rail have been installed.

Pick up an obvious path bearing left away from the wall. Follow this east initially, then north-north-east before curving east again. After 430m turn left along a perfectly **straight bog track**. Follow the bog track north for 540m to where it meets a stony track. Turn right along this and follow it east-south-east, curving left to north-north-east. After 500m, ascend onto the rocky outcrop of **Pierce's Castle** (467m).

Continue north over its high point and look for a safe descent through the rocks on the left. Alternatively, retrace your steps south off the rock and contour north around its west side. Descend north along an obvious path. After 600m, keep straight across a col and ascend north towards Tornamrock. After 300m, pass over Tornamrock's south top. Continue north along the ridgeline for 500m to the unmarked rocky summit of **Tornamrock** (390m). After a further 50m, turn left to descend north-west. Follow a path for 360m to a 325m col.

Continue straight across the Mourne Way and ascend along a worn path for 300m to the summit cairn on **Rocky Mountain** (405m). Turn left to descend west off the summit along a grassy path. This becomes rocky in places as it zigzags its way down. After 720m, meet a stone track. Bear right and descend along the track for 250m to a junction. If finishing at Yellow Water car park, bear left here. Turn right along the track and retrace your steps north-west to finish at **Leitrim Lodge car park**.

Variant 1: north-east loop to Pierce's Castle

At the first junction, bear left to follow a track signposted as the 'Mourne Way'. Ignore all turn-offs, including one where the Mourne Way departs to the left. Stick

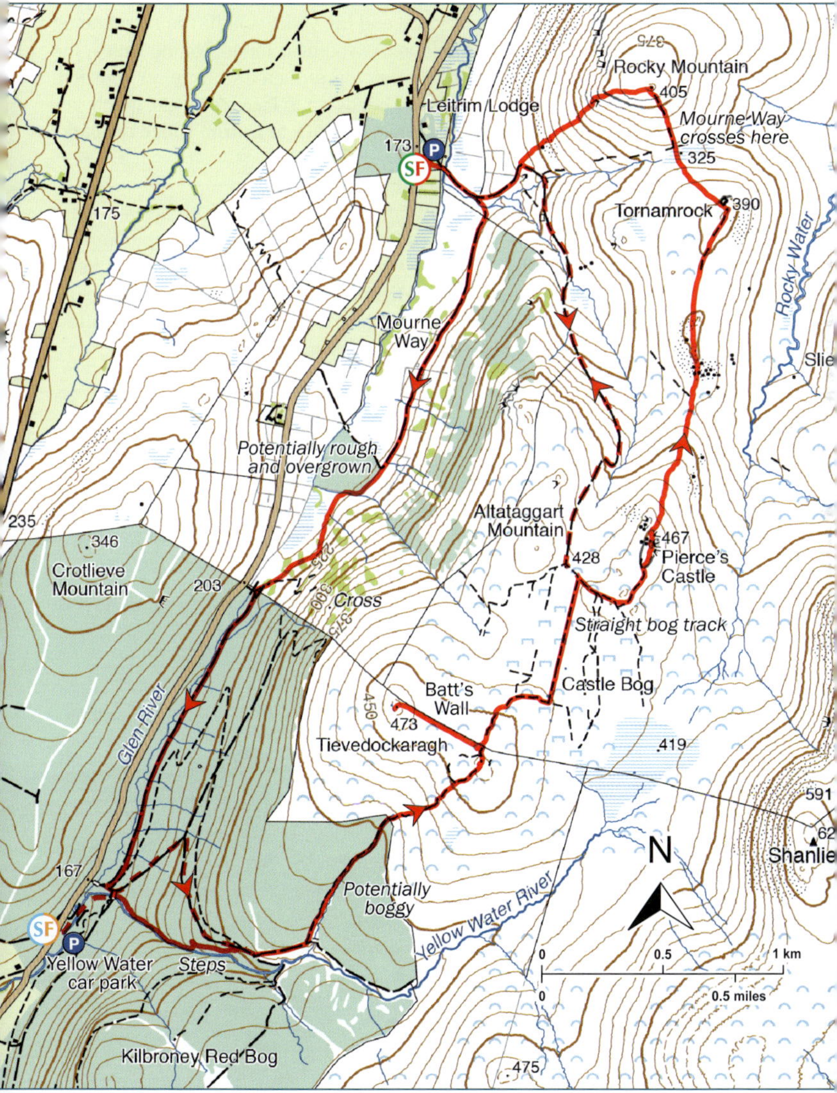
Rocky Mountain
405
375
Mourne Way crosses here
325
Leitrim Lodge
173
P
SF
Tornamrock
390
Rocky Water
175
Mourne Way
Slie
Potentially rough and overgrown
235
Altataggart Mountain
467
Pierce's Castle
346
Crotlieve Mountain
428
203
Cross
Straight bog track
Castle Bog
Batt's Wall
473
450
Tievedockaragh
419
Glen River
591
62
Shanlie
N
167
Potentially boggy
Yellow Water River
SF
P
Yellow Water car park
Steps
0
0.5
1 km
0
0.5 miles
Kilbroney Red Bog
475

to the main track as it curves right to ascend the valley south. The ridgeline on your left is the return section of the loop. As you near the top of the valley, the track begins an orbit around the rocky outcrop of Pierce's Castle on your left. Ignore all turn-offs on the right as the track bends left to **Pierce's Castle**. If only visiting Pierce's Castle, retrace your steps down the track to **Leitrim Lodge car park**.

Variant 2: start/finish at Yellow Water car park

Starting from the north end of Yellow Water car park, take a path north-east for 280m, beside Yellow Water River, to a junction with a footbridge nearby. Turn left here and cross the **footbridge**. After a few metres, before you meet a forest track, turn right along a path, ascending east to tie into the main route. When you return to this point later, continue straight across the footbridge, bear right after a few metres and retrace your steps south-west to finish at **Yellow Water car park**.

Variant 3: south-west loop

At the end of the **straight bog track**, turn left and follow the stony track all the way down the valley. Continue along the track as it bends left past a side path where the Mourne Way joins from the right. Come to a track junction. If using an alternate start/finish at Yellow River car park, bear left here and follow the Mourne Way south. Turn right along the track and retrace your steps north-west to finish at **Leitrim Lodge car park**.

Take this straight line through Castle Bog then a right to Pierce's Castle

ROUTE 23

Rocky River Horseshoe

Start/finish	Hen Mountain car park
Time	6hr 30min
Distance	18.3km
Ascent/descent	1175m
Grade	Very hard
Options	East loop (-7.6km/-530m/-2hr 45min); west loop (-1.5km/-290m/-45min)

Challenge yourself on one of the Mournes' lesser-walked big horseshoe routes. Following the ridgeline enclosing the Rocky River's highest tributaries, Rocky Water and Rowan Tree River, you will pass over eight summits, including two official mountains. The route also takes in one of the boggiest cols in the Mournes, which is why you should save this walk for the end of a long spell of dry weather.

The southern high section of the route follows Batt's Wall, a notable property boundary in the Mournes.

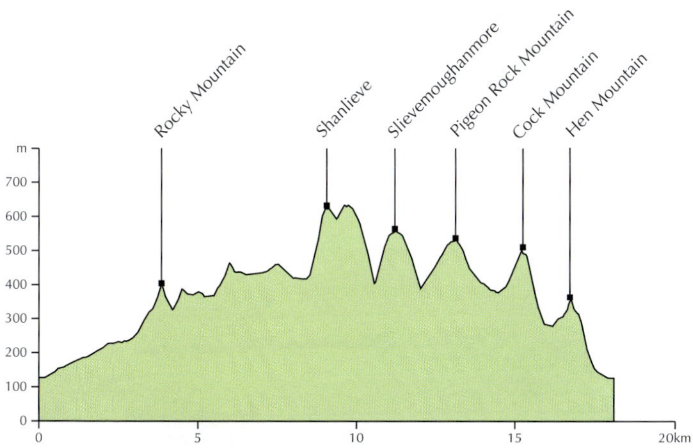

From the entrance of Hen Mountain car park, cross **Sandbank Road** to access the track directly ahead. Proceed east along the track for 600m, keeping the granite tors of Hen Mountain directly ahead. Arrive at a gate where the track enters open mountain land. Turn right along the **Mourne Way**. Follow the track south-east for 1.6km, keeping a close eye on the Mourne Way marker posts. Pass a couple of these pointing straight ahead. Just after fording a stream, come to a Mourne Way marker post pointing right along a faint side path.

Variant for east loop

Continue straight here to where the track ends. From there, follow a faint and sometimes muddy path along the left-hand side of **Rowan Tree River** to meet Batt's Wall at a **393m col**. Turn left here to join the main route.

Main route continues

Turn right along the side path here to follow the Mourne Way south-west for 450m to where it crosses **Rowan Tree River**. At the time of writing, there was no bridge here. Cross carefully using the rocks, bearing in mind they could be slippery. Continue south beside **Rocky Water** for 120m to a footbridge. Turn right across this and ascend a potentially muddy path west for 800m to a **325m col**. Turn right off the Mourne Way and ascend along a side path for 300m to the summit cairn on **Rocky Mountain** (405m).

Retrace your steps down to the col. Continue straight across the Mourne Way and ascend south-east along a path for 360m to the rocky summit of **Tornamrock** (390m). Turn right and follow a clear ridgeline path south. After 870m, keep straight across a col then ascend for a further 680m towards the rocky outcrop of Pierce's Castle. Approach the outcrop on its right-hand side, where you will find a route up through the rocks. Alternatively, continue past it and ascend from the south. Arrive at the top of **Pierce's Castle** (467m).

Hen Mountain and Cock Mountain

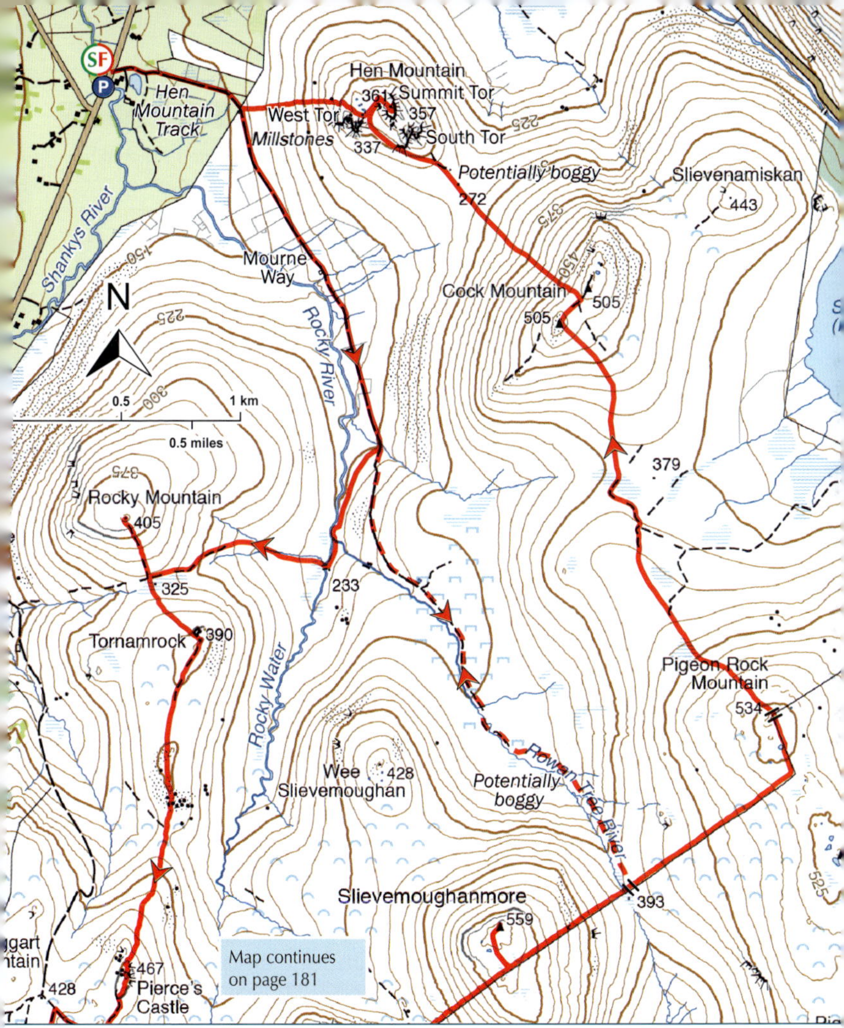

Map continues on page 181

Descend south off the rock and pick up a track. Follow this for 430m as it curves right, ignoring the first few turn-offs on the left. Look for a perfectly straight sidetrack on the left. Take this and follow it south for 540m to a junction. Turn right along a path heading west, curving left. After 430m, meet **Batt's Wall**. Turn left and follow the wall east. Ahead of you lies one of the boggiest cols in the Mournes.

BATT'S WALL

This impressive dry-stone structure runs almost uninterrupted for 8.3km from the Mourne Way near Sandbank Road to intercept a corner of the much younger Mourne Wall at the summit of Slieve Muck. Along the way, it crosses over, or very close to, the summits of Tievedockaragh, Shanlieve, Eagle Mountain, Slievemoughanmore and Pigeon Rock Mountain (north summit). The wall marks the southern boundary of Batt's Estate, comprising more than 1200 acres of mountain land purchased by Belfast banker Narcissus Batt in the 1830s. Detailed information about the wall is hard to come by, but it is believed to have been constructed in the mid-19th century during the Famine. It is unknown if the Batt's Wall we see today is all that remains of a more extensive wall that enclosed the entire estate. If that were the case, it is possible that eastern sections of Batt's Wall beyond Slieve Muck could have been rebuilt decades later to become part of the Mourne Wall.

The wall becomes a fence after 130m. Follow the fence – and another brief re-appearance of the wall – east as far as you can before the ground gets too boggy to continue. The soft area in front of you is called **Shanlough**, even if it does not look much like a lake. If you want to stay dry, turn left, away from the fence, now. Take the driest route you can find to bypass Shanlough around its north side. You might even pass over the 419m col along the way. Curve south to meet the fence again.

Turn left along the fence to where Batt's Wall restarts for the tough Shanlieve ascent. In the absence of a stile here, you need to find a suitable location to cross the fence without damaging it. Keeping Batt's Wall close on your left, ascend steeply east for 640m to where the wall bends left. Bear right, south, away from the wall, for 60m to the summit cairn on **Shanlieve** (626m).

Retrace your steps to the corner on the wall. Turn right to follow the wall north-east for 500m across a 591m col to where the wall bends left at a stile. Turn right here, south-east, away from the wall, for 60m to the summit cairn on **Eagle Mountain** (637m). Retrace your steps to the corner on the wall and cross the stile. Continue straight ahead beside the wall for 310m, then turn right with it to descend north-east for 520m.

This descent is quite steep, so you may have to zigzag a bit, staying close to the wall. Arrive at **Windy Gap** (407m). Ascend north-east for 470m to a high point along the wall. Bear left away from the wall along a faint path north for 210m to the summit cairn on **Slievemoughanmore** (559m). There are a couple of cairns on the summit area. You want the most north-easterly one. Return south to rejoin the wall and turn left. Descend north-east for 590m to a **393m col**.

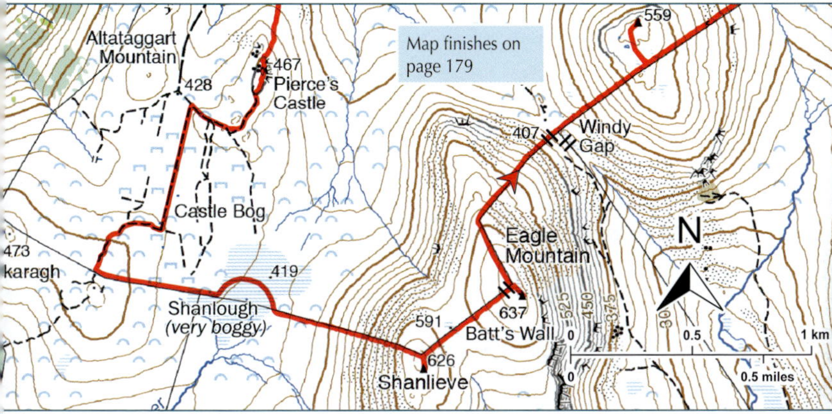

Variant for west loop

Turn left away from the wall here. With **Rowan Tree River** on your left, follow a faint and sometimes muddy path to meet a track further down. Follow this to a gate you passed through earlier. Pass through it again and retrace your steps west to finish at **Hen Mountain car park**.

Main route continues

Continue straight ahead and ascend north-east for 900m to a left-hand bend in the wall. Bend left with the wall, then bear left from it to pass over the unmarked north summit of **Pigeon Rock Mountain** (534m). Rejoin the wall and continue to a right-hand bend beside a cairn. Bear left away from the wall and descend north-west along a faint path. This becomes a track further down. With Cock Mountain ahead of you, take a moment to survey the ridgeline and boggy col you need to cross to get there.

The strict horseshoe challenger will tackle this in a mirrored S-shape to pass through the 379m col. If you want the driest possible route, stick to the one described here. Expect some wetness underfoot. After 1.2km of descent, bend right along a raised straight section of bog track. Turn left off this at its midpoint 60m further on. Ascend north for 740m along a faint path. Bear left near the top to approach the south-west summit of **Cock Mountain** (505m). Its north-east twin is 270m away.

Descend north-west from the col along a faint path between the twin summits, directly towards the rocky tors of Hen Mountain. This is quite a steep descent. After 740m, continue straight across a **272m col**, which may be muddy.

Hen Mountain from Cock Mountain's south-west summit

A further 260m on, keep left around the base of the south tor (357m). In 150m, curve right to ascend between the summit tor and the west tor (337m). Head north-north-east, past a small pool, to ascend the left-hand side of the summit tor, then turn right to reach the summit of **Hen Mountain** (361m).

When you decide to leave Hen Mountain, pass the north side of the west tor, where a path descends west towards an obvious stone track lower down. After 500m, meet the track at a gate you passed through earlier. Pass through it again and retrace your steps west for 600m to finish at **Hen Mountain car park**.

ROUTE 24

Hen Mountain, Cock Mountain and Slievenamiskan

Start/finish	Hen Mountain car park
Time	2hr 45min
Distance	7.8km
Ascent/descent	450m
Grade	Moderate
Option	Hen Mountain only (-5.1km/-250m/-1hr 30min)

This trio of hills to the west of Spelga Dam packs a variety of character and views into a relatively short walk. Hen Mountain, the lowest of the three, with its rocky tors, is particularly interesting. Although classified as a small hill, it has the feel and look of a real mountain. If you are stretched for time, a short out-and-back to explore the tors crowning Hen's summit area is a magical experience on its own. Cock Mountain and Slievenamiskan offer excellent views back down to Hen and across Spelga Dam to the mountains lining the western edge of Silent Valley. A lovely section of the Mourne Way completes the loop.

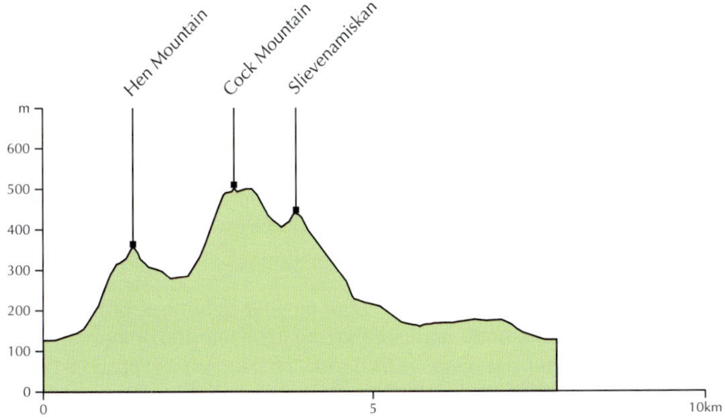

Spelga Dam from the summit of Slievenamiskan

From the entrance of Hen Mountain car park, cross **Sandbank Road** to access the track directly ahead. Proceed east along the track for 600m, keeping the granite tors of Hen Mountain directly ahead, to a gate where the track enters open mountain land. Cross the **Mourne Way** and continue straight towards Hen Mountain to ascend an obvious grassy path, keeping left of the west tor, which appears as the highest point from this angle. After 500m, arrive on Hen's flattish grassy summit area, which is decorated with an array of rocky tors.

Hen Mountain is one of the most interesting summits in the Mournes. Taking half an hour to explore its rocky tors is highly recommended. There are some big drops off the tors so please explore them carefully, especially in the wet. Always keep children under close supervision.

Continue, passing the west tor (337m) on your right, then bear left past a small pool and ascend north-north-east up the left-hand side of the summit tor. Take extra care as you zigzag up the final rocky section. As you approach the top, turn right to reach the summit of **Hen Mountain** (361m). Retrace your steps to Hen Mountain car park if not visiting any further summits.

Continue back down to the pool and bear left to contour east-south-east around the base of the south tor (357m), on your left. Descend for 260m to cross a **272m col**, which may be muddy. Ascend south-east along a worn path, aiming for the low point between Cock Mountain's twin summits directly ahead. The terrain becomes steeper as you ascend and the path may be hard to see where it passes through heather. After 740m, reach a col midway between the twin summits, where Spelga Dam comes into view ahead. Turn right to visit the south-west summit of **Cock Mountain** (505m).

Return to the col and continue straight across to the north-east twin. Descend east-north-east for 500m to a col, then ascend straight ahead for 200m to the unmarked summit of **Slievenamiskan** (443m).

Bear left from the summit and head north initially to keep right of a small rock face. Descend north-north-west along the pathless high line of Slievenamiskan's shoulder for 790m to meet a contouring path. This is the **Mourne Way**. Turn left here along the path. Hen Mountain and Cock Mountain are directly ahead of you.

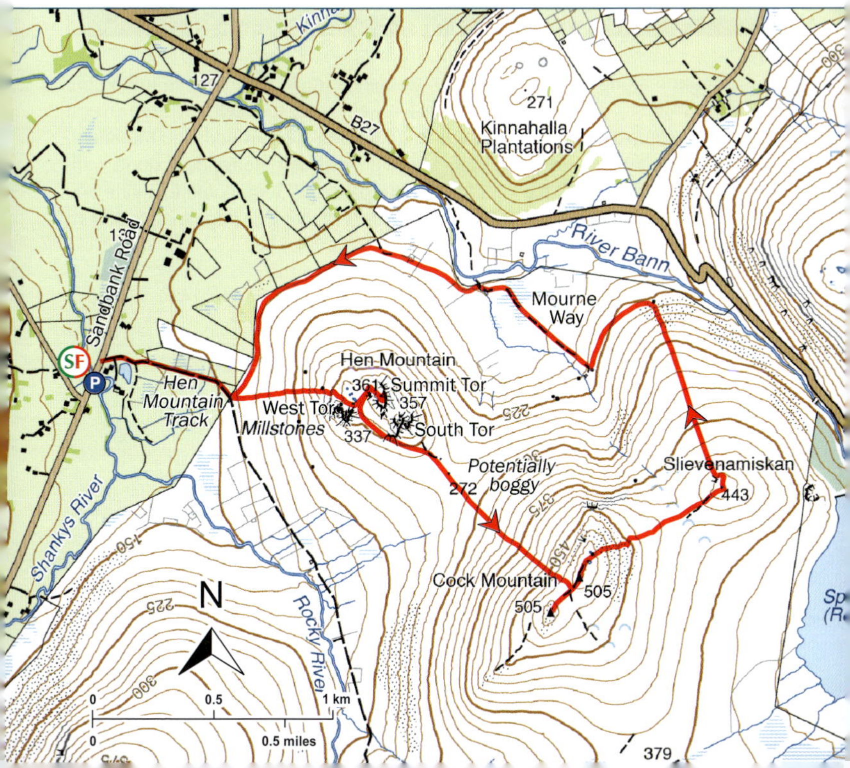

Looking over the South Tor from Hen Mountain's summit to Cock Mountain

Continue along the path for 400m to meet a track. Turn right to follow the track north-west. After 580m, just before a field gate, turn left and step over a stream to pick up a path. Follow this to contour north-west around Hen Mountain. After 500m, continue along the path where it bends left alongside a stone wall. Keep a few metres left of the wall for a better path. In 950m, come to a gate you passed through earlier. Pass through it again and retrace your steps west for 600m to finish at **Hen Mountain car park**.

THE MOURNE WALL

Descending off Slieve Donard towards the Saddle, alongside the Mourne Wall

The summit cairn on Meelmore, with the stile and stone shelter beyond

What is the Mourne Wall?

The Mourne Wall – commonly referred to by hillwalkers simply as 'The Wall' – is a 31.4km (19.5 miles) dry-stone structure marking the perimeter of Northern Ireland Water's largest chunk of land in the Mourne Mountains, which measures approximately 36km^2 (14 square miles). Writers occasionally compare it to the Great Wall of China, which is a bit of a stretch; both are built of stone and pass over mountains, but that is where the similarities end.

Commissioned by Belfast City and District Water Commissioners (BC&DWC), the Wall was built by locals between the months of April and October over an 18-year period (1904–22). Its primary purposes were to define BC&DWC's property boundary and to keep livestock out of Silent Valley and Annalong Valley, thereby maintaining the standard of the groundwater within the catchment area and minimising purification processes. The water would later be collected in two new reservoirs – Silent Valley (completed 1933) and Ben Crom (completed 1957) – to then be piped for consumption in the growing city of Belfast.

The Mourne Wall passes directly over 10 official summits (including 6 of the range's 14 mountains) and within 300m of 3 others: Slieve Commedagh, Slieve Bearnagh and Rocky Mountain. It also passes over four notable tops that do not qualify as summits due to them having less than 30m prominence: Slieve Bearnagh East Tor, Slieve Corragh, Carn Mountain North Top and Moolieve. The Wall is roughly the height of an adult (you may not be able to see a passing walker on the other side), is just under a metre thick (please do not walk along its flat top – the Wall is very delicate) and includes three integrated stone shelters along its northernmost section.

Although a primary purpose was to keep livestock out of the rainfall catchment area, the Wall deviates on occasions from the ridgeline that defines the catchment boundary. These deviations occur along the following sections of the Wall: Wee Binnian to Moolieve; the west side of Silent Valley Mountain Park to Slieve Muck; and where the Wall misses Rocky Mountain. It is unknown why these deviations occurred, but they are most likely the result of land-purchase negotiations during the 1890s. Route 7 (Annalong Valley Horseshoe) and Route 13 (Silent Valley Horseshoe) refer to these deviations but direct walkers along the ridge sections where it would have been more logical to build the Wall.

One might wonder why the Wall-enclosed catchment area extends so far south in the Annalong Valley, given that the Binnian Tunnel redirects water from the river 1.4km upstream from where the Wall crosses. This is due to the original plan to build a reservoir in the Annalong Valley before the construction of the Wall had even started. That idea was later abandoned because of difficulties encountered during the Silent Valley Reservoir project, by which time the entire Wall had long been completed. If the Binnian Tunnel had been part of the original masterplan, the Wall's path across the Annalong Valley might be very different today.

The Mourne Wall has been a Listed Historical Building since 15 March 1996. In its listing details, the Wall is described as 'the longest upstanding man-made structure in Ireland'. Regular maintenance is undertaken by local stonemasons commissioned by Northern Ireland Water.

Walking the Mourne Wall

With the Mourne Wall being one of the most iconic human-built features in the Irish uplands, to walk its full length is a long-established and popular challenge among hillwalkers. Along most of the Wall, especially the higher sections, conditions often permit walking on both sides. Navigation along these sections is generally straightforward: just follow the Wall. However, things get significantly trickier along a couple of lower sections where the Wall cuts across Annalong Valley and Silent Valley.

As a result of these tricky sections, Mourne Wall Challenge walkers tend to deviate away from the Wall twice. The most popular version of the challenge, described in Route 25, is an updated version of the old challenge route, which previously crossed Silent Valley via the lower dam wall. New paths in Silent Valley Mountain Park now permit a more southerly crossing of the valley. A couple of variations are also described for walkers wishing to maximise the length of Wall they walk.

Route descriptions

To provide you with options on how much of the Wall's length you want to include in your Mourne Wall walking adventure, three versions of the route are described in Route 25 and its two variations.

The Challenge Route

This version is the most popular route for walking the Mourne Wall. It includes 26.6km of the Wall's 31.4km length, has no out-and-back sections, takes a shortcut across Silent Valley Mountain Park and contains a diversion away from the Wall with 1.5km of road walking.

The Maximised Route

This version is for challenge hillwalkers wanting to maximise the length of Mourne Wall they walk without entering private land. It includes 29.4km of the Wall's 31.4km length, has two out-and-back sections, takes a shortcut across Silent Valley Mountain Park and contains a diversion away from the Wall with 90m of road walking (described in Route 25 and Variant 1).

The Entire Mourne Wall

This version is for the strictest of challenge hillwalking purists. It includes all 31.4km of the Wall's length, has one out-and-back section (i.e. the access track start and finish), takes no shortcuts or diversions away from the Wall and includes three short sections skirting the edge of privately owned, low-level agricultural land along the outer side the Wall. What would it take for this to become the official Mourne Wall Challenge route it deserves to be? Less than 4km of path development, no more than 10 new stiles/gates and some access arrangements. With a bit of luck, this may have already happened by the time you arrive to walk the Wall (described in Route 25 and Variant 2).

Fitness and safety

Given the length of the Wall and the amount of ascent/descent involved, a high level of fitness is required for one-day attempts. Two-day attempts with a night under canvas are popular among walkers looking for a more leisurely option. In the interests of safety, it is recommended that complete circuits of the Wall be undertaken during the summer months, when daylight hours are longest.

A group of Mourne Wall challengers beginning their descent off Slieve Muck (Routes 13, 14, 19 and 25)

Camping

There are no formal camping facilities along the course of the Wall. The closest campsite can be found at Meelmore Lodge, which is roughly 3km off route near the halfway point. This can be accessed from three consecutive cols in the vicinity of Slieve Meelmore and Slieve Bearnagh, as identified in Route 25. If you depart from the Wall to camp at the end of day one, you must return to that same departure point to continue the walk on day two. Wild camping beside the Wall is a popular option for two-day challengers. If you want to enjoy a sunrise/sunset from your tent, consider the northernmost chain of summits from Slieve Meelmore and Slieve Donard. Please leave no trace of your overnight stop. Always take a final look back when departing from your camping spot to make sure you leave nothing behind.

Water sources

There are no tap water supplies along the Wall. In Silent Valley Mountain Park, it may be possible to ask for a refill at the café. Given that much of the Wall follows ridgelines, there are very few flowing streams to serve as clean-water sources on the route. Much of the H_2O encountered along the ridgeline is likely to be standing water in isolated boggy areas (and probably rain). Some fast-flowing surface streams can be found by descending either side of ridges. The Wall crosses a stream on the south-east slopes of Slieve Muck, although the water quality is unknown. It would be worth carrying a water filtration system if you are trying to keep the weight down.

A freshwater pipe is located on the upper slope of Slieve Commedagh to the west of the stone shelter. This pipe is very easy to find, close to the Wall on its south side, and is conveniently positioned near the halfway point of Route 25. Another pipe is also present on the east slope of Slieve Meelmore on the south-west side of the Wall. This one is a bit further away from the Wall, making it not so easy to spot.

How long is the Mourne Wall?

Answer: 31.4km (19.5 miles)

This figure has been determined from high-precision measurements taken from multiple printed and digital mapping sources and further checked using GPS tracking devices in the field.

It is worth noting that many online sources mistakenly quote the Wall as being 22 miles long. This error is believed to have originated from a misinterpretation of the length of a Mourne Wall walking route described in an earlier guidebook, which included a section of access track at the start and finish (as has also been done in Route 25 of this book). The incorrect figure appears to have stuck and continues to do the rounds online.

The 22-mile conundrum

In 2016, a survey was undertaken along the entire stretch of the Mourne Wall. One of the objectives of this survey was to solve what has been referred to as the '22-mile conundrum'. This involved surveying the full 19.5 miles of Mourne Wall and assessing the condition of nearby adjoining dry-stone walls to find the missing miles. Without any detailed records from the time of construction to refer to, and with a specified target of 22 miles to prove, the study comes across as a guesswork exercise.

The resulting report conveniently identified just enough candidate branch-wall sections – including some that appear to predate the 19.5-mile Wall by several decades – to claim a total length that almost matches the study's 22-mile target. Bearing in mind that the Wall was built to mark the water company's property boundary and to keep livestock out of the catchment area, the deliberate construction of unnecessary branch-wall sections seems highly unlikely. Even if the course of the Wall had to be readjusted due to property expansion during its 18-year construction, any redundant branch-wall sections would have been demoted instantly and no longer considered part of the Mourne Wall.

A freshwater pipe on the ascent to Commedagh

ROUTE 25

The Mourne Wall Challenge

Start/finish	Dunnywater parking spot
Alt starts/finishes	Carrick Little car parks and Silent Valley car park
Time	12hr 30min
Distance	32km
Ascent/descent	2555m
Grade	Very hard
Options	Maximised route (+3.8km/+60m/+1hr 30min); entire Wall route (+1.1km/+20m/+30min)
Bus stops	The Mourne Rambler summer bus service stops at Carrick Little car park, 220m from the Dunnywater parking spot and 600m from Silent Valley car park

Completing a full circuit of the Mourne Wall over one or two days ranks among Ireland's most iconic hillwalking achievements. Are you up for the challenge? The current standard route (which deviates from the Wall in a couple of places) is described here, along with optional sections (including some wild ones) to help you maximise the length of Wall walked. You can read more about the Mourne Wall on the preceding pages.

Standing at the Dunnywater parking spot with the ornate walled red gates behind you, turn right along Head Road and follow it west. If maximising the length of the Wall walked, or walking the full length of the Wall, turn around and start through the ornate walled red gates instead (Variant 1A). There is no footway so be careful along the road as it is quite narrow with a few blind bends. Take extra care at a twisting section where it drops to cross Annalong River at the single-lane **Dunnywater Bridge**. After 1.4km, arrive at **Carrick Little car park** on the right, opposite Oldtown Road. This can be used as an alternate start/finish. Turn right up the track just before the car park.

Follow the track north for 1km to where it passes through the **Mourne Wall** at a gate. Continue through this and past a small gate on the right. A short distance directly ahead, pass through another gate to enter open mountain land. When the path splits 200m further along, bear left alongside the Wall. Ascend north-west

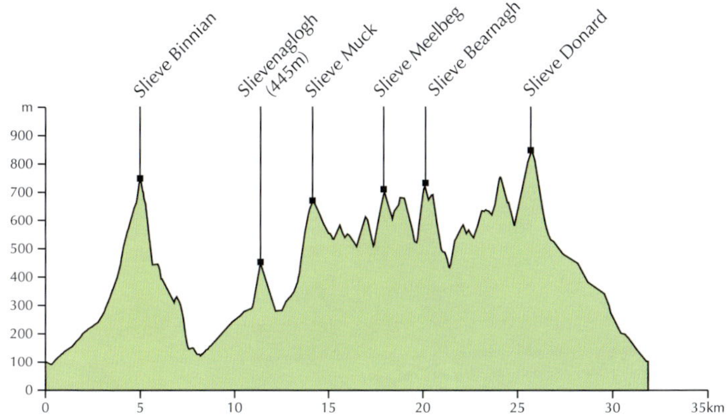
Slieve Binnian
Slievenaglogh (445m)
Slieve Muck
Slieve Meelbeg
Slieve Bearnagh
Slieve Donard
m
900
800
700
600
500
400
300
200
100
0
0
5
10
15
20
25
30
35km

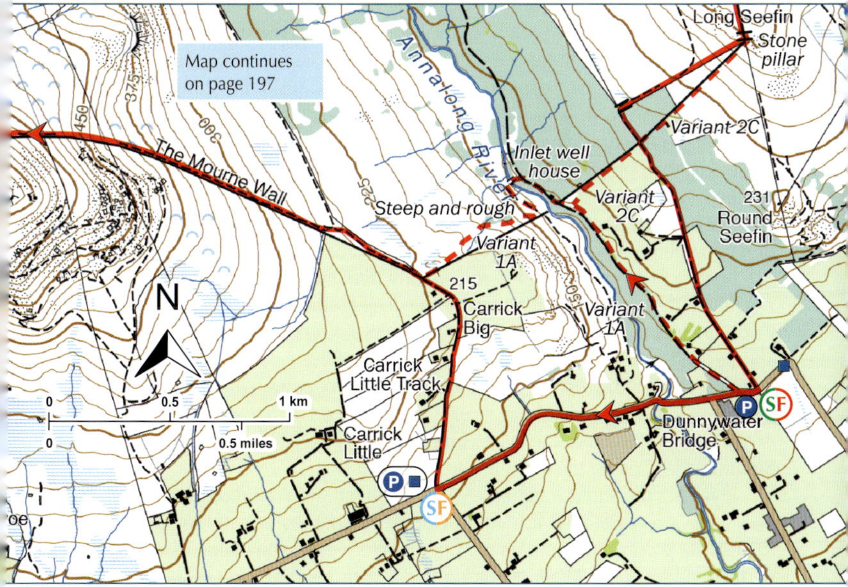
Map continues on page 197
Long Seefin
Stone pillar
Annalong River
Variant 2C
Inlet well house
The Mourne Wall
Steep and rough
Variant 2C
231
Round Seefin
Variant 1A
215
Carrick Big
Variant 1A
N
Carrick Little Track
0
0.5
1 km
0
0.5 miles
Carrick Little
Dunnywater Bridge
SF
SF

Walk to where the Wall meets Slieve Binnian's summit tor, then skirt right to the mini col

close to the Wall for 1.9km as it gradually curves left to a stile. Continue past the **stile**, without crossing, for 150m to where the Wall meets the base of Slieve Binnian's granite summit tor.

Turn right and skirt around this to a mini col near the summit of **Slieve Binnian** (747m). From here you can look down the other side, over Silent Valley Reservoir. (The actual summit is marked by a metal post on the rocks to your left. It is accessible, but care is needed.) Continue straight ahead at the mini col and descend west down the Silent Valley side, bearing left immediately and staying close to the tor's base on your left, to where the Wall restarts. Brace yourself for a steep downhill section.

Bear right along the Wall and carefully descend alongside it. The worn zigzagging path has short straights and some deep rock-and-earth steps to negotiate. If you are a confident user of walking poles on this type of descent, your legs will appreciate them here. After 500m, pass a stile at the next col and keep straight on to ascend south-west for 150m. Note the path bearing right from the stile and any others heading right on the ascent. You may need to follow one of these soon. Arrive at a point where the Wall is interrupted once again. The summit of **Wee Binnian** (459m) is on the rocks just to your right.

If visiting the summit, return to where you left the Wall moments earlier. You now have a few options. You could exit by passing just left of the summit rock to descend west on a path. A safer option is to retrace your steps by descending north-east beside the Wall. If you spotted a path heading right when ascending

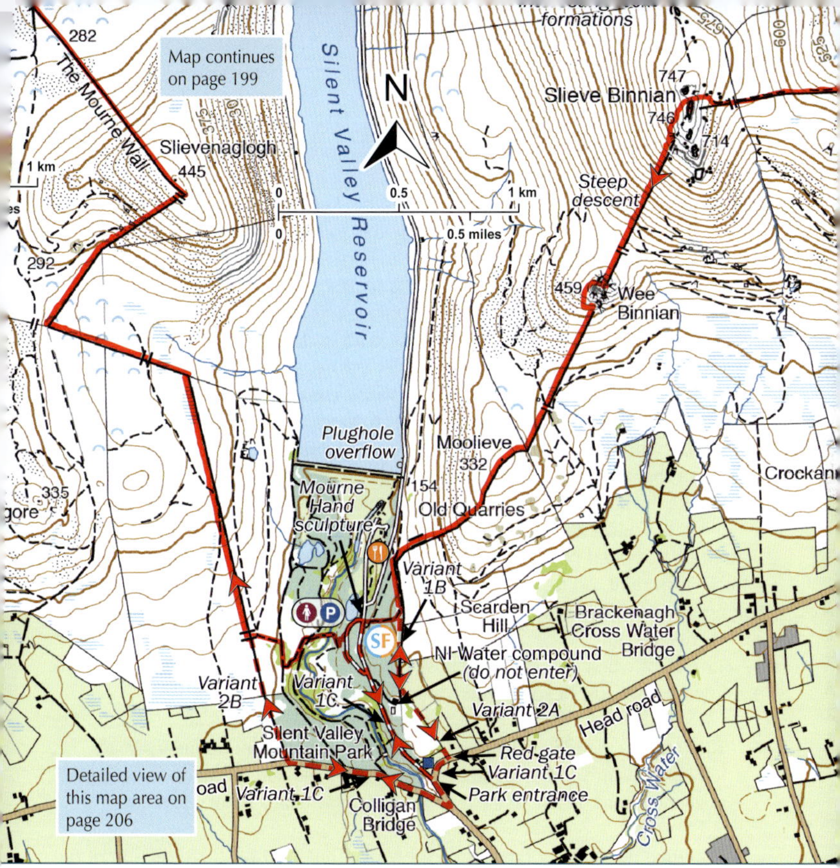

this part minutes earlier, it will be on the left as you descend. If you cannot find it, continue to the one at the stile in the col. Whichever path you choose, follow it left, away from the Wall, to contour around the right-hand side (west) of Wee Binnian.

When the Wall reappears south-west of Wee Binnian, bear left and make your way to where it restarts. Turn right and follow the Wall south-west as it deviates more than 200m left of the ridgeline. After 600m, pass through a broken side wall where the Mourne Wall itself bends right to rejoin the ridgeline at the subsidiary top of **Moolieve** (332m). Continue south-west beside the Wall for a steep descent towards Silent Valley Mountain Park. From here you can see some of the early 20th-century water-related buildings downstream of the reservoir embankment.

After 550m, arrive at a stile over a fence. Take care when crossing this stile because the flight you descend is considerably longer than the one you ascend. When safely across, continue down the path for 30m. You have now entered **Silent Valley Mountain Park**. Bear left at a fork, keeping the Wall close. Bear left again after 80m onto a better path. Follow this south for 200m to where it bends right into the forest. Continue straight ahead here if maximising the length of Wall walked (Variant 1B). Follow the path right and descend through the trees for 190m to meet an access road beside *The Mourne Hand* sculpture. Turn left here along the access road if maximising the length of Wall walked (Variant 1C).

Check for traffic then continue straight across, along an access road bending left past a toilet block, to enter **Silent Valley car park**. This can be used as an alternate start/finish. Bear right immediately towards the west edge of the car park, where you will find the start point for some waymarked trails. Following black arrows for the 'Mountain Trail', take the path descending south.

Where the path turns right after a short initial straight, take a sharp right down a side path. Follow this for 350m, across a bridge over Kilkeel River, past the bottom of a stepped path ascending on the right, then alongside a fence to meet a track. Turn right, north, along the track for 100m, then turn left up a side path. Follow this west for 140m, ignoring any turn-offs, to meet the **Mourne Wall** at a stile. Cross the stile.

Turn right when you step off the stile and follow the Wall north for 800m to pass over a ridge just beyond where a track briefly comes close.

The ridgeline defining **Silent Valley Reservoir's catchment boundary** heads left here towards Slievenagore. The Wall's unexplained deviation from the ridgeline means 0.8km^2 of the reservoir's catchment area is not enclosed.

Continue north for 300m beside the Wall. This short off-ridge section of the Wall crosses a few hard-to-see water channels, so walking poles may help to identify boggy spots. Turn left at a bend in the Wall and follow it west for 190m to a **stile**. Cross the Wall here.

Turn left off the stile and continue west for 440m to a wall junction. The Wall turns right here. Step straight over it at a low point near the wall junction and turn right immediately. Navigation and directions become relatively simple from here. However, there is still a significant amount of ascent left to do. With the Wall on your right, ascend north-east beside it for 820m to a **stile**. Cross this and turn left around the corner of the Wall. Once around the corner, bear right, away from the Wall, to the summit cairn on **Slievenaglogh** (445m).

Bear left to rejoin the Wall and descend north-west for 1km. Cross a **282m col** to where the Banns Road track passes through the Wall. The catchment boundary

ridgeline switches from the left-hand side to the right-hand side of the Wall here. With the Wall still on your left, continue straight ahead to ascend north-west for 1.8km. At a couple of short rocky sections, bear right from the Wall to bypass these before returning to it above them. Arrive at a stile near the summit of **Slieve Muck** (674m). The summit trig is 40m away on the other side of the Wall.

Departing Slieve Loughshannagh en route to Meelbeg

With the Wall still on your left, follow it north for 1km. Just before the Wall bends right, negotiate a short rocky section. Bear right to descend around this to a 531m col. Ascend east for 300m to a wall junction beside the summit cairn on **Carn Mountain** (585m). Ignore the stile, pass through a gap in the adjoining wall and turn left to follow the Wall north-east. Keeping the Wall on your left, pass over **Carn Mountain North Top** (557m). After 880m, arrive at a **510m col**.

Continue straight through and ascend for 500m to the summit cairn on **Slieve Loughshannagh** (617m). Descend north-east, with the Wall still on your left, for 360m to a **511m col**. Cross the stile here. With the Wall now on your right, ascend north-east for 620m to the summit cairn on **Slieve Meelbeg** (701m). Follow the Wall as it bends right and descend north-east for 330m to a 590m col. Keep straight on and ascend for 600m to the summit cairn on **Slieve Meelmore** (688m).

Continue north along the Wall for 110m to a stone shelter built into a sharp corner. Cross a stile just before the shelter. With the Wall now on your left again, descend south-east for 620m towards the jagged tors of Slieve Bearnagh directly ahead. Fresh water flows from a pipe in the heather a few metres right of the Wall along this descent. Keep straight through a 516m col and brace yourself for the

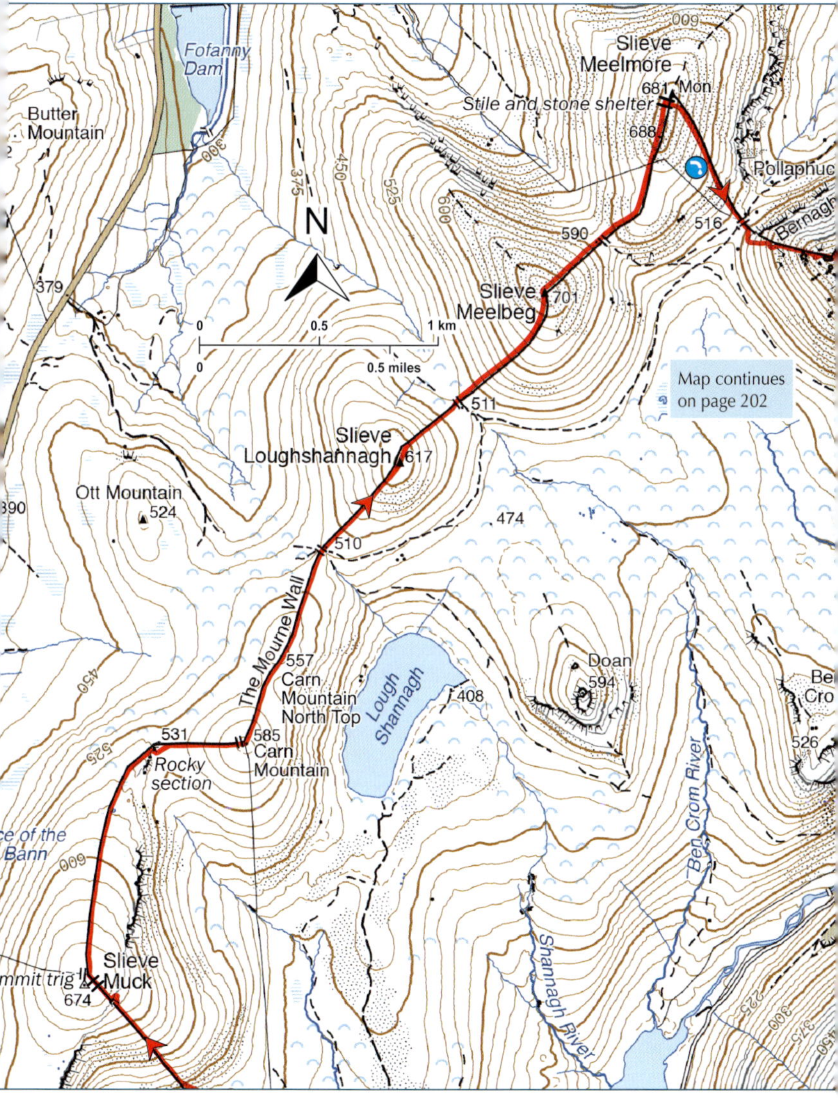

Map continues on page 202

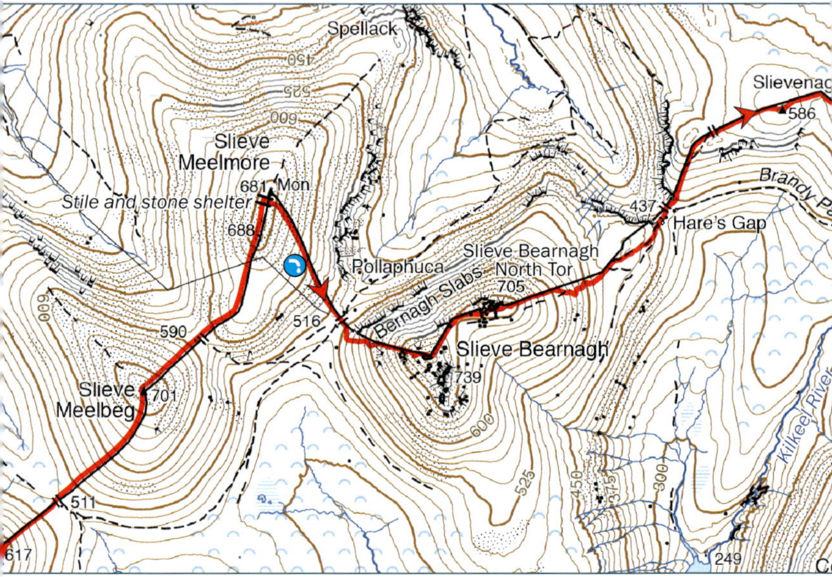

imminent steep ascent. Bear slightly right of the Wall initially to ascend one of the worn paths. The ground here is steep and quite eroded. Carefully zigzag your way up through this area, always keeping the Wall in sight.

When ground conditions improve, move back to the Wall. After ascending for 470m, come to a sharp left-hand bend on a rocky subsidiary top near the summit of **Slieve Bearnagh** (739m). (The actual summit is located on a granite tor 100m south of here. It is accessible, but care is needed.) Work your way anticlockwise around the south side of the rocks on this subsidiary top to rejoin the Wall as it descends north-east.

Continue close to the Wall for 280m to where it is interrupted by **Slieve Bearnagh North Tor**. Skirt around the rock to pick up the Wall again where it restarts, then do the same again a few metres further on. Continue east-north-east beside the Wall for 880m. The descent steepens along here for a bit, then flattens before a constructed flight of rock steps leads down to **Hare's Gap** (437m).

Continue straight across the col and up some more rock steps. Keeping the Wall on your left, follow it eastwards for 2.6km, over the summit cairn on **Slievenaglogh** (586m) and the subsidiary top of **Slieve Corragh** (641m), until you arrive at a stone shelter. Note the freshwater pipe you passed to the right of the Wall on the climb.

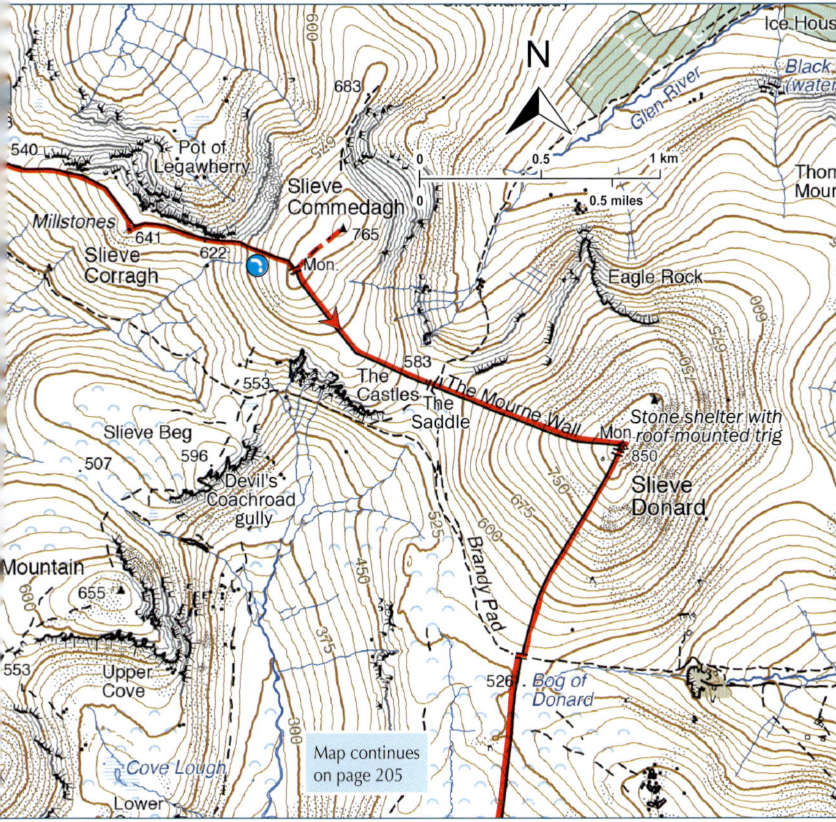

Map continues on page 205

Cross the stile beside it. The summit cairn on Slieve Commedagh (765m) is just 270m to the north-east of here if you fancy the short out-and-back detour. Turn right alongside the Wall, past the shelter, and descend south-east to the **Saddle** (583m).

Continue straight across this col with the Wall on your right. Ascend east along a constructed path, past a stone shelter, to arrive immediately at the summit cairn on **Slieve Donard** (850m). Turn right past the stone shelter. For the descent south-west, decide which side of the Wall to be on and use the stile if necessary. Descend for 1km beside the Wall to a col stile in the **Bog of Donard** (526m). If the Wall is on your right, cross the stile.

On the home straight, heading past the stile at Rocky Mountain

With the Wall now on your left, continue south for 1.8km to a **stile** just after Rocky Mountain. Ignore this and continue straight on for 1.2km, past another stile, to a corner in the Wall embellished with a small ornate pillar at **Long Seefin**.

To proceed along the Mourne Wall from here would require special permission from the landowner (see Variant 2C). Turn right and carefully descend south-west beside a wall for 600m to a **stile**. Cross the stile, turn left and follow a track south-east for 160m. Pass through the Mourne Wall at a gate. Variant 2C passes left to right across here. Continue straight along the track.

A walled area on the right encloses a **straining well** on the Belfast-bound Mourne Conduit. This was an important junction where water piped separately from Silent Valley and Annalong Valley was brought together for the onward journey to Belfast.

After 1.1km, meet Head Road. Turn right along the road for 90m to finish at **Dunnywater parking spot**. If using an alternate start/finish, continue straight here.

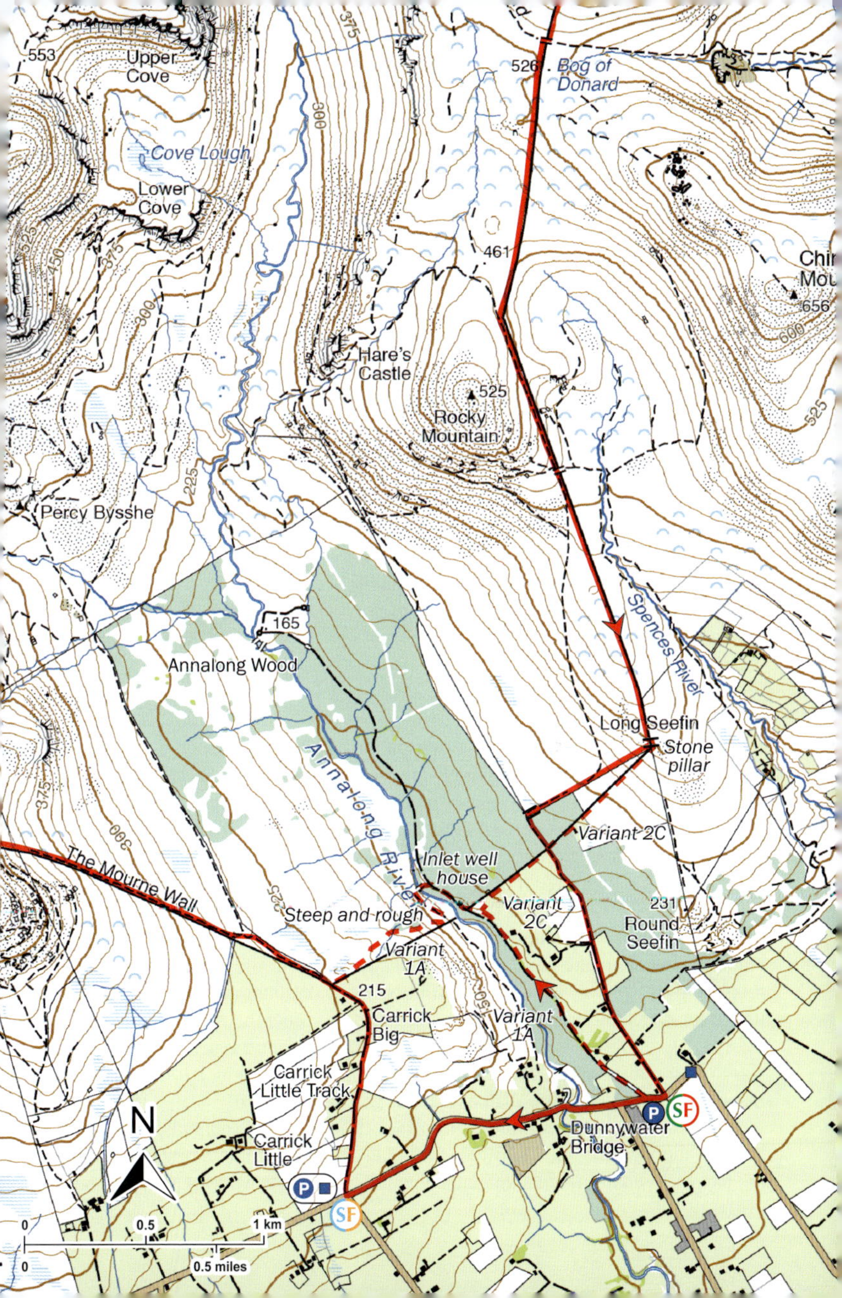
Upper Cove
Cove Lough
Lower Cove
Bog of Donard
Hare's Castle
Rocky Mountain
Percy Bysshe
Annalong Wood
Annalong River
Spences River
Long Seefin
Stone pillar
Variant 2C
Inlet well house
Steep and rough
Variant 1A
The Mourne Wall
Round Seefin
Carrick Big
Carrick Little Track
Carrick Little
Dunnywater Bridge
SF
P
N
0
0.5
1 km
0.5 miles

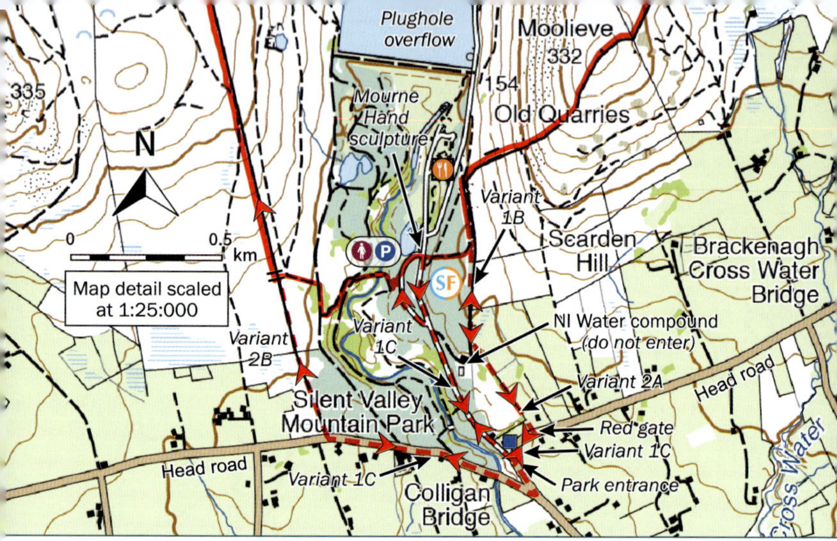

Variant 1: maximised route including all public sections

The following three sections allow you to maximise the length of Mourne Wall walked. None require you to access private agricultural land, so there are no access issues.

1A: Dunnywater to Carrick Big

From the start/finish at the Dunnywater parking spot, pass through a gate in the ornate stone-walled entrance to the Dunnywater Track. Proceed north-west along the track, passing a couple of houses on the right along the way.

After 1.1km, just before reaching a stone **inlet well house**, look for the Mourne Wall on both sides where it crosses the track. Strict challengers walking the full route of the Wall would join here later by descending from the right (Variant 2C).

Continue for 170m along the track and turn left down a short path leading to a footbridge over **Annalong River**. Cross this and ascend the opposite bank. Turn left and carefully make your way downstream for 200m. The ground here can be rough and overgrown, so be mindful of every step. Walking poles would be very useful for checking the ground along this section. Meet the **Mourne Wall**. Turn right and ascend west-south-west alongside the Wall. Dense vegetation may force you to bear quite far right of the Wall on this short steep section. If this is the case, make your way back to the Wall as soon as you get a chance.

After 300m, when conditions improve and the incline decreases, bear left towards the Wall for another 300m. You may encounter cattle along here which are part of an environmental management initiative so be aware of their potential presence and of electric fences. Come to a gate through an adjoining wall. Pass through this to access the **Carrick Little Track**. Turn right here.

1B: east side of Silent Valley Mountain Park

Divert from the main route by continuing straight on. Keeping the Wall on your left, walk as far south as you can. This corridor between the Wall and the forest on the right may be quite overgrown with long grass and brambles. After about 300m, look for a **wall junction** where the Mourne Wall bears left. This may be hard to see from eye level. To proceed any further south along here would require special permission from Northern Ireland Water (Variant 2A). Turn back as soon as you see buildings directly ahead and retrace your steps to rejoin the main path. Take a sharp left into the forest here.

1C: south side of Silent Valley Mountain Park

At *The Mourne Hand* sculpture, turn left to follow the access road south for 780m. As you pass a booth in the middle of the road, let the attendant know you are walking the Mourne Wall and will be re-entering the park again shortly. Hopefully they will not charge you admission later. Pass the superintendent's house on the left, exit through the red gates and turn left along Head Road. Take care on the bendy road. Follow the Wall on your left for about 120m north-east to another **red gate**. The Mourne Wall bends left immediately after the gate to serve as a field boundary.

Turn around and follow the road south-west back to the Silent Valley entrance gates. Continue past the gates and follow the road for 120m as it bends left to a junction. Turn right here and descend north-west to cross **Colligan Bridge** over

Variant 1C exits and re-enters Silent Valley Mountain Park through its main gate

Kilkeel River. Ascend the road with the Wall on your right and the forest beyond it. Continue past an entrance with red gates on the right. After 720m, arrive at a right bend on the Wall where the forest ends. To proceed north-west along the Wall from here would require special permission from the landowner (Variant 2B).

Turn around and retrace your steps east along Head Road, then turn left at the junction and re-enter Silent Valley Mountain Park, past the booth. Bear left into the car park and descend north along its left-hand side. Near the lower end of the car park, locate the start point for some waymarked trails. Turn left here.

Variant 2: entire Mourne Wall, including private sections

The following three sections would be required to complete a full circuit of the entire Mourne Wall. However, please note that these all pass through private agricultural land where there is no formal permission for public access. It is your own personal responsibility to obtain the necessary permission from landowners in advance. There are no gates or stiles for crossing fences and walls on these sections, and dogs are not permitted.

2A: south-east corner of Silent Valley Mountain Park

Having followed Variant 1B to a wall junction, the Mourne Wall bears left in a straight line south-east for 370m to meet Head Road beside a **red gate**, where it ties into Variant 1C. You should only undertake this section after being granted permission by Northern Ireland Water. Even then, you may also need to be accompanied by a member of staff.

2B: west side of Silent Valley Mountain Park

Having followed Variant 1C to a corner of the Wall where the **forest ends** on Head Road, the Mourne Wall turns right in a straight line north-west for 550m to a stile, where it ties into the main route. You should only undertake this section after being granted permission by the landowner. Even then, you may also need to be accompanied by the landowner.

2C: Dunnywater descent

Having arrived from the north at a stile, continue a few metres south to a corner of the Wall embellished with a **small ornate pillar**, where it turns right. As marked on all maps, the Mourne Wall is the left (south) one descending south-west for 620m from the pillar to cross a track. It continues along the edge of a dense forest for another 400m to meet Dunnywater Track, where it ties into Variant 1A near a stone **inlet well house**. You should only undertake this section after being granted permission by the landowner. Even then, you may also need to be accompanied by the landowner.

THE MOURNE ULTRA

A stile at Windy Gap, with Batt's Wall ascending Slievemoughanmore (Route 29)

The Mourne HRT starts/finishes near the Cone of Light *sculpture*

What is the Mourne Ultra?

The Mourne Ultra (TMU) is the ultimate double coast-to-coast crossing of the Mourne Mountains, combining the signposted Mourne Way and the unsignposted Mourne HRT routes into a single 75.6km-long challenge. The five interconnected day loops described over the following pages allow walkers to complete the full challenge over five separate days or walk whichever sections of it they choose. One-day and two-day options can also be attempted by experienced challenge hillwalkers and runners.

What is the Mourne Way?

The Mourne Way is a signposted 37km-long Quality Section of the Ulster Way. Starting near the tourist information centre in the town of Newcastle, where it ties into the Lecale Way, it passes through Tollymore Forest Park, around the range's northern and western fringes, and finally through Rostrevor Forest to finish at Kilbroney Park in the village of Rostrevor. The Mourne Way is mostly a low-level route, its highest point being the 504m summit of Slievenamuck near the halfway point.

Two-way signposting facilitates walking in either direction, although markings are sparse in a couple of places. The Way is described in five sections in this book, across Routes 26 to 30, starting from Newcastle and finishing in Rostrevor.

If walking the entire Mourne Way from Newcastle to Rostrevor, follow the relevant sections described across the five routes in the following order: Route 26 > Route 27 > Route 28 > Route 29 > Route 30

What is the Mourne High Ridge Traverse (HRT)?

The Mourne HRT is a hillwalking challenge route identified and developed by the author in 2024 and first published in this book in 2026. It is the longest linear ridge walk in the Mourne Mountains. Starting from the Carlingford Lough coastline at the village of Rostrevor, its 38.6km length follows the range's primary ridgeline over 16 official summits (including 9 of the range's 14 mountains) before dropping down to the Dundrum Bay coastline finish at the town of Newcastle. In this direction, the route separates the catchment areas of Rostrevor River, the River Bann and Shimna River on the left (north and west) from those of Ballincurry River, Cassy Water, White Water, Kilkeel River, Annalong River and Bloody Bridge River on the right (south and east). The highest point on the route is the 850m summit of Slieve Donard. The Mourne HRT is not signposted and can be walked in both directions. It is described in five sections in this book, across Routes 26 to 30, starting from Rostrevor and finishing in Newcastle.

If walking the entire Mourne HRT from Rostrevor to Newcastle, follow the relevant sections described across the five routes in the following order: Route 30 > Route 29 > Route 28 > Route 27 > Route 26

Walking the Mourne Ultra

Time

This very much depends on how you are planning to undertake the Mourne Ultra. An ultra runner or adventure racer may aim to complete the full out-and-back route in a single day, while a challenge hillwalker may choose to do it over two consecutive days with an overnighter in Newcastle or Rostrevor. If you prefer a more leisurely approach, five interconnected loops covering the full Mourne Ultra are described in Routes 26 to 30.

Start/finish points

The five interconnected loops have start/finish points at Donard Park in Newcastle, Meelmore Lodge, Ott car park, Leitrim Lodge car park, Yellow Water car park and Kilbroney Park in Rostrevor. These and alternate start/finish points are all identified in Routes 26 to 30. One-day and two-day options start and finish at Donard Park and/or Kilbroney Park, depending on which direction you choose.

Route descriptions

The five interconnected loops of the Mourne Ultra are described in Routes 26 to 30. To assist one-day and two-day challengers, relevant connection points have been highlighted in the route descriptions. These points also allow challengers to easily merge two or more adjoining loops into a longer one-day route.

Fitness and safety

One-day completions should only be attempted by experienced ultra runners. Two-day completions should only be attempted by highly experienced, fit hill runners and challenge hillwalkers. It must be emphasised that loops one, three and four (Routes 26, 28 and 29) could each be considered a standalone challenge walk. In the interests of safety, it is recommended that complete circuits of the Mourne Ultra or the full HRT be undertaken during the summer months when daylight hours are longest.

Camping

Designated campsite facilities can be found at Tollymore Forest Park (near Route 26), Meelmore Lodge (Route 27 start/finish) and Kilbroney Park on Route 30. Wild camping is widely tolerated in the Eastern Mournes, especially alongside the Mourne Wall and within the 36km^2 area it encloses. In the Western Mournes, permitted wild camping opportunities are sparse. Some suitable informal spots do exist along the Mourne Way; however, these cannot be identified in this book. You will just have to find them as you walk and use your own best judgement. Please leave no trace

Nearing the finish along Newcastle's South Promenade

Pick your way through boulders as you come off Donard toward Millstone Mountain (right)

of your overnight stop. Always take a final look back when departing from your camping spot to make sure you leave nothing behind. Other types of accommodation are also available in Newcastle and Rostrevor.

Water sources

Along the Mourne Way, tap water is available at the campsite locations mentioned above, as are cafés and kiosks, where you could ask for a refill. For more information, see 'Water sources' in the Mourne Wall chapter.

The perfect Mourne Mountains hillwalking challenge

If you choose the five interconnected one-day loops described in Routes 26–30, you will get to experience most of the range's finest hillwalking and viewing opportunities. This makes for an excellent five-day hillwalking challenge in the Mourne Mountains. An out-and-back detour to the summit of Doan (see Route 15) when walking Route 27 is also highly recommended. If you have an extra day or two at your disposal, adding a full circuit of the Annalong Valley Horseshoe (see Route 7) and a day exploring Silent Valley (see Route 13) would be the perfect recipe for an unforgettable week-long hillwalking challenge holiday in the Mourne Mountains.

ROUTE 26

Newcastle to Trassey Track (TMU1)

Start/finish	Donard car park
Alt start/finish	Trassey car park
Time	8hr 30min
Distance	24.3km
Ascent/descent	1240m
Grade	Very hard
Options	Trassey car park (same stats); Commedagh extension (+0.6km/+10m/+15min); combine with Route 27 (+9.3km/+625m/+3hr 15min)
Bus stops	Year-round local Ulsterbus services and the Mourne Rambler summer bus service stop 100m from Donard car park. The Mourne Rambler stops 1.4km from Trassey car park

This challenging anticlockwise loop takes in the easternmost ends of the Mourne Way and Mourne HRT walking routes. The terrain is mostly well-defined parkland and woodland paths, with clear upland sections beside the iconic Mourne Wall. There is also a short road section and a stretch of wild upland, which can be quite boggy. Directions for linking with Route 27 (TMU2) are included.

From the south end of Donard car park, head east towards Central Promenade. Carefully cross the **A2** road. The Mourne Coastal Route is a waymarked scenic drive that mostly follows the A2 road between Belfast and Newry. Continue past the *Cone of Light* sculpture and turn left. Follow the walkway north for 350m with the beach to your right. Bear left from the walkway onto the roadside footpath to arrive in front of Newcastle tourist information centre. Carefully cross the road here and continue north for about 100m to a road bridge over Shimna River. The Mourne Way starts here.

Turn left at the south end of this bridge and follow the river west for 200m towards another road bridge. Follow the path left then right through a gate to a controlled road crossing. Cross here and enter the park on the other side. Turn right along a path. After 30m, bear right to cross a footbridge over Tullybranigan River, keep straight, then curve left to follow a path beside **Shimna River**. Turn right

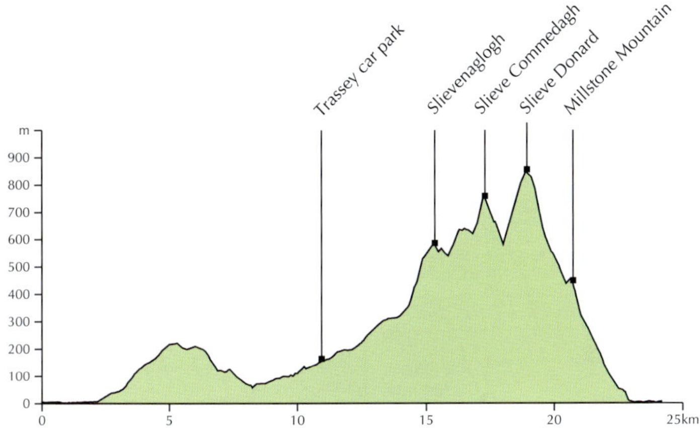

across the Shimna, then left immediately after. Curve right with the river for 180m, then bear left at a path junction to curve left past a play park to meet another road 270m further along. Turn left beside the road as it passes over Shimna River.

Immediately after the bridge, carefully cross the road to the entrance of Riverside Park. Access the walled path starting just to the right of this entrance. Follow this parallel to Tipperary Lane for 70m to meet the east corner of **Tipperary Wood**. Continue straight, north-west, along the forest track (Tipperary Lane) then curve left with it for 430m to exit forest. Continue south-west along Tipperary Lane for 670m to meet **Tullybrannigan Road**. Turn right to follow the road west for 280m. Carefully cross to the left-hand side of the road before arriving at a right-hand bend, where a cul-de-sac branch of Tullybrannigan Road forks off to the left.

Bear left and ascend north-west along the side road, past an underground reservoir on the left. Further along, pass a stone house with beige brick quoins and opening surrounds.

> This is the first of **six identical cottages** that were built between 1899 and 1901 along the route of the Mourne Conduit – a historical water supply line from Silent Valley to Belfast.

After 320m, arrive at a gate that spans the road ahead. Cross the stile beside the gate and continue straight up the road to a pair of gates. Pass through the small one on the left and continue straight into **Tollymore Forest Park**.

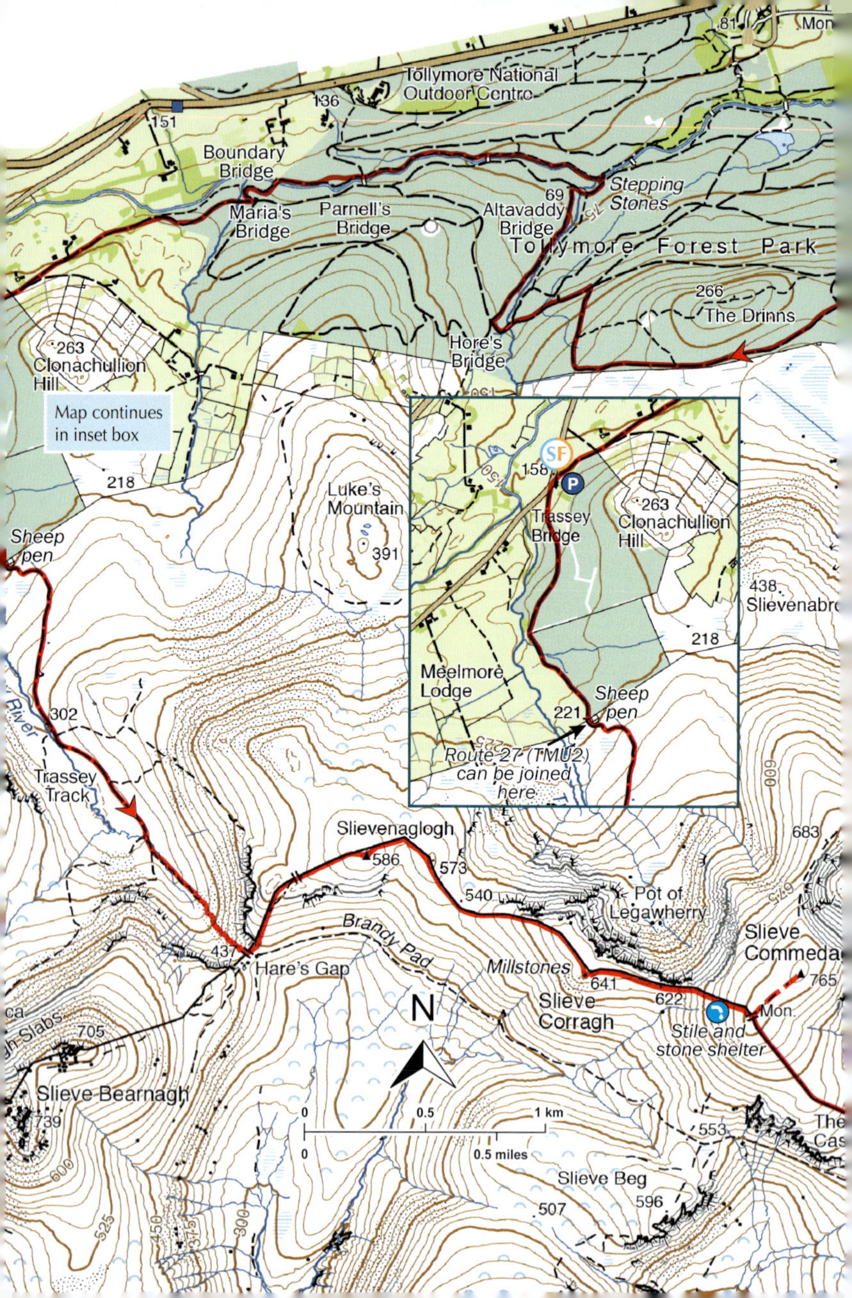

Tollymore National Outdoor Centre
136
151
81
Mon
Boundary Bridge
Maria's Bridge
Parnell's Bridge
Altavaddy Bridge
69
Stepping Stones
Tollymore Forest Park
266
The Drinns
Hore's Bridge
263
Clonachullion Hill
Map continues in inset box
218
Luke's Mountain
391
Sheep pen
158
Trassey Bridge
263
Clonachullion Hill
438
Slievenabro
218
Meelmore Lodge
221
Sheep pen
Route 27 (TMU2) can be joined here
River
302
Trassey Track
Slievenaglogh
586
573
540
Pot of Legawherry
683
Slieve Commeda
765
437
Hare's Gap
Brandy Pad
Millstones
641
622
Mon.
Slieve Corragh
Stile and stone shelter
705
Slabs
Slieve Bearnagh
739
N
0
0.5
1 km
0
0.5 miles
553
Slieve Beg
596
507
600
525
450
375
300

Shimna River
Tollymore
A50
A2
Tipperary Wood
Tipperary Lane
Cottage
Gate
Tullybrannigan Road
255
24
7
Newcastle
Mourne Way start/finish
Mourne High Ridge Traverse start/finish
Cone of Light sculpture
A2 South Promenade
Drinnahilly Mast
254
Donard Forest
A2 Kilkeel Road
Slievenamaddy
Ice House
Black Stairs (waterfalls)
Glen River
Thomas's Mountain
Eagle Rock
Millstone Mountain
460
The Mourne Wall
Stone shelter with roof-mounted trig
850
Slieve Donard
Crossone
544
150
225
300
375
450
525
600
675
750

Follow the forest track for 490m as it zigzags uphill to meet another track. Turn left to stay on the Mourne Way. Follow the track south initially then curve right with it to head north-west. Ignoring all right turns, follow the track bending left to descend west. The boundary wall comes in close on the left for a while before the track descends again more steeply and bends right, heading north. After 2.8km, arrive at a major track junction with various waymarkers. Take a sharp left here to follow a forest track south-west for 480m, ignoring all turn-offs. Shortly after crossing **Hore's Bridge**, curve right to another major junction with waymarkers.

Turn right and descend along a track, with Spinkwee River on your right, for 690m to a junction. Turn right here and cross the river at **Altavaddy Bridge**. Curve left with the track for 150m, then descend left to carefully cross a set of purpose-built stepping stones (see Route 1).

Turn left upstream for 1km with Shimna River on your left, past bridges and the second set of stepping stones, to meet a wide forest track at **Parnell's Bridge** (built 1842). Continue straight across the track onto another path, with the river still on your left. After 360m, cross **Boundary Bridge**, then ascend for 220m to a track junction. Turn right here to follow the Mourne Way west. Follow this path

Boundary Bridge across Shimna River in Tollymore Forest Park

west, passing the King's Grave and avoiding all turn-offs. Continue through several boundaries, using the gates and stiles provided. After 1.3km, meet Trassey Road close to **Trassey car park**. This can be used as an alternate start/finish.

Turn left and follow Trassey Road uphill for a few metres to where it bends right. Follow the Mourne Way, passing through the gate on the left at this bend. There is also an option to cross the wall to the left of the gate, using built-in stone steps. You are now on **Trassey Track**. Continue south along the track for 1.1km, passing through a couple of pedestrian gates to enter open mountain land beside a stone **sheep pen**. If combining with Stage TMU2 or walking the full Mourne Way to Rostrevor, divert to Route 27 here. Leave the Mourne Way, pass the sheep pen on your left and continue along Trassey Track as it gently ascends the Trassey River valley.

With Spellack's cliffs on your right, proceed towards the dramatic steep-sided col of Hare's Gap directly ahead. Stick to the track, avoiding all turn-offs. After 1.5km, ford a shallow stream, then keep left at two forks in the track. As the valley narrows, the track splits into faint paths, which all lead steeply through rough ground. Take care along this 500m section, especially if the ground is wet. Choose your own path south-east, keeping close to the centreline, to meet the Mourne Wall at **Hare's Gap** (437m). Cross the stile and turn left.

The approach to Hare's Gap

You are now on the Mourne HRT. Heading north-east, ascend some rock steps. Keeping the Wall on your left, follow it eastwards for 310m to the summit cairn on **Slievenaglogh** (586m).

Continue beside the Wall for 1.9km, over the subsidiary top of **Slieve Corragh** (641m), until you arrive at a stone shelter. Note the freshwater pipe you passed to the right of the Wall on the climb. Cross the stile beside it. The summit cairn on Slieve Commedagh (765m) is just 270m to the north-east of here if you fancy the short out-and-back detour. Turn right off the stile along the Wall , past the shelter, and descend south-east for 780m to the **Saddle** (583m).

Continue straight across this col with the Wall on your right. Ascend east along a constructed path, past a stone shelter, to arrive immediately at the summit cairn on **Slieve Donard** (850m). Turn left past the cairn and head north-east across the plateau for 230m to another large cairn, which offers great views over the town of Newcastle. Down on the coast to the north-east, the piers of the harbour can be seen just over the left shoulder (north) of Millstone Mountain – your next target. Use this opportunity to study the descent ahead.

Continue straight on from the cairn, descending north-east, initially, towards Thomas's Mountain. As the descent steepens, the ground becomes rougher with scattered granite boulders and slabs, so proceed carefully. Be aware that some of these rocks may be unstable and could move when stepped on. There may also be deep gaps between the rocks, some of which could be hidden by heather.

Curve very gradually right to maintain the high line of the ridge leading to Millstone Mountain. After 1.3km, find the driest route you can across a shallow boggy col, then ascend east for 170m to a cairn marking the subsidiary top of **Millstone Mountain** (460m). Continue straight past the cairn, bearing slightly left to descend towards the coast off Millstone Mountain's steeper side. Look for an old quarry below you at Drinneevar. Zigzag down, aiming slightly left of the quarry to pick up an old works track. After 500m, come to a gate through a wall just beyond the quarry.

About 170m beneath your feet lies a tunnel section of the **Mourne Conduit** – a historical water supply line running from Silent Valley to Belfast. Nowhere along its entire length does the Mourne Conduit pass deeper below the surface.

Pass through the gate and continue east onto a clear track heading for the coast. Follow this east for 400m and pass through a gate to enter **Donard Forest**. Keep straight ahead along the track at all junctions, descending through the forest

Descend past Drinneevar Quarry from Millstone Mountain

THE BOGIE LINE

This steep, straight path descending through Donard Forest to the harbour is now referred to as the Bogie Line. In the past, it formed the route of a mineral railway that transported stone in bogies from Thomas's Mountain Quarry above the treeline down to the harbour, where it was loaded onto boats. Several related relics and replicas (including a bogie near the harbour end) are on display along the route. A second line also ran from Millstone Mountain Quarry, entering the forest 60m east of where a replica timber shoddy hut is now on display. The Bogie Line is part of the Granite Trail.

Turn right to descend along the lowest section of the Bogie Line for 80m, passing through a stone arch to meet King Street in Newcastle. Cross the road and descend diagonally on a stepped path on a grassy slope and a tarmac driveway for 60m to meet South Promenade near the Harbour Inn. There is a choice of places around here for post-walk beverages, snacks and meals. Carefully cross the **A2 South Promenade** and follow the footway north for 1km to the *Cone of Light* sculpture, then using the nearby ramp, step onto the **beach**. The Mourne HRT ends here.

If the tide is not too far out, walk to the water's edge and dip the toe of your boot in the surf. Retrace your steps up the ramp to the *Cone of Light*. If finishing at Trassey car park, turn right here. Carefully cross Central Promenade to finish in **Donard car park**.

ROUTE 27

Trassey Track to Ott Track (TMU2)

Start/finish	Meelmore Lodge car park
Alt starts/finishes	Trassey car park, Happy Valley car park and Ott car park
Time	5hr 15min
Distance	14.9km
Ascent/descent	885m
Grade	Hard
Options	Trassey car park (+1.3km/+25m/+30min); Happy Valley car park (-0.6km/+5m); Ott car park (-1.1km/-25m/-15min); combine with Route 28 (+15km/+720m/+5hr 15min); combine with Route 26 (+19.6km/+1010m/+6hr 45min)
Bus stops	The Mourne Rambler summer bus service stops at Ott car park, 600m from Happy Valley car park and 1.4km from Trassey car park

This challenging anticlockwise loop takes in the eastern midsections of the Mourne Way and Mourne HRT walking routes. The terrain is a mix of well-defined tracks and clear upland sections beside the iconic Mourne Wall, including a short section at the top of Ott Track that can be quite boggy. Directions for linking up with Route 26 (TMU1) and Route 28 (TMU3) are included.

From Meelmore Lodge (see Route 17), proceed south through the car park behind Hare's Gap Bistro. At the lower end of the car park, access a track and follow it south-south-east for 500m to a dry-stone wall. Cross using the stile and turn right to follow the **Mourne Way** west-south-west for 1.6km to a stile and stream. Cross these, then ascend the far bank to a path junction. Happy Valley car park start/finish ties in here (Variant 1).

Turn left and ascend south for a few metres then turn right. Continue west along the Mourne Way for 750m, then curve south with it. Cross a stile and footbridge to pass alongside **Fofanny Dam** (see Route 16) for 450m. At the south end of the reservoir, the Mourne Way bends right and ascends south-west for 300m to a stile beside Slievenaman Road. Cross the stile and turn left up the road for 690m to **Ott car park**. This can be used as an alternate start/finish. If combining with TMU3 or walking the full Mourne Way to Rostrevor, divert to Route 28 here.

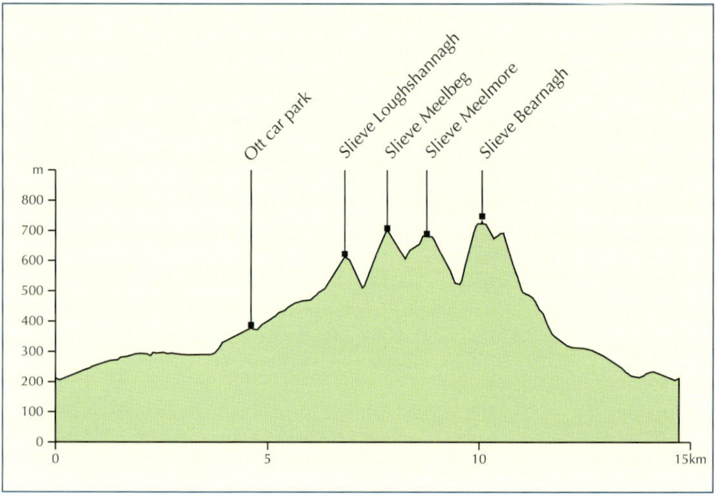

Meelmore (left) and Bearnagh (right) from Meelbeg's summit via the Mourne Wall

Just slightly before the car park entrance, turn left across a stile to access **Ott Track**. You have now left the Mourne Way. Follow the track south-east for 160m to a fork. Turn right here and ascend the track for 1.2km to its end. Continue east along a worn path for 400m, through peat hags, to meet the Mourne Wall at a **510m col**. Cross a stile and turn left.

You are now on the Mourne HRT. Ascend alongside the Wall for 500m to the summit cairn on **Slieve Loughshannagh** (617m). Descend north-east for 360m to a 511m col. Cross the stile here. With the Wall now on your right, ascend north-east for 620m to the summit cairn on **Slieve Meelbeg** (701m).

Follow the Wall as it turns right and descend north-east for 330m to a 590m col. Keep straight ahead and ascend for 600m to the summit cairn on **Slieve Meelmore** (688m). Continue north along the Wall for 110m to a stone shelter built into a sharp corner.

Cross a stile just before the shelter. With the Wall now on your left again, descend south-east for 620m, with the jagged tors of Slieve Bearnagh directly ahead. Fresh water flows from a pipe in the heather a few metres right of the Wall along this descent. Keep straight on through a 516m col and brace yourself for the imminent steep ascent. Bear slightly right of the Wall, initially, to ascend one of the worn paths. The ground here is steep and quite eroded. Carefully zigzag your way up through this section, always keeping the Wall in sight. When ground conditions improve, move back to the Wall.

After ascending for 470m, come to a sharp left-hand bend on a rocky subsidiary top near the summit of **Slieve Bearnagh** (739m). (The actual summit is located on a granite tor 100m south of here. It is accessible, but care is needed.) Work your way anticlockwise around the south side of the rocks on this subsidiary top to rejoin the Wall as it descends north-east. Continue close to the Wall for 280m to where it is interrupted by **Slieve Bearnagh North Tor**.

Skirt around the rock to pick up the Wall again where it restarts, then do the same again a few metres further on. Continue east-north-east beside the Wall for 880m. The descent steepens for a bit, then flattens before reaching a constructed flight of rock steps down to **Hare's Gap** (437m). If combining with TMU1 or walking the full Mourne HRT to Newcastle, divert to Route 26 here.

Turn left and cross the stile. You have now left the Mourne HRT. Descend north-west along an initial rough section of the valley. Choose your own path through this section, keeping close to the centreline. After 500m, pick up a track at the bottom of the slope. Follow this north-west for 1.6km down the Trassey River valley to a gate beside a stone **sheep pen**. The Trassey car park start/finish ties in here (Variant 2).

Turn left here to follow the Mourne Way west-south-west alongside a wall for 500m, over a couple of streams, to a stile you crossed earlier. If using an alternate

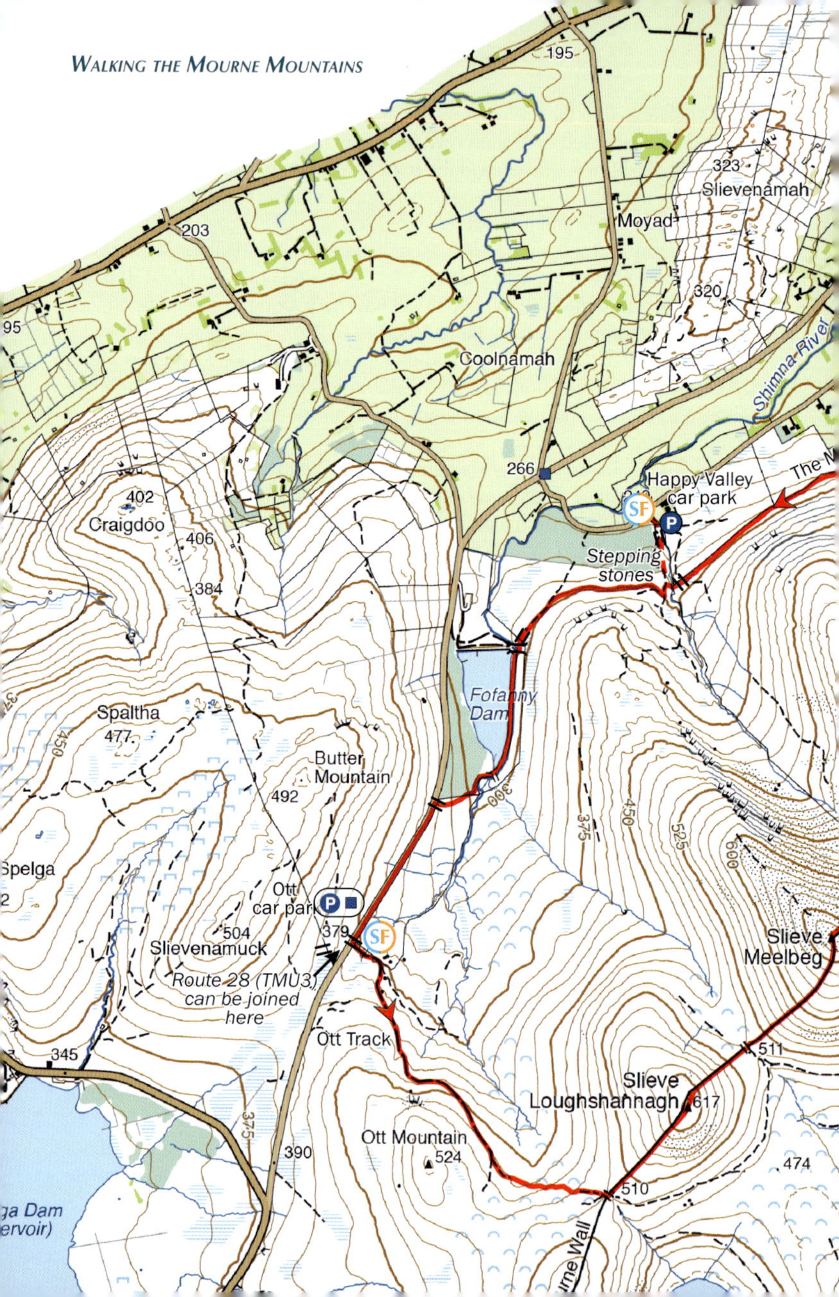
195
323
Slievenamah
Moyad
203
320
95
Shimna River
Coolnamah
266
Happy Valley
car park
The M
402
Craigdoo
406
Stepping
stones
384
Fofanny
Dam
Spaltha
477
450
Butter
Mountain
492
300
375
450
525
600
Spelga
Ott
car park
379
504
Slievenamuck
Route 28 (TMU3)
can be joined
here
Slieve
Meelbeg
Ott Track
345
511
Slieve
Loughshannagh
617
375
Ott Mountain
524
390
474
510
ga Dam
ervoir)
rne Wall

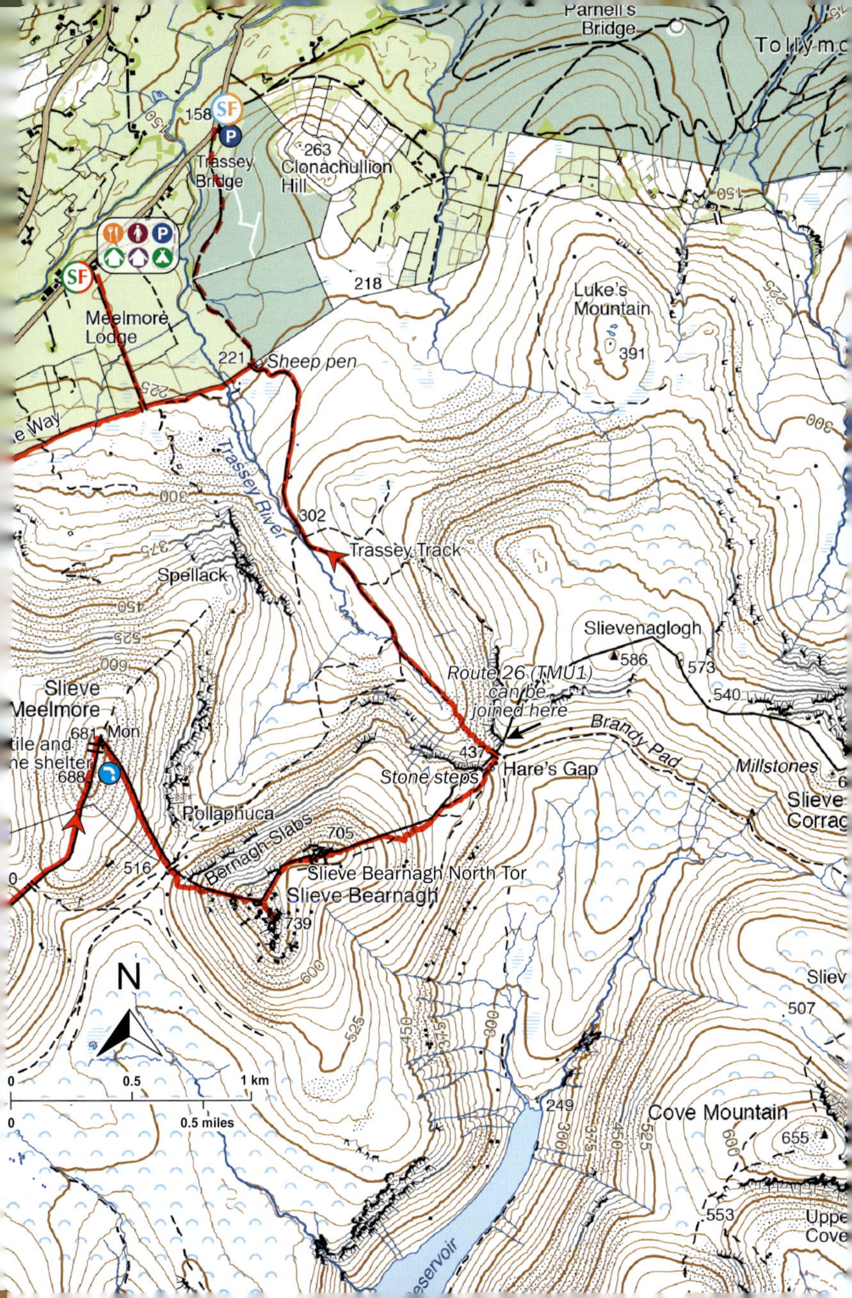

Parnell's Bridge
Tollymo
158
SF
P
Trassey Bridge
263
Clonachullion Hill
SF
Meelmore Lodge
218
Luke's Mountain
391
221
Sheep pen
Way
225
150
300
Trassey River
302
Trassey Track
375
Spellack
450
525
600
Slievenaglogh
586
573
540
Slieve Meelmore
681
Mon
tile and
ne shelter
688
Route 26 (TMU1) can be joined here
437
Hare's Gap
Brandy Pad
Millstones
Stone steps
Slieve Corrag
Pollaphuca
Bernagh Slabs
705
516
Slieve Bearnagh North Tor
Slieve Bearnagh
739
N
0
0.5
1 km
0.5 miles
507
249
Cove Mountain
655
553
Uppe Cove
eservoir

Along the lower section of Trassey Track

start/finish, continue straight on here. Turn right, cross the stile and retrace your steps north-north-west along the track to finish at **Meelmore Lodge**.

Variant 1: start/finish at Happy Valley car park

Starting from the south end of Happy Valley car park, take the path ascending south, crossing a stile along the way. After 300m, meet the **Mourne Way** at a junction near a stile and stream. Turn right here to join the main route. When you return to this point later, turn right and retrace your steps north to finish at **Happy Valley car park**.

Variant 2: start/finish at Trassey car park

Starting from the entrance of Trassey car park, turn left to follow Trassey Road uphill for 100m to where it bends right. Follow the Mourne Way through the gate on the left at this bend. If the gate is closed, make sure to close it again after you. There is also an option to cross the wall to the left of the gate, using built-in stone steps. You are now on **Trassey Track**.

Continue south for 1.1km along the track, passing through a couple of pedestrian gates, to enter open mountain land beside a stone **sheep pen**. Turn right here to join the main route. When you return to this point later, pass through the gate and retrace your steps north to finish at **Trassey car park**.

ROUTE 28

Ott Track to Rocky River (TMU3)

Start/finish	Ott car park
Alt starts/finishes	Hen Mountain car park and Deer's Meadow parking spot
Time	6hr 15min
Distance	18.5km
Ascent/descent	860m
Grade	Very hard
Options	Hen Mountain car park (+1.2km/+30m/+15min); combine with Route 29 (+14.6km/+695m/+4hr 45min); combine with Route 27 (+10.2km/+710m/+3hr 45min)
Bus stop	The Mourne Rambler summer bus service stops at Ott car park

This challenging anticlockwise loop takes in the central sections of the Mourne Way and Mourne HRT walking routes. The terrain is a mix of well-defined tracks and clear upland sections beside prominent stone walls. Directions for linking up with Route 27 (TMU2) and Route 29 (TMU4) are included.

From Ott car park, proceed north-west away from the road to the rear of the car park. Locate a path departing from here through the trees. This is the Mourne Way. Follow the path uphill for 60m to a stile. Cross this and bear right to ascend north-west on a grassy path for 450m onto a ridgeline. Bear left for 40m to the unmarked summit of **Slievenamuck** (504m). Turnaround and follow a grassy path north-east for 450m keeping slightly right of the ridge's high line to meet a fence. Turn left along the fence.

There are a couple of boggy sections along here. At some of these, a mesh path has been placed to help you get across. In other places you will have to move to the left of the fence to find a suitable point to jump over the boggy sections. After 700m, just before you reach a mound with exposed rocks on the left, locate a grassy path heading south-west. Turn left, away from the fence, and follow the path for 820m, keeping the ridge's high line on your right. Ignore any side paths until you cross the high line and arrive at a fork. Bear right here to descend east-north-east on the other side of the ridge.

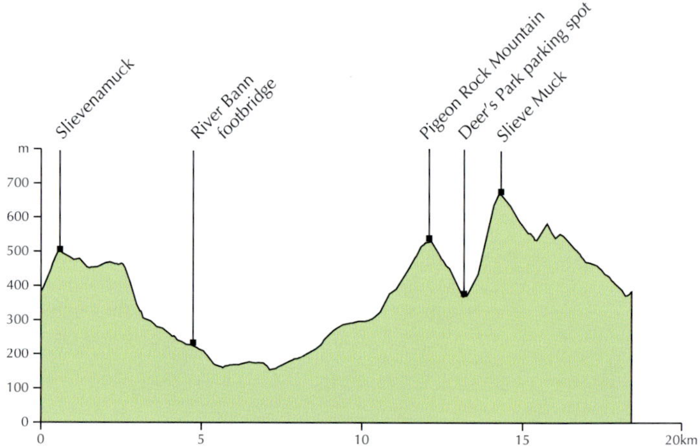

As you descend a small valley, keep as close to the middle of it as you can. When you see deep channels cut by the streams, aim to pass them on the left. After 620m, meet a wall with a fence in front of it beside a Mourne Way marker post. Turn left along the **fence** and follow it south-west, curving south for 850m to a stile beside the **B27 Kilkeel Road**. Cross the stile and carefully cross the road. Turn left to follow it uphill for 20m to where a stone wall begins.

Turn right here and pass through a small gate, then turn left along a grassy path descending south-east for 150m to a footbridge over the **River Bann**. Switchback to cross the bridge, then bear right. Cross over some rocks to pick up a worn path heading north-west. Follow this and ignore any side paths ascending on the left. In 100m, pass the corner of a fence. Continue for 130m, with the fence on your right, to a Mourne Way marker post pointing left. Turn left, away from the fence, and ascend a few metres to find a parallel path.

Turn right along this and contour with it around the north-west slope of **Slievenamiskan**. The smaller hill in front with the rocky summit is Hen Mountain. The higher one to its left is Cock Mountain. Continue along the path for 560m to meet an old track. Turn right to follow the track north-west. After 600m, just before the track reaches a field gate, turn left and step over a small stream to pick up a path. Follow this to contour north-west around **Hen Mountain**. After 500m, bend left with the path alongside a stone wall. Keep a few metres left of the wall for a better path.

Mourne Way marker post on approach to B27 Kilkeel Road

Continue for 930m beside the wall to gates where the Hen Mountain Track accesses open mountain land. The Hen Mountain car park start/finish ties in here (Variant 1). Bear left to follow the track south-east, keeping a close eye on the Mourne Way marker posts. Pass a couple of these pointing straight ahead. A further 1.5km along the track, just after fording a stream, come to a **Mourne Way marker post** pointing right along a faint side path. If combining with TMU4 or walking the full Mourne Way to Rostrevor, divert to Route 29 here.

Continue straight along the track, past the marker post. You have now left the Mourne Way. As you ascend the valley, the track comes close to Rowan Tree River on the right. In 1.4km, after fording the river twice, the track comes to an end. With the river on your right, ascend south-east for 950m along a worn path, which gets boggy and slippery in places. This brings you to **Batt's Wall** (see Route 23) at a 393m col.

Turn left to ascend north-east beside the wall for 850m. You are now on the Mourne HRT. Follow the wall when it bends left, then bear left from it to pass over the unmarked north summit of **Pigeon Rock Mountain** (534m). Rejoin the wall and continue to a corner after 250m. Turn right with the wall here and descend north-east beside it for 1km. Cross a stile at the **Deer's Meadow parking spot**. This can be used as an alternate start/finish. Carefully cross the B27 Moyad Road, cross the stile and ascend east-south-east beside the wall for 1km to the summit trig on **Slieve Muck** (674m).

Kinnahalla
296
127
B27
271
Kinnahalla Plantations
Wall and fence
130
River Bann
Sandbank Road
SF
P
Hen Mountain Track
Hen Mountain
361
357
337
Millstones
225
B27 Kilkeel Road
300
272
Slievenamiskan
443
375
Shankys River
150
450
Cock Mountain
505
505
Rocky River
225
300
Route 29 (TMU4) can be joined here
Mourne Way marker post
379
375
Rocky Mountain
405
Lodge
325
233
Tornamrock
390
Rocky Water
Pigeon Rock Mountain
534
Fords
Potentially very boggy
Rowan Tree River
Wee Slievemoughan
428
Batt's Wall
Slievemoughanmore
559
393
Chimney Rock Mountain
428
467
Pierce's

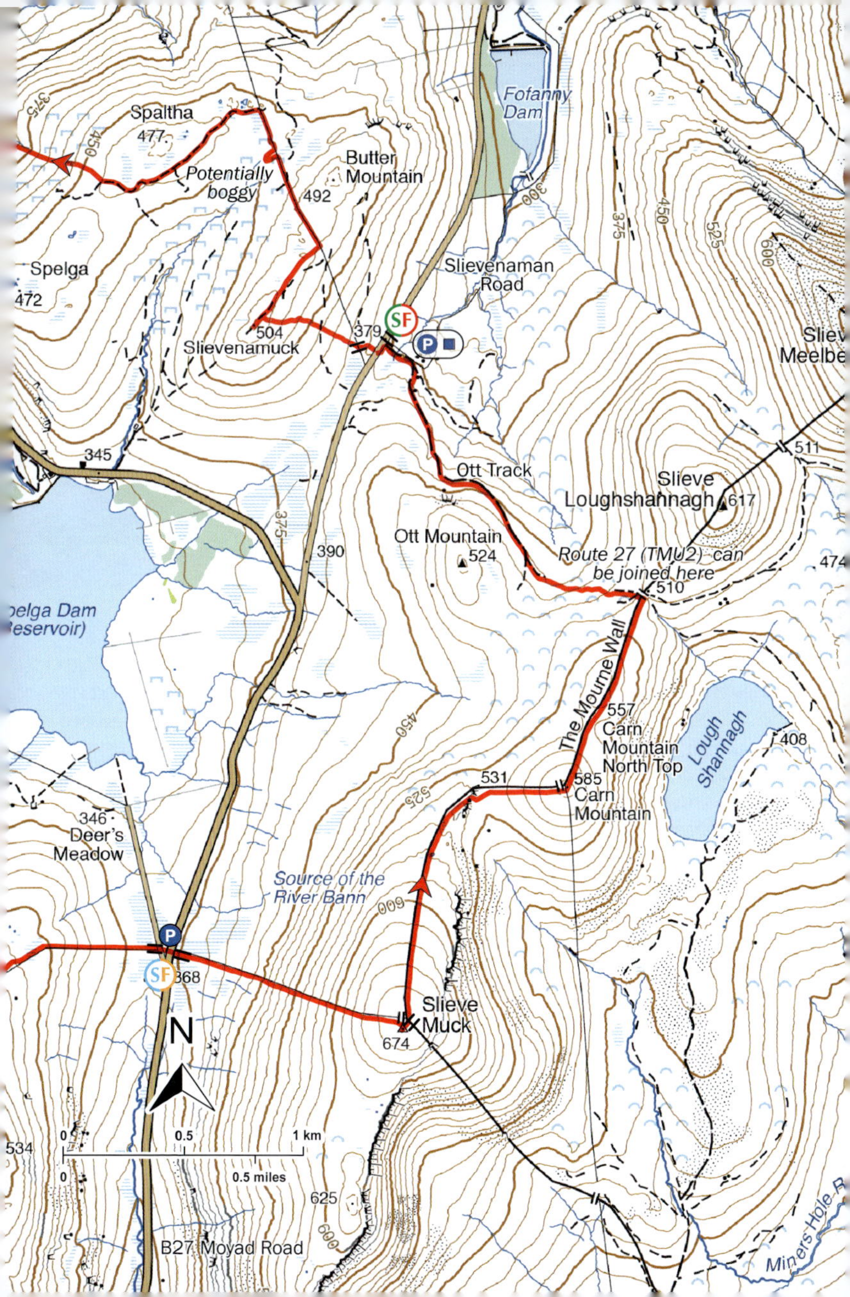

Spaltha
477
Potentially boggy
Butter Mountain
492
Fofanny Dam
Spelga
472
Slievenaman Road
504
Slievenamuck
379
SF
P
Ott Track
Slieve Loughshannagh
617
511
Ott Mountain
524
Route 27 (TMU2) can be joined here
510
474
345
390
Spelga Dam (Reservoir)
The Mourne Wall
557
Carn Mountain North Top
Lough Shannagh
408
531
585
Carn Mountain
346
Deer's Meadow
Source of the River Bann
368
Slieve Muck
674
N
0
0.5
1 km
0.5 miles
534
625
B27 Moyad Road
Miners Hole R

Walkers making their way down from the 510m col towards Ott Track

Head 40m north-east from the trig pillar, cross the right-hand stile, then turn left to follow the Wall north for 1km. Just before a bend to the right, negotiate a short rocky section. Bear right of the Wall to descend this section to a 531m col. Ascend east for 300m to a wall junction beside the summit cairn on **Carn Mountain** (585m). Ignore the stile and pass through a gap in the adjoining wall. Turn left along the Wall and pass over **Carn Mountain North Top** (557m). After 880m, arrive at a 510m col. If combining with TMU2 or walking the full Mourne HRT to Newcastle, divert to Route 27 here.

Turn left and cross the stile. You have now left the Mourne HRT. Proceed away from the Wall to descend west for 400m along a path through peat hags to meet the top of **Ott Track**. Follow this north-west for 1.3km to finish at **Ott car park**. If using an alternate start/finish, continue through Ott car park to access a path behind it.

Variant 1: start/finish at Hen Mountain car park

Starting from the entrance of Hen Mountain car park, cross **Sandbank Road** to access the track directly ahead. Proceed east along the track for 600m, keeping the granite tors of Hen Mountain directly ahead, to a gate where the track enters open mountain land. Turn right here to join the main route. When you return to this point later, turn right and retrace your steps west to finish at **Hen Mountain car park**.

ROUTE 29

Rocky River to Yellow Water River (TMU4)

Start/finish	Leitrim Lodge car park
Alt start/finish	Yellow Water car park
Time	6hr 30min
Distance	19.8km
Ascent/descent	880m
Grade	Very hard
Options	Yellow Water car park (same stats); alternate Yellow Water River ascent (+0.3km); combine with Route 30 (+11.9km/+440m/+4hr); combine with Route 28 (+13.8km/+690m/+5hr)

This challenging anticlockwise loop takes in the western midsections of the Mourne Way and Mourne HRT walking routes. The terrain is a mix of well-defined forest tracks and exposed upland, including some wild sections that can become very rough and boggy in places. Due to the difficulties posed by this terrain, this section of the route should be saved for a clear summer day after a long period of dry weather. Directions for linking up with Route 28 (TMU3) and Route 30 (TMU5) are included.

From the south end of Leitrim Lodge car park, follow the path south-east for 270m, passing through a gate, and join a track crossing **Shankys River** to arrive at a junction. Turn right here to follow the Mourne Way south. About 1.3km further along, the track narrows to a path, which can become quite rough and overgrown by ferns in places. Pay attention to waymarkers along this 800m section. Come to a stile crossing **Batt's Wall** (see Route 23).

Cross the stile to enter Rostrevor Forest the stile and continue south-west along the track for 1.4km to a junction. Turn left along a forest track for 40m, then head right a few metres to where the Mourne Way crosses a footbridge. Just before you reach the footbridge, locate a side path on the left heading uphill. The Yellow Water car park start/finish ties in here (Variant 1). If combining with TMU5 or walking the full Mourne Way to Rostrevor, divert to Route 30 here.

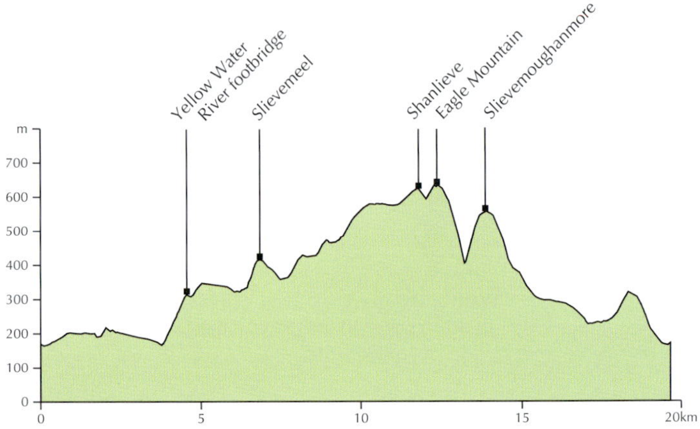

Potential diversion

If the side path heading uphill is closed for any reason, turn around and retrace your steps north a few metres, then turn right to ascend the forest track north-east. At a track junction, take a sharp right and continue uphill to rejoin the main route.

A tributary of Shankys River flowing across the Mourne Way

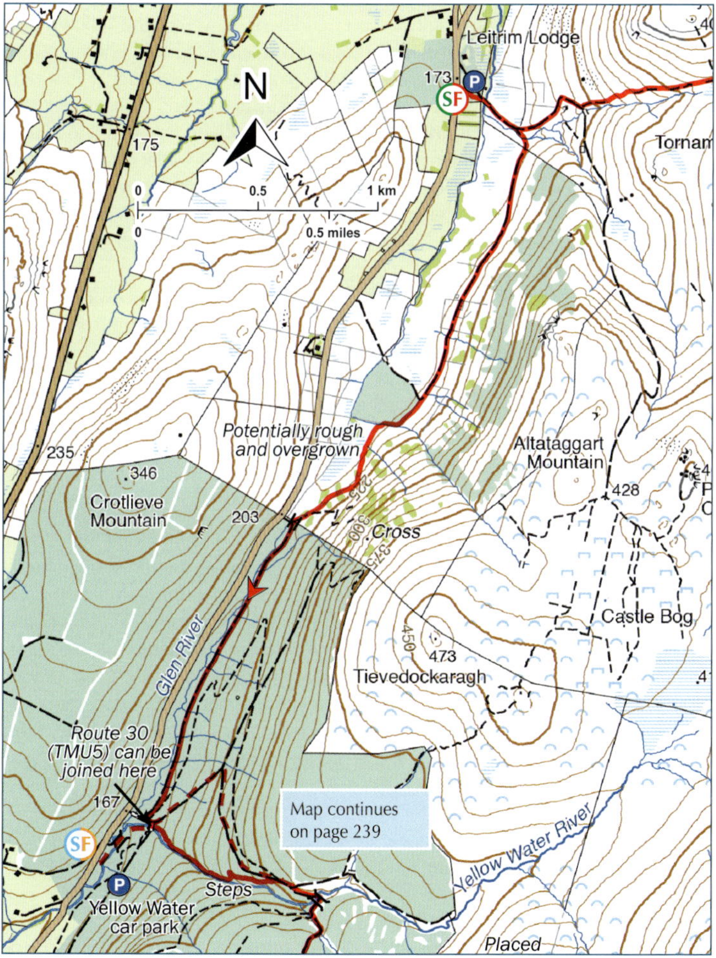

Map continues
on page 239

Main route continues

Turn left to ascend east along the side path for 680m. This is a section of the Fallows Trail, which, at the time of writing, was waymarked for walking in the opposite direction only. Take care when walking over the exposed tree roots and rocks along this section, especially in wet conditions. To your right, Yellow Water River can be heard cascading its way down this steep-sided valley. After a long flight of steps, you will soon emerge from the path onto a forest track. Turn right here along the track for 70m, then bear right at a fork to descend along a sidetrack.

After 120m, cross a footbridge over **Yellow Water River**. Bend right to ascend south-west for 340m along the path, ignoring all turn-offs, to a flat, straight section through Kilbroney Red Bog. Continue straight on, heading south-west for 700m, passing a large **pond** on the left along the way. Continue south-west for 500m along the path as it descends into the trees. At a junction, bear left onto a path. Ascend south along this for 360m to exit the forest through a gate.

Turn left off the path as soon as possible after the gate and ascend east-south-east for 280m through pathless heather. You are now on the Mourne HRT. Arrive at a post marking the summit of **Slievemeel** (420m). The next section is one of the toughest on the Mourne HRT: 5km of rough and mostly pathless ground, which can be boggy in places. Thankfully, the low heather under foot poses no major obstacle and allows you to interpret the surface beneath. Walking poles would be useful along this section for identifying holes or soft spots, as would gaiters in case you step into them.

From Slievemeel, descend north-east for 640m across rough ground to the right-hand corner of the forest. Continue north-east for 170m along the edge of the forest, passing close to a 355m col. Bear right where the forest edge heads left and ascend east-north-east for 480m to an unmarked **430m** spot height. From here, bear left to follow the high line north-east for 300m towards a low dome-shaped top with the summit of Shanlieve visible directly behind it. Negotiate channels and soft spots along the way. Cross a rough col and ascend straight ahead for 350m. Keep left of a small boggy section to meet a boundary fence.

Beside a large boulder on the north end (left) of a broken wall section, cross the fence where two rocks serve as a stile. Be aware of the barbed-wire top strand.

Take a few moments to find the words 'Ross' and 'Killmory' carved into the **boulder and its neighbour**. If these refer to the Ross family and the Kilmorey Estate, it is likely that the broken wall marked a significant landownership boundary.

Ascend north-east for 70m to locate an unnamed, unmarked minor top (**475m**).

Now for the tricky part. As you face south-east, the next 1km of the Mourne High Ridge takes on an odd shape that is hard to identify from ground level. Even on a map, this section of ridgeline is not immediately obvious. Good map-reading skills are required, especially an ability to visualise topography by studying local

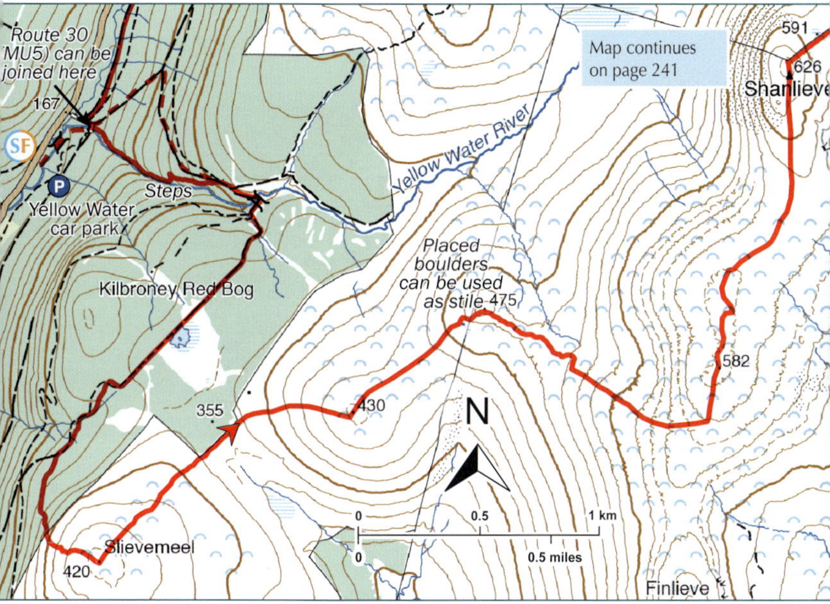

contours and watercourses. In addition to this, the presence of soft spots and channels makes a direct path through almost impossible.

From the 475m minor top, head south-east on a grid bearing of approximately 120° towards the Shanlieve–Finlieve ridge, bypassing any peat hags and soft spots. Maintain the highest line you can across the shallow col. If you encounter a soft linear channel, bear left and walk alongside it, keeping it on your right. Negotiate any branch channels. These should be easier to cross than the main channel. The aim is to find the driest route without straying too far left of the high line. After 450m, meet a contouring path crossing your ascent.

Locate a nearby point on the uphill side of this path where a boulder sits below the end of a large peat hag. Ascend away from the path on a grid bearing of approximately 125° through elongated peat hags, which are aligned roughly in the direction you want so you can walk along the top or follow the channels in between. The going improves further up as the channels become progressively rockier and wider. After ascending for 650m, arrive on the Shanlieve–Finlieve ridgeline. Turn left and follow the high line north through the unmarked **582m** spot height.

Looking across the shallow col to Eagle Mountain from Shanlieve's summit cairn

After negotiating some peat hags, continue north along the high line on a faint path, curving north-east then north again for 1.7km to the summit cairn on **Shanlieve** (626m). Continue straight on for 60m to a corner on Batt's Wall. If walking the full Mourne HRT, you will be relieved to know that the next 18.5km follows stone walls over dry terrain. Expect longer and steeper ascents and descents from here on. Turn right and follow the wall north-east for 500m, passing over a shallow col along the way to where the wall bends left at a stile. Turn right, away from the wall, and head south-east for 60m to the summit cairn on **Eagle Mountain** (637m).

Return to the wall and cross the stile. Continue straight beside the wall for 310m, then turn right with it to descend north-east for 520m. This descent is quite steep so you may have to zigzag a bit, staying close to the wall. Continue straight across **Windy Gap** (407m) and ascend north-east for 470m. When you reach the high point of the wall, bear left away from it, heading north along a faint path for 210m to a summit cairn on **Slievemoughanmore** (559m). There are a couple of cairns on the summit area. You want the most north-easterly one.

Return south to rejoin the wall and turn left. Descend north-east for 590m to a **393m col**. If combining with TMU3 or walking the full Mourne HRT to Newcastle, divert to Route 28 here. Turn left here to leave the Mourne HRT. Proceed away from Batt's Wall and descend north-west, keeping to the right-hand side of the stream. This section gets boggy and slippery in places. After 950m, pick up a track when the descent flattens. Follow the track north-west for 1.4km, fording **Rowan Tree River** twice along the way.

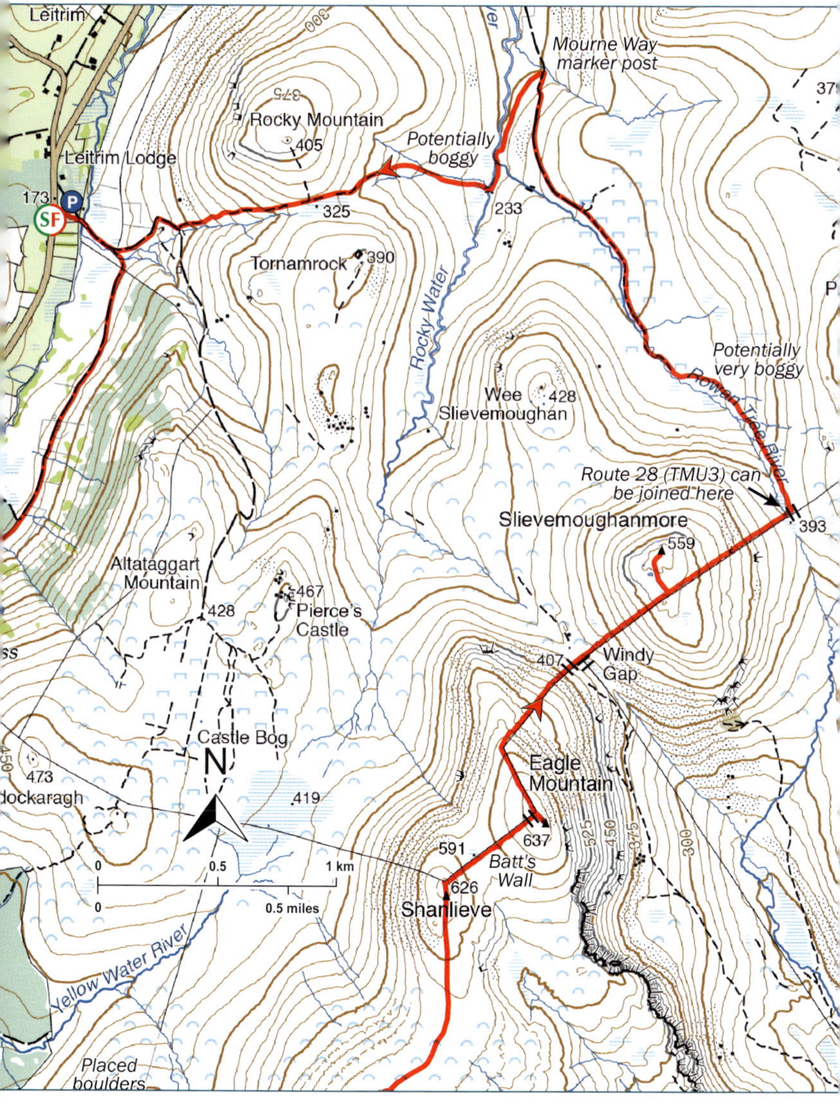
Leitrim
Mourne Way marker post
Rocky Mountain
405
Potentially boggy
Leitrim Lodge
173
P
SF
325
233
Tornamrock
390
Rocky Water
Wee Slievemoughan
428
Potentially very boggy
Rowan Tree River
Route 28 (TMU3) can be joined here
Slievemoughanmore
393
559
Altataggart Mountain
428
467
Pierce's Castle
407
Windy Gap
Castle Bog
N
Eagle Mountain
473
419
637
591
Batt's Wall
626
Shanlieve
0
0.5
1 km
0.5 miles
Yellow Water River
Placed boulders

> Some older maps show the **Mourne Way** crossing Rowan Tree River about 400m after these fords. Please note that this no longer matches what is on the ground. The Mourne Way has since been re-routed slightly and now crosses the river further downstream as described in the next paragraph.

Come to a post-mounted Mourne Way arrow pointing west (left as you approach). From this direction the information plate may only appear on the opposite side of this post. Turn left along the side path here to follow the Mourne Way south-west for 450m to where it crosses Rowan Tree River again. At the time of writing, there was no bridge here. Cross carefully using the rocks, bearing in mind they could be slippery.

Continue south beside **Rocky Water** for 120m to a footbridge. Turn right across this and ascend west along a potentially muddy path for 800m to a **325m col**. Ignore the path crossing here and descend west for 600m along a better path to meet a track. Turn right along this and follow it for 350m to another track junction. If finishing at Yellow Water car park, bear left here. Turn right along the track for 270m, crossing Shankys River and passing through a gate along the way to finish at **Leitrim Lodge car park**.

Variant 1: start/finish at Yellow Water car park

Starting from the north end of Yellow Water car park, take a path north-east for 280m beside Yellow Water River to a junction with a **footbridge** nearby. Turn left here and cross the footbridge. After a few metres, before you meet a forest track, turn right along a path ascending east to tie into the main route. When you return to this point later, continue straight across the footbridge, bear right after a few metres and retrace your steps south-west to finish at **Yellow Water car park**.

ROUTE 30

Yellow Water River to Rostrevor (TMU5)

Start/finish	Yellow Water car park
Alt start/finish	Kilbroney car park
Time	5hr 45min
Distance	18km
Ascent/descent	680m
Grade	Moderate
Options	Kilbroney car park (-0.6km/-5m/-15min); alternate Yellow Water River descent (+0.3km); combine with Route 29 (+13.7km/+635m/+4hr 45min)
Bus stops	Year-round local Ulsterbus services stop in Rostrevor village and along the A2 Shore Road

This anticlockwise loop takes in the westernmost ends of the Mourne Way and Mourne HRT walking routes. The terrain comprises well-defined forest tracks and constructed upland paths. Directions for linking up with Route 29 (TMU4) are included.

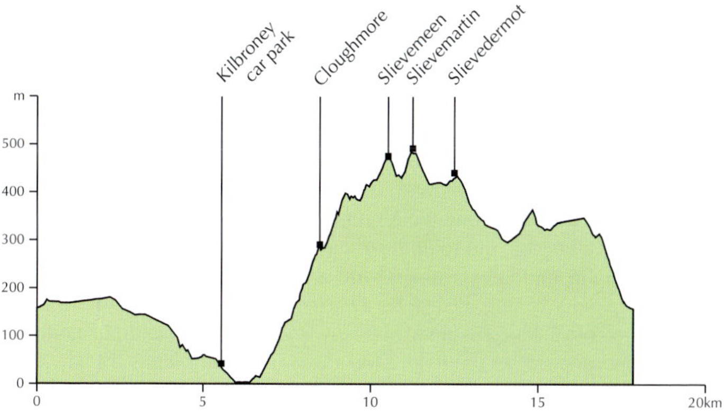

The Mourne Way starts/finishes beside the Cloughmore Centre in Kilbroney Park

From the north end of Yellow Water car park, take a path north-east for 280m beside Yellow Water River to a junction with a footbridge nearby. Turn right along the Mourne Way and the Fallows Trail (purple arrows), heading south-west. After a few metres bear right at another junction. Stick to this track, ignoring all turn-offs, as it descends south-west through **Rostrevor Forest** (more about Kilbroney Park and Rostrevor Forest in Route 21). After 5km, keep straight on where the track joins the forest drive to arrive at **Kilbroney car park**. This can be used as an alternate start/finish. The Mourne Way ends here.

From the entrance of Kilbroney car park, descend south-west along the tarmac road. Take care here because there is no footway, limited verge and vehicles are moving in both directions. Note the red-brick building 270m along on the left and a path entering the forest just downhill from it behind a small parking area. You will be returning to this location in a few minutes. For now, continue straight for 180m to the main **A2** coast road. The Mourne Coastal Route is a waymarked scenic drive that mostly follows the A2 road between Belfast and Newry.

Turn right alongside the road, heading north-west. Cross when it is safe to do so, bearing in mind any walkers who are with you or others who may be influenced by your timing. Please be aware of vehicles emerging from nearby side roads and other accesses along this busy stretch of road. Continue north-west along the opposite side of the road. Over the wall on your left is the sea inlet of Carlingford Lough, with the Cooley Mountains rising beyond in County Louth. Directly ahead is the village of Rostrevor, with the port town of Warrenpoint further along the coast.

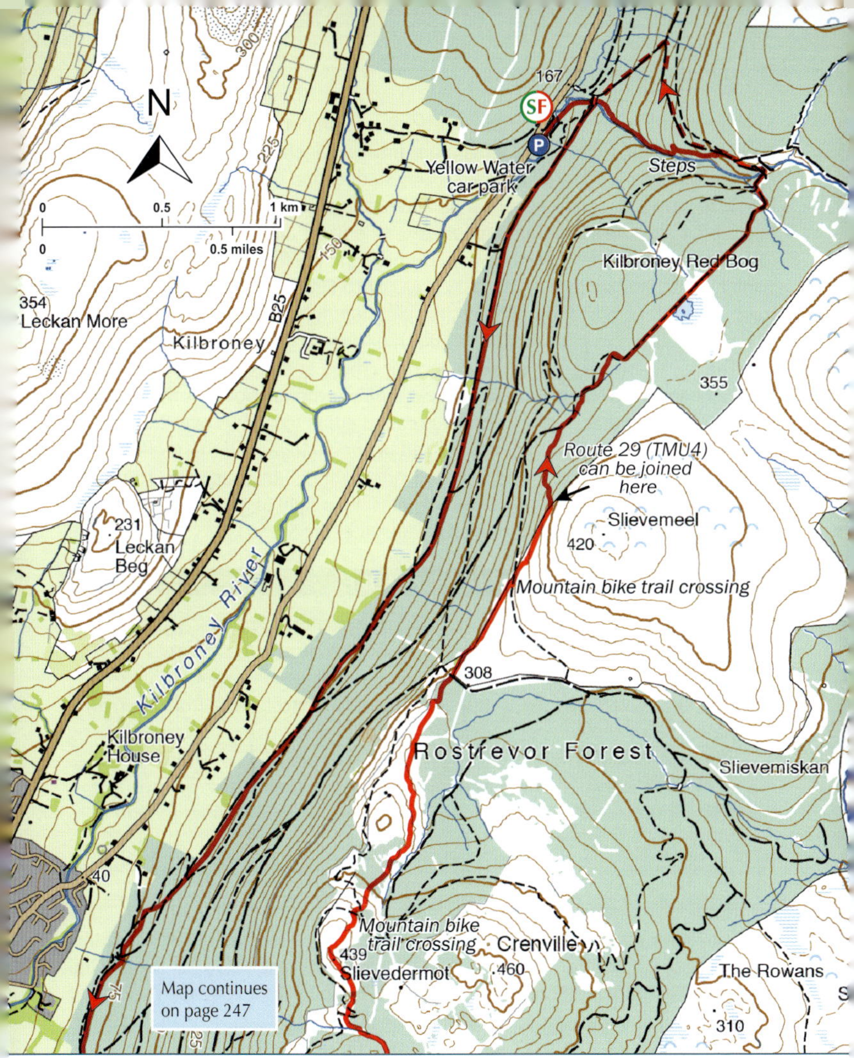

After 180m, turn left through a gap in the wall to descend a ramp onto the beach. Tread carefully as it could be slippery. The **Mourne HRT** starts here. If the tide is not too far out, walk to the water's edge and dip the toe of your boot in the surf. Retrace your steps up the ramp, alongside and across the road and up the

Kilbroney Park access road to the red-brick building you passed a few minutes earlier. From here follow the Cloughmore Trail anticlockwise. At the time of writing, this trail was waymarked in the clockwise direction only.

Turn right through the small car park here and pass through a gap in the fence to access a path heading south. Ignore any side paths and ascend for 530m to a fork. Bear left onto the higher of two paths here and continue to ascend for 350m, winding your way up through a grassy area called **Fiddlers Green** to meet a forest track. Turn left here and follow the track north for 280m to where a path forks off to the right. Take this path and ascend north-east for 260m.

The path starts off good but soon becomes rocky and tree rooty. At a junction, turn right and keep straight for 90m to a walled viewpoint known as the **CS Lewis Bench**. This is a great spot for a quick break to enjoy the views over Carlingford Lough. Retrace your steps a few metres and bear right to ascend east along a path. Follow this for 300m, ignoring any turn-offs, to meet another path. Turn right along this for 30m to a junction of broad paths. Bear right to ascend south-east on a grassy path for 40m to the **Cloughmore** (aka the 'Big Stone').

CLOUGHMORE

Often referred to as the 'Big Stone', this 50-tonne granite erratic is perched on 400-million-year-old sandstone at the southern end of the Mournes' main ridge, high above the village of Rostrevor. It is believed to have been carried there from Scotland by ice 10,000 years ago. In contrast, a tale from the rich tapestry of Irish mythology provides a more instantaneous account of Finn McCool throwing it from the Cooley Mountains, across Carlingford Lough, to its current location while battling a rival giant. Some also believe that circling the stone seven times brings good luck. Just a few things for you to ponder while admiring this impressive boulder.

Retrace your steps north-west to the junction. Turn right here along a good path marked as the 'Fallows Trail' (purple arrows). Ascend south-east along this path for 480m, ignoring the well-marked bike trails crossing it. Do not loiter at the bike crossings. Turn right onto a side path and continue along a stepped section of the Fallows Trail to emerge above the treeline after 120m. With a small grassy top ahead, continue for 250m to a junction. Continue straight through a gap in a broken stone wall and ascend south for 70m along a clear path to the **Ballynagelty** viewpoint. From here you can see the full length of Carlingford Lough.

Retrace your steps to the junction and turn right. Continue along the path as it zigzags up, then follow a boundary fence and wall east. After 890m, keep an eye out for a grassy path on the left to visit the nearby summit cairn on **Slievemeen**

Looking north across the Western Mournes from Slievedermot

(471m). Return to the main path and turn left along it. Descend north beside the fence, with Slievemartin and a mast directly ahead. After 400m, reach a col where several paths meet beside a stile. Keep straight on and ascend for 320m beside the fence and up some stone steps to the summit trig on **Slievemartin** (485m).

A bench is located 20m beyond the trig if you want to spend a few minutes taking in the views over Rostrevor, Warrenpoint and the lough. Return to the main path and bear left to follow it north. Descend for 540m to enter the forest. It is worth noting that the constructed path strays slightly from the high line of the ridge along here, but it is close enough. Continue north along the Fallows Trail for 860m as it winds its way through the forest to the unmarked subsidiary top of **Slievedermot** (439m).

Descend north-east, keeping straight ahead where a mountain bike trail crosses after 250m. Check for passing bikers and do not loiter at the junction. Follow the path north for 1.2km to meet a track at the edge of the forest, near a **308m** spot height. Keep straight along a path for 200m to a gate. Pass through this and continue north-east along the path, with forest on your left. After 400m, pass another bike trail, then 250m further on arrive at a gate into the forest. If combining with TMU4 or walking the full Mourne HRT to Newcastle, divert to Route 29 here.

Continue straight through the gate into the forest. You have now left the Mourne HRT. Descend north for 360m along the path through trees to a junction. Bear right along a path, ascending north-east for 500m to a flat, straight section through Kilbroney Red Bog. Continue north-east along this 700m straight, passing a large **pond** on the right along the way. Descend for 340m to a footbridge. Cross **Yellow Water River** here and continue 120m north-west to a track junction.

Bear left along the forest track for 70m to where a side path branches off to the left.

Potential diversion

If you arrive here to find the next section of the Fallows Trail (purple markers) is closed, keep straight for an alternative descent along the forest track. At a track junction, take a sharp left and continue downhill to another junction near a **footbridge**.

Main route continues

Turn left here to descend the path west. Take care when walking over the exposed tree roots and rocks along this section, especially in wet conditions.

To your left, Yellow Water River can be heard cascading its way down this steep-sided valley. A set of **steps** brings you closer to the river as you follow it down-stream. After 680m, come to a path junction. Turn right here and cross the **foot-bridge** over Yellow Water River to a fork. If finishing at Kilbroney car park, bear left here. Bear right and follow the path 280m to finish at **Yellow Water car park**.

APPENDIX A

Car parks

The table below lists all of the 19 car parking locations that feature in this book. For each location, a QR code and a selection of coordinates are provided, along with a list of routes that start and/or finish there. *Please note that*:

*The Mourne Rambler bus service stops here during summer months.

**The Mourne Rambler bus service stops nearby during summer months.

***Start and finish at same car park unless noted otherwise

****Coordinates are in this order: *Irish grid ref*; **Lat/long**; ///what3words

Car park	Routes***	Notes	Coordinates****	QR code
Banns Road car park*	13 (near route), 14		*J 28426 21399* **54.125741, -6.036073** ///hamper.essays.tigers	
Bloody Bridge car park*	4, 5 (start)		*J 38867 27146* **54.174631, -5.873825** ///swims.months.fashion	
Carrick Little car park*	7, 8, 9, 25 (on route)	If car park is full, paid parking is available nearby along Carrick Little Track and on the Oldtown Road	*J 34474 21893* **54.128625, -5.943393** ///chose.contracting.flesh	
Deer's Meadow parking spot	19 (on route), 28 (on route)		*J 27095 25237* **54.160535, -6.054811** ///pinch.deal.typically	
Donard car park**	2, 3, 26	Mourne Rambler bus stop on Central Promenade is 100m away	*J 37440 30547* **54.205544, -5.894105** ///bloodshot.young.custodian	
Dunnywater parking spot**	6, 7 (on route), 25	Mourne Rambler bus stop on Head Road is 220m away	*J 35760 22308* **54.132021, -5.92355** ///tucked.dabbling.qualify	

Car park	Routes***	Notes	Coordinates****	QR code
Happy Valley car park**	16, 17 (near route), 27 (near route)	Mourne Rambler bus stop on Slievenaman Road is 650m away	*J 29264 29704* **54.2001, -6.019704** ///swift.piled.branched	
Hen Mountain car park	23, 24, 28 (near route)		*J 23304 27743* **54.183956, -6.111795** ///sprinter.disprove.educated	
Kilbroney car park	21 (near route), 30 (on route)	Parking fee to be paid on arrival	*J 18621 17968* **54.097281, -6.187339** ///spindles.unearthly.amid	
Leitrim Lodge car park	22, 29		*J 22389 25599* **54.164928, -6.12668** ///packing.shut.replying	
Meelmore Lodge car park	2 (near route), 5 (near route), 17, 18, 27	Parking fee to be paid on arrival	*J 30552 30773* **54.209371, -5.999516** ///reboot.occupiers.trial	
Ott car park* (aka Blue Quarry)	15, 16 (on route), 19 (on route), 27 (on route), 28		*J 27994 27855* **54.183821, -6.039938** ///revived.freshest.glimmers	
Rostrevor Forest car park	21	Parking fee to be paid on arrival to access the forest drive	*J 19549 17452* **54.092429, -6.173358** ///prospers.change.spenders	
Sandy Brae parking spot	20		*J 26332 20528* **54.118437, -6.068456** ///refer.guides.factories	

Car park	Routes***	Notes	Coordinates****	QR code
Silent Valley car park**	10, 11, 12, 13, 25 (on route)	Parking fee paid on arrival. Mourne Rambler bus stop at Silent Valley Mountain Park entrance on Head Road is 600m away	*J 30677 20922* **54.12089, -6.001863** ///newer.saga.shorter	
Spelga Dam car park**	19	Mourne Rambler bus stop on Slievenaman Road is 1.2km away	*J 26823 27316* **54.179266, -6.058098** ///cleansed.singer. nurtures	
Tollymore car park**	1	Parking fee to be paid on arrival. Mourne Rambler bus stop on B180 in Bryansford Village is 400m away	*J 34497 32669* **54.22538, -5.938238** ///challenge.scarred. firelight	
Trassey car park**	2 (on route), 5 (finish), 17 (near route), 18 (near route), 26 (on route), 27 (near route)	If car park is full, paid parking is available nearby at Meelmore Lodge. Mourne Rambler bus stop on B180 Bryansford Road is 1.4km away	*J 31100 31406* **54.214923, -5.990841** ///aquatic.outhouse. download	
Yellow Water car park	22 (near route), 29 (near route), 30		*J 20843 22248* **54.135201, -6.15168** ///pioneered.recur. situates	

APPENDIX B

Glossary

Definitions of some of the words, phrases and terminology used in this book are provided below.

Access road – a surfaced private or semi-private route built to accommodate modern vehicles for the purpose of providing access to a specific facility. Some access roads can be used by recreational walkers.

Castle – an exposed rugged rock formation.

High line – the highest possible route along a ridge line or spur.

Hill – an Irish summit lower than 609.6m (2,000ft) above sea level.

Horseshoe – a circular hillwalking route that follows the ridgeline enclosing the highest section of a river catchment area, deviating from it only where affected by access issues or hazardous terrain.

Mountain – an Irish summit of at least 609.6m (2,000ft) above sea level that features in Ireland's official list of mountains – the Irish Hewitts. There are 14 of these summits in the Mournes.

Slieve – an anglicised version of the Irish word *sliabh*, meaning mountain.

Subsidiary top – the highest point of a raised piece of land close to a higher summit from which it is required to drop less than 30m of elevation along the surface before ascending to that higher summit.

Summit – the highest point of any raised piece of land from which it is required to drop at least 30m of elevation along the surface before ascending to any higher location.

Tor – a large smooth rock outcrop at a summit or notable subsidiary top.

Track – an unsurfaced route constructed primarily to accommodate work vehicles. They allow mountain rescue teams to drive four-wheel-drive vehicles deep into the Mournes. Private vehicles are generally not permitted on tracks.

Trail – a formal named route with physical direction waymarkers positioned at strategic locations to enable users to navigate without needing a map.

Wild section – part of a route that does not follow a road, track, path or trail.

APPENDIX C

Useful links

If you require further information, the following links will direct you to relevant online content. You can access this either by typing the URL into your device or by scanning the QR code.

The Ireland Walking Guide

The Mourne Mountains
theirelandwalkingguide.com/mourne-mountains

Walking in Ireland
theirelandwalkingguide.com/general-information

Transport in Ireland
theirelandwalkingguide.com/transport

Staying safe in the Mournes

Met Office
weather.metoffice.gov.uk/specialist-forecasts/mountain/mourne-mountains

Mourne Mountain Rescue Team
mournemrt.org

what3words
what3words.com

Looking after the Mournes

Northern Ireland Water
niwater.com/silent-valley

National Trust
nationaltrust.org.uk/visit/northern-ireland/the-mournes

Forest Service Northern Ireland
nidirect.gov.uk/forests

Mourne Heritage Trust
mournelive.com

Leave No Trace
leavenotraceireland.org

Our formats

App

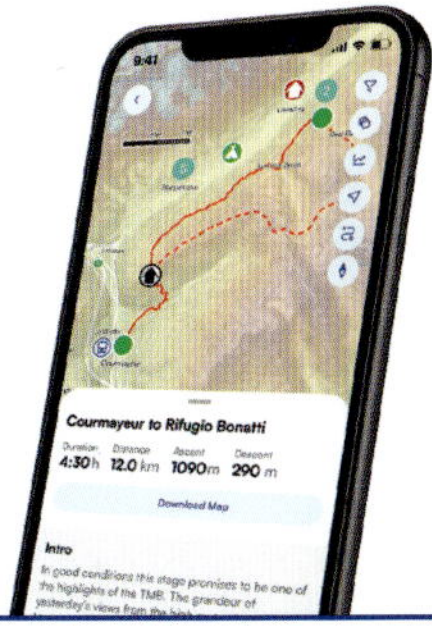

A digitised version of the guidebook's expert-curated routes, with interactive maps, detailed facilities information and offline GPS navigation

Guidebook

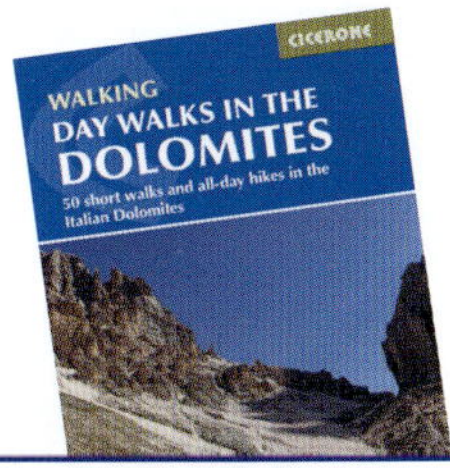

The complete guidebook with detailed descriptions, route and facilities information, profiles and maps in an easy-to-use printed format

eBook

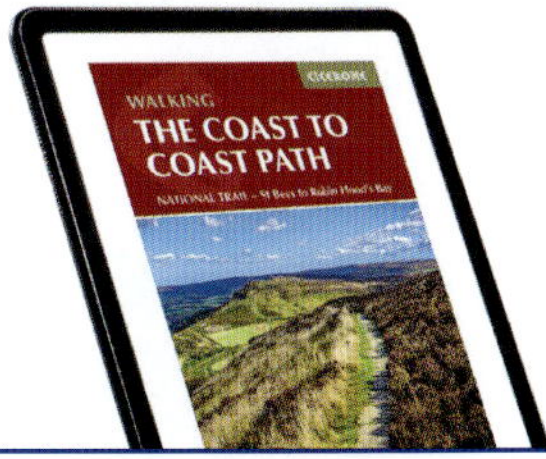

The digital edition of the guidebook with detailed descriptions, route and facilities information, profiles and maps, ready to use on any device

GPX files

Download GPX route files from your account to use on compatible devices for easy navigation and planning

See available formats for this book at **cicerone.co.uk/1262**